The Christian Science Monitor

The Christian Science Monitor

An Evolving Experiment in Journalism

Linda K. Fuller

 PRAEGER

AN IMPRINT OF ABC-CLIO, LLC
Santa Barbara, California • Denver, Colorado • Oxford, England

Library of Congress Cataloging-in-Publication Data

Fuller, Linda K.
  The Christian Science Monitor : an evolving experiment in journalism /
Linda K. Fuller.
    p. cm.
  Includes bibliographical references and index.
    ISBN 978–0–313–37994–9 (hard copy : alk. paper) — ISBN 978–0–313–37995–6
(ebook)
1. Christian Science monitor.   I. Title.
PN4899.B65C55   2011
071′.44—dc23   2011019632

ISBN: 978–0–313–37994–9
EISBN: 978–0–313–37995–6

15 14 13 12 11   1 2 3 4 5

This book is also available on the World Wide Web as an eBook.
Visit www.abc-clio.com for details.

Praeger
An Imprint of ABC-CLIO, LLC

ABC-CLIO, LLC
130 Cremona Drive, P.O. Box 1911
Santa Barbara, California 93116-1911

This book is printed on acid-free paper ∞

Manufactured in the United States of America

This book is dedicated to all truth-seekers,
nonjudgmental journalists prime among their numbers.

Contents

"Engage with Your World": Preface and Acknowledgments

This project had a gift as its genesis. In the 1960s, when my job title was executive director of our local (Springfield, Massachusetts) World Affairs Council, my husband and I participated in one of its programs: *Great Decisions*, a discussion series begun by the Foreign Policy Association in 1954. One day, out of the blue, we received word that Madeline and Bill Wright, an elderly couple in the group, had given us a complimentary subscription to *The Christian Science Monitor* (CSM) You can only imagine what happened next.

For starters, it turns out that Madeline Ball Wright herself was a journalist, her 1975 autobiography *How I Broke the Sex Barrier* delightfully chronicling how, in 1918, she became the first female reporter at the *Springfield Republican*. Beginning as a stenographer earning $15 a week for the city's War Chest, she eventually worked her way into the city room to cover World War 1 and its Armistice Day, the flu epidemic, passage of the 19th Amendment giving women the right to vote, strikes and scabs, being the first person to cross Memorial Bridge (over the Connecticut River), interviewing members of a rattlesnake club, checking out rum runners with the Coast Guard, even joining a group of nudists to be able to report about them. "Plucky" barely describes her as a pioneering female journalist, and it certainly is prescient that she was the one who got me going as a faithful *Monitor* reader.

In full disclosure, it should be known that I am not of the Christian Science faith, although some of our family members are; in fact, my mother was Protestant and my father Catholic, so my sister and I were required to go to both churches every Sunday. Add to that how involved I was with one of my Jewish friends as she studied for her bas mitzvah and how, as an adult, I have lived in Buddhist (Singapore) and Muslim (Senegal) countries, and perhaps it becomes clear that my religious experiences grant me a certain removed credibility to write this book.

Two events that occurred during grad school spurred this book onward. First, introduced to methods of media criticism, I was very taken by Edward Jay Epstein's *News from Nowhere: Television and the News*, a 1973 expose of how evening news programs were produced on ABC, CBS, and NBC. Interested in organizational theory, Epstein insinuated himself in these corporations enough to study their internal and external pressures and see how personal values became part of the process. Pulling out my browned paperback, the same feelings crept up about how what ran on the evening news shows depended on what photos and/or film crews were available, how limited amounts of information could be blown up into full "stories," how stereotypes tended to self-perpetuation, how immediacy is illusory, and how *time* determined everything. From then on, as a social scientist, I have seen television differently. During this time, I was employed as town correspondent to a freely circulated newspaper delivered door-to-door every Tuesday, and decided to do a study on its worker harmony. The *Recorder*, the name chosen for my study (Fuller 1983), had an approach just the opposite of Epstein's: Interviewing 19 people who worked there; observing procedures at the newspaper at the beginning, middle, and end of the week as well as at different times of day; and performing a content analysis of one month's news. Because I was a known figure at the office, it was easy to obtain permission from the owner and to gain access to interviewees, assuring them that their reportage would be held in strict confidence. My main mission was trying to find out why the place was so pleasant, and soon the answer came through loud and clear: Flex time, such that employees were happy to help one another—especially knowing that favors would be reciprocated. Autonomy and "free reign" were also factors, my conclusion stating how it had been "an excellent opportunity for a community newspaper to be incorporated into the educational/theoretical setting" (page 32).

All that time, of course, I had been reading *The Christian Science Monitor*, at one point realizing that it was my major source of news. When I was invited to deliver a paper at The Olympic Movement and the Mass Media Conference at Calgary, Canada in 1987, Marilyn Hoffman's article "Women sports stars tackle broadcast journalism" (*CSM* 8/2/84, 27) inspired me to check it out further. The immediate result was my presentation, "Olympics access for women: Athletes, organizers, and sports journalists." Next came my report on "The business of sportscasting" in 1989, at the International Conference on Sports Business, University of South Carolina, and eventually the presenting, editing, and writing of numerous articles and books in this field, as evidenced on my website, www.LKFullersport.com. Something similar occurred when I was invited to the Media and Crisis Conference in Quebec City, Canada in 1990, with George Gerbner as keynote speaker. Not only did my analysis of *CSM*'s treatment of Tiananmen send me into an entirely new area of research, it also began a long friendship with Gerbner as he established the Cultural Environment Movement.

As an information source and research tool, then, the *Monitor* has been invaluable in my life. So it only seemed natural—inevitable, perhaps— that I needed to get at the bottom of why, and how, this organization has such a unique approach to journalism. My files contain correspondence with managing editor David Anable (1/24/86) relative to research on "Press concentration and media monopoly"; editor Katherine Fanning (9/26/88) on her receipt of my study on how *CSM* had covered terrorism from 1977 to 1987 (Fuller 1988b); Rushworth Kidder (3/7/88) on media ethics; Donald E. Feldheim, director of public affairs (6/14/90), on my meeting with Alf McCreary, the *Monitor*'s Ireland correspondent; editor Richard J. Cattani on circulation statistics (9/21/91); and editors David T. Cook (9/20/95), Paul Van Slambrouck (6/12/04), and Richard G. Bergenheim (1/15/07) about my wanting to write a book about the *Monitor*. Although the process got started several times, there always seemed to be complications, though—lawsuits, shake-ups, and such at headquarters—and I was encouraged to hold off. Then came the "perfect storm": John Yemma as editor and their decision to diversify onto the web (CSMonitor.com) 24/7, electronically, with *CSM* weekly in print and the *Daily New Briefing* by email. The idea instantly had merit: Analyze *CSM* for a year (April 2009 to April 2010) to see what happened.

Greenwood/Praeger seemed like a logical choice as publisher, but just as the contract was signed they were sold to ABC-CLIO. Having already published my books *The Cosby Show* (1992), *Community Television in the United* States (1994), *Dictionary of Quotations in Communications* (1997), and *National Days/National Ways* (2004), they became as excited as I was. It is nice to be working with acquisitions editor Dan Harmon again, and Lynn Jurgensen, an ABC-CLIO editor who used to work at the *Monitor*, has gone out of her way to be helpful.

There are many people who need to be thanked for their cooperation such that this book could come to light: the late George Gerbner, for supplying me with an early draft of his "instant history" reflection on the

Moscow coup; Charlie Craine, general manager of the *Deseret News*; Kevin King of the Christian Science Reading Room in Boston and Robert Pozos of the Christian Science Reading Room in Springfield/Longmeadow; and Mark Montgomery, reference librarian in the Christian Science Reference Library.

New England is known for its brutal winters, and it seemed that every one of my trips to Boston brought snow, sleet, hail, and several rainstorms that turned umbrellas inside out—but nothing could deter me from this project. Because it was my haven when I had to stay overnight to do research and interviews, let me thank the staff at The College Club of Boston (founded in 1890, the oldest women's college club in the country): Edith Toth, Donald Farwell, Lee Tarr, and chef extraordinaire Jesse Wolkiewicz.

It is with deep appreciation also that I thank the following *Monitor* folks for reading various sections of the book: *Daily News Briefing*—Ross Atkin; Mary Baker Eddy library— Judy Huennecke; the Culture section of the weekly—Susan Leach; Journalism in the twentieth century—Leigh Montgomery; various appendices and such—Ed Blomquist; and, if you can believe it, editor John Yemma for proofing early drafts of this manuscript for *Monitor*-related facts—but in no way should he be held responsible for what appears here. Any errors, of course, are mine.

Monitor staff who were not interviewed but who sent along messages of support also need special mention, including Ron Scherer, New York national bureau reporter; Dan Murphy, world news; Carol Huang, world news; Christa Case Bryant, world news; and others whose schedules simply could not accommodate mine. It has been critical, and comforting, to have the cooperation and blessing of the Board of Trustees of the Christian Science Publishing Society—particularly Judy Wolff, chair.

While some people like to open presents, my greatest joy comes from opening conversations and getting to know people. The essence of what is revealed here comes from interviews with 61 *Monitor* staff who were willing and/or able to talk to me either in person or on the telephone. Listed here chronologically, enormous thanks goes to them all: Brad Knickerbocker, senior writer/editor; Peter Ford, Beijing bureau chief; Marshall Ingwerson, managing editor; David C. Scott, world editor; Mark Sappenfield, deputy national news editor; Judy Lowe, environment editor; Ross Atkin, *Daily News Briefing* editor; Abe McLaughlin, product manager; Jimmy Orr, online editor; Melanie Stetson Freeman, photographer; Mark Guarino, national bureau (Chicago); Gordon Lubold, reporter, Washington, D.C. (Pentagon); Chris Gaylord, innovation editor; Amelia Newcomb, world news; Marjorie Kehe, book editor; Clay Jones, chief editorial writer; Rosalie Dunbar, news editor of Christian Science magazines; Gregory Lamb, *People Making a Difference* editor and reporter; Stacy Teicher Khadaroo, education reporter; Dave Cook, bureau chief, Washington, D.C.; Gillian Charters, copyeditor; Kendra Nordin, *Weekly* assistant editor; Leigh Montgomery, librarian; Eoin O'Carroll, online producer; Alfredo Sosa, photo editor and director of multimedia; David R. Francis, economic columnist; Josh Burek, Op-Ed; Peter Grier, *Decoder* writer and reporter, Washington, D.C., bureau; John Kehe, design director; Mike Farrell, San Francisco bureau; Peter Rainer, film critic; Amanda Paulson, national bureau (Chicago) and education reporter; Ed Blomquist, copyright administrator; Linda Feldmann, Washington, D.C., bureau; Walter Rodgers, columnist; Patty Collingsworth, circulation marketing director; Haide Bolanos, marketing manager, CSM; Amanda Gustin, researcher, MBE Library; Francine Kiefer, editorial writer; Donal Toole, finance and strategy director; Clare Turner, *Monitor* religious article; Jonathan Wells, managing publisher; Peter Spotts, reporter; Clara Germani, senior editor; Owen Thomas, deputy *Weekly* editor; Heather Ehmke, copyeditor; Pat Murphy, deputy online editor; Laurent Belsie, economy editor; Cindy Anderson, manager, planning and administration; Cheryl Sullivan, national news editor; Judy Huenneke, MBE Library senior archivist; Rex Nelles, executive assistant; John Yemma, editor; Bob Hanna, ad sales director; Howard LaFranchi, diplomatic correspondent; Mark Trumbull, reporter; Susan Hackney, marketing director; Gloria Goodale, Los Angeles features bureau chief; Clayton Collins, *Weekly* editor (by email); John Hughes, columnist, and Alexandra Marks, reporter and blogger.

Some of these names need to be singled out. Rex Nelles and Cindy Anderson facilitated my many interviews at *Monitor* headquarters, as well as answering so many questions and accommodating so many requests, and Cindy made sure I got early issues of the *Daily News Briefings*. But most of all, this book could never have been written without the unconditional support of editor John Yemma. He enthusiastically accepted my proposal, facilitated it such that I could attend production meetings, and kept an open door and an open mind, even suggesting a change to my original title of this book. Most amazing, though, has been his willingness to review what I have written; his feedback has been invaluable.

My husband, Eric Fuller, went above and beyond for this go-around, putting up with all those crates and cartons, having dinners at weird times, and proofing all the chapters. All three of our sons, and their families, are delighted to have received copies of *CSM Weekly*, and it has been fun sharing this information with them. As is clear, then, this book owes a debt to many considerate people—starting with Madeline and Bill Wright's gift.

At one point, when I was feeling the panic of putting all these findings together, it came to me what an incredible trust it has been, transcribing and translating personal and professional reportage of what it is like to be part of *Monitor* journalism. But then it also struck me that this is a treasure, too—documenting one year of a venerable institution's decision to experiment, to evolve.

Linda K. Fuller
Wilbraham, Massachusetts

Chapter 1

Introduction to the *Monitor*: CSMonitor.com (24/7 Website); *CSM Weekly* (Print: Email); *Daily New Briefing* (Email)

For 100 years, The Christian Science Monitor *has been changing and elevating the global conversation with its humane, hope-filled approach to reporting on the world. During its first century, the paper won seven Pulitzer prizes and developed a world-class reputation. Its website has 1.8 million unique visitors per month—people who are highly educated, wealthy, and deeply engaged in their communities.*

—http://knol.google.com/k/the-christian-science-monitor

What follows here is the story of how a newspaper, founded in 1908 by a woman in her 88th year, evolved into a unique, highly respected journalistic venture and then, in 2009, decided to go digital with a Web-first format supplemented for subscribers by a weekly edition and a daily email version. This is an assessment, a year later, of that experiment.

If this saga were made into a movie, it might start with an establishing shot of the prestigious Bay Back neighborhood in Boston, Massachusetts, near the 52-floor Prudential Tower ("The Pru") and Symphony Hall, then zeroing in on the majestic façade of Romanesque granite world headquarters of the First Church of Christ, Scientist. A 14-acre complex located in a plaza alongside Huntington Avenue with an address at 210 Massachusetts Avenue, it includes the original Mother Church, built in 1894, with an annex added in 1906; the Christian Science Publishing House, built in 1934, with the Mapparium (a three-dimensional perspective of the world of 1935), where *The Christian Science Monitor (CSM)*[1] is produced; The Mary Baker Eddy Library for the Betterment of Humanity,[2] a 28-story administration building; Horticultural Hall; a colonnade; and a reflecting pool with fountain designed by I. M. Pei in the 1960s.

Do a close-up of *CSM*'s newsroom, though, and you will find journalistic popular culture images off kilter. Classic Hollywood depictions of newsrooms typically show smoke-filled rooms with frantic, noisy men rushing around cubicles, phone in hand and anxiety written all over their faces (Good 1989; Robards 1990; Ehrlich 2006)—"those loathsome misconceptions that journalists are hard-drinking, foul-mouthed, dim-witted social misfits concerned only with twisting the truth into scandal and otherwise devoid of conscience, respect for basic human dignity or a healthy fear of God" (Rowe 1992, 27). That would not be the *Monitor*. There has never been any smoking, and the place has always been neat and tidy—Erwin D. Canham (1958, 68) reminding us at the newspaper's 50th anniversary that, "There aren't any spittoons." Of course most newsrooms today prohibit smoking, but right away we see that *Monitor* reality differs from mediated perceptions.

For an award-winning[3] international news organization that, as indicated by the title to this introduction, appears on a 24/7 website (CSMonitor.com), weekly in print (*CSM Weekly*), and daily Monday through Friday by email (*Daily New Briefing* or *DNB*), *The Christian Science Monitor*'s evolution since its 1908 beginnings as the purely print newspaper of the Church of Christ, Scientist, has, as one of the more amazing parts of its story the fact that the organization does not evangelize; instead, it only includes a single religious article—usually news- or topic-relevant. You will learn here about its history, its philosophical underlay, its financial situation, and, mainly, its concern for people around the world.

Appendices included at the end of this book—many alluded to in the text—provide extra material for both the scholar and the interested reader to learn more about the uniqueness of *CSM*'s decision to go digital. Below, you will see a brief literature review of the few publications dealing with what has been consistently cited as an "elite" newspaper—one that I, in "monitoring the *Monitor*" for nearly a half century, have found invaluable both as a personal resource and an academic staple. Having long wanted to write its story, the opportunity arrived when in October 2008 the *Monitor* announced that it would cease printing Monday through Friday (M–F) editions and would instead go Web-first as of April 2009, along with print and email supplements. While economics were naturally part of that decision—the *Monitor* citing losses of $18.9 million even after $12.5 million in annual revenue—there was much more to it, as you will learn.

Analyzing what happened during that year—April 2009 to April 2010—informs this book.

While the CSMonitor.com website offers constant, continually changing news updates in the same journalistic tradition that *Monitor* readers and viewers had come to expect, the *DNB*—and, technically, the website—maintain a dictum by *CSM*'s founder, Mary Baker Eddy (MBE), that daily reports be available, and the Weekly Edition consolidates a wide range of topics—world, nation, people, newsmakers and decision-makers, money, science, environment, culture, religious perspective, specials and series, and editorial views—that staff deem *de rigueur*.

In her first editorial in the first edition of her now more than 100-year-old newspaper (November 25, 1908), MBE made clear a journalistic mandate that has held firm throughout: "To injure no man, but to bless all mankind." The newspaper's purpose never was to convert people to the Christian Science faith; rather, the mission, according to its first editor, Archibald McLellan (1908), was "To publish the real news of the world in a clean, wholesome manner, devoid of the sensational methods employed by so many newspapers. There will be no exploitation or illustration of vice and crime, but the aim of the editors will be to issue a paper which will be welcomed in every home where purity and refinement are cherished ideals."

For more, check out a video featuring current editor John Yemma and then editor-at-large Richard Bergenheim on the occasion of *CSM*'s centennial, "The *Monitor*'s timeless mission" (December 16, 2008), on YouTube.[4] Yemma has a PowerPoint titled "Who we are, what we do" that easily explains how the newspaper sees itself:

- We expose injustice, celebrate progress, find people making a difference;
- Non-profit based in Boston. 8 overseas bureaus, 8 domestic bureaus, 8-person Washington staff;
- Strengths: foreign policy, Washington, environment, innovation, money/values, culture;
- Seven Pulitzers in 100 years.

"One of the world's most distinguished and respected news organizations, the *Monitor* has achieved a unique position in journalism history," according to a *knol*,[5]

By striving to report the news in an objective, constructive way and by interpreting events to show them in relation to societal progress, it is credited with important contributions to progress, peace, and world thought. It pioneered in presenting national and international news, and persists in reporting international news at a time when foreign news coverage is declining more than any other subject. It also seeks to provide analytic, informative, clean and entertaining news for every member of the family.

At one point boasting a circulation of 200,000—eventually eroded to about 60,000 by 2005, albeit drawing at that time some 1.8 million visitors per month to its website (CSMonitor.com)—in its heyday, the *Monitor* was delivered to some 120 nations and geographical areas of the world, more than any other newspaper. Today, with the Internet, its reach continues, if in a different venue. Throughout this history, it has been difficult to ascertain how many *Monitor* readers and subscribers are of the Christian Science faith, but what is known—both by income figures and anecdotally—is that it has endured in hometown and university libraries, institutions, public offices, private homes, and organizations.

As noted in the subtitle to this study, evolution is key to understanding *CSM*'s metamorphosis. Both its news coverage and its handling of the topic itself shows that it sits in the center of modern thinking, unhindered by faith-based notions of creationism or "intelligent design" (see Fuller 2010c). Relative to the movement, Robert Peel (1984, 108) noted that, "For one thing, Darwinism had shaken the foundations of evangelical faith and biblical literalism more seriously than the whole Age of Reason had been able to do. By the end of the nineteenth century, traditional Christianity was clearly in retreat before the increasing claims of a basically materialist science." Mary Baker Eddy, he points out, had written in 1875: "Mr. Darwin is right with regard to mortal man or matter, but should have made a distinction between these and the immortal, whose basis is Spirit." As the notion of "Social Darwinism" emerged—incorporating and co-opting notions of natural selection and survival of the fittest, it becomes clear that interpretations vary. The *Monitor* has not hesitated to take the subject head-on: Peter Grier and Josh Burek (12/21/05) co-authored "Banned in biology class: Intelligent design" relative to the 2005 *Kitzmiller v. Dover* trial, declaring that teaching creationism in public schools violates our constitutional right separating church and state; Greg Lamb (10/23/06) has reported on evolutionary biologist Richard Dawkins's views of religion as unscientific and dogmatic, Jeremy Kutner (2/12/09) on the continuing debate about evolution, and Robert C. Cowen (2/19/09) on "Science advances beyond what Darwin did not know (DNA)"; Todd Wilkinson (3/17/09) reviewed Jerry A. Coyne's *Why Evolution is True*, and Peter N. Spotts (4/5/10) featured Francisco Ayala, an evolutionary biologist who won the 2010 Templeton Prize for affirming spiritualism.

So it is clear that, from the start, as the *Monitor* itself evolves, so too does its balanced reportage. As a reporter, Mark Trumbull has a broad perspective on the big picture that *CSM*'s recent transition will have for readers. Having joined in 1987, he told me (personal communication, 4/8/10) that, "Things have evolved in various incarnations." "Change is a constant at the *Monitor*," then editor David T. Cook wrote in "A note from the editor" (11/10/98), discussing design changes as "evolutionary, not revolutionary." As you will see, evolution also has included its fair share of experimentation. Add to these themes some other recurrent ones imbedded in this account—media and journalistic overviews, stories and storytelling, ethical perspectives, and real voices by participants, all at a juncture when many people are curious to see how this all plays out.

My basic premise is two-dimensional: Realizing that the production of news is a result of historical, sociopolitical, economic, and—unique to *The Christian Science Monitor*—religious considerations, as well as reactions to it by consumers, "news" (which stands for North, East, West, South) needs to be analyzed and interpreted. Clearly, the evolution of *CSM* as a cultural and organizational product, mostly manufactured by journalists who hold to a similar journalistic ethic, makes for a fascinating story. To make that case, what follows is a discussion of how and why this is a unique case study, *CSM*'s role in the world of media, its uniqueness, "Only in the *Monitor*" examples, methodology, a literature review, and an introduction to the website (CSMonitor.com), *CSM* weekly, and the *Daily News Briefing* (*DNB*) that inform *Monitor* journalism.

CSM: A UNIQUE CASE STUDY

Over its more than 100 years of highly esteemed journalism, *The Christian Science Monitor* has steadily earned and maintained a reputation and a respect enviable within the profession. Fair or not, though, it is best known for the following: Objective reportage on the Middle East; *Monitor* breakfasts with newsmakers; the first female editor of a national newspaper (Kay Fanning, 1983–1988); limited libel issues; and two hostage-related incidents: Staff writer David Rohde's 1996 discovery of graves confirming the Bosnian massacre and then his 10-day captivity, and freelancer Jill Carroll's 2006 kidnapping in Baghdad for 82 days. Preeminently, as you will read here, *CSM* is the first major newspaper to move to a Web-first format.

Many media observers are aware that *Monitor* staff have been recipients of seven Pulitzer Prizes, although some of the uninitiated still think that it is a religious newspaper, and others—whether long-time readers or recent Web viewers—realize that it is an amazing news resource.

Wide-Ranging Uniqueness

This reportage on *CSM* is unique in many ways. For starters, it is the culmination of my half century of research; further, it turns out that having unbiased objectivity toward an unbiased media source is unusual. Consider: The *Monitor* has never had any partisan political affiliations and/or commitments, but has dedicated itself to public service and reportage of news, with special emphasis on globalism.

By way of example relative to its international coverage, my content analysis of datelines (locations where news stories originate) for the first year just in the *Weekly Edition* identified 122 countries. While datelines do not always coincide with places being discussed, they nevertheless are a good marker for figuring out where stories were written and/or filed. At the top of the list, quite naturally, is the United States, at about 450 datelines,[6] followed by the United Kingdom (45), China (43), Germany (37), India (36), Israel (33), Mexico (33), Afghanistan (32), Japan (31), Russia (29), and South Africa (27) as the top 10. Next in order comes a tie between South Korea and Canada (26 each); Pakistan (25); France and Egypt (23 each); Iraq (22); Kenya and Turkey (21 each), Lebanon and Italy (19 each), Brazil (18), Thailand and Australia (14 each); Colombia, Gaza, and Ireland (12 each); United Arab Emirates and Sri Lanka (11 each); Argentina, Haiti, Chile, Jordan, the West Bank, and Sweden (10 each); Spain and Syria (8 each); Cuba, the Czech Republic, Nigeria, and Venezuela (7 each) Indonesia, Qatar, and Uruguay (6 each); and Austria and Uganda (5 each). These countries had four datelines: Cambodia, the Democratic Republic of the Congo, Dominican Republic, Ecuador, Equatorial Guinea, Greece, Honduras, the Netherlands, Peru, Poland, Rwanda, Saudi Arabia, Singapore, Switzerland, and Zimbabwe; these, three: Finland, Hong Kong, Mali, Myanmar, North Korea, Tanzania, Tibet, and Yemen; two: Portugal, Serbia, Sierra Leone, Sudan, Tajikistan, and Trinidad; and one: Angola, Bosnia-Herzegovina, Costa Rica, Denmark, Ethiopia, Georgia, Hungary, Kosovo, Kuwait, Kyrgyzstan, Madagascar, Namibia, Niger, and Norway.

Here is *CSM*'s statement regarding its policy on not endorsing political candidates: "The *Monitor*'s editors believe readers should decide for themselves who is best qualified for public office. Through our extensive political coverage from Capitol Hill and in races around the country, we strive to provide all the information necessary for voters to make political decisions most appropriate for them, their communities, and the nation, whether choosing a local candidate or the next president of the United

States."[7] Front-page coverage of "Obama's new political era" (Feldman 11/6/08), for example, read: "Barack Obama's historic election as America's first black president has ushered in a new political era at a time of tremendous challenge, both at home and abroad." Other articles dealt with what the win might mean abroad, how voter turnout was "historical in numbers and diversity," wondering about an economic lift, varying views of it all, an editorial reminder that Obama had said he would bring Doris Kearns Goodwin's book *Team of Rivals* (about Abraham Lincoln's inclusive leadership style) to the White House, opinions on whether he could deliver and what his global to-do list should contain, the Democratic agenda, and many small related articles. Although it was easy to catch the optimism, the reader would still be left wondering where the newspaper's vote went.

"The *Monitor* truly is unique. Boston-published in the elegant civil style of Yankee Brahmins, its strength is an intangible quality of thought and excellence," columnist Walter Rodgers told me in an interview (2/24/10). "It represents journalistic courage, excellence and integrity perhaps higher on the integrity scale than any other paper. The industry and the country would be much poorer if this paper were to disappear."

As a publication of The Mother Church (TMC), *CSM* nonetheless has never been a proselytizing or preaching tool, even if it does contain a daily religious article or perspective in each issue and/or on its website. It "aims never to make religion obtrusive, but does not hesitate to point out that a better awareness of spiritual values and duties is the essential preliminary to action for the salvation of society," Canham (1958, xxiv) has explained. He added: "To emphasize such facts is to get at the real meaning of events. It is journalism of the highest order." Mormons began the *Deseret News* in 1847, and to this day it remains geared to church members and citizens of Utah; and the Vatican publishes *Osservatore Romano*; but to this day the *Monitor* is the only nondenominational, widely circulated, church-produced newspaper focusing on world issues, the *Washington Times*, published by the Unification church, being too insular to be competition. While it might include reports about annual meetings of TMC, the occasional text from a Christian Science lecture, news about management changes, or such, the underlying declaration that *CSM* is a "real newspaper" predominates.

Although in the 1930s Rufus Steele had a column called "March of the Nations" and Henry E. Williams wrote "Tower Views," *The Christian Science Monitor* has deviated from traditional newspapers' dependency on regular columnists. Instead, it aims to provide a wide range of opinions. John Hughes and Walter Rodgers comment on international issues, Peter

Grier does *Decoder*, David R. Francis has *Economic Scene*, Peter Rainer writes film reviews, Ruth Walker has *Verbal Energy*, and John Yemma does *Open Source*, but the *Monitor* prides itself on encouraging disparate views.

With a news-gathering, reporting, and editing staff of about 85, supplemented by eight domestic and eight international news bureaus, *CSM*'s organizational structure also includes some stringers and freelancers—keeping it free of dependency on wire services. "It provides news purely as a public service. Here is why: If the basic theology of that church says what reaches and affects thought shapes experience, it follows that a newspaper would have significant impact on the lives of those who read it," claims its website.[8] "The idea is that the unblemished truth is freeing (as a fundament human right); with it, citizens can make informed decisions and take intelligent action, for themselves and for society."

"The *Monitor* openly advocates all things green and has a tilt to positive, solution-oriented reporting," Rick Edmonds of *Biz Blog* (2009) has noted. "It is serious but not totally above the fray of pop culture. The *Monitor* did Letterman, did balloon boy and has been heavy on the Fox News-Obama administration feud . . . (It) also covered Kanye West's rant at the Grammies and related incidents of incivility."

Gloria Goodale, a *Monitor* reporter for the Los Angeles bureau, started with the organization back in 1982—when she and Cheryl Sullivan helped teach local Boston children ballet. Kay Fanning was the idol of all the younger staffers, she recalled (4/11/10). "Mostly, she is 'with it,' I told her, from her varied reportage—fashion, WebTV, novel architecture, photojournalism, Hollywood, Obama as fodder for laughs, but her response was simply, 'I live in L.A.!'—pop culture capital of the country."

CSM's Reputation

The Christian Science Monitor is often included and studied as an "elite" (e.g., Strout 1999; Patrick 2002) or "prestige" newspaper, "one of the world's best-known" (ProQuest 2003), "a great publication respected by newsmen and other discerning readers of current affairs" (Charles Guy, civic activist of Lubbock, TX), "both factual and hopeful" (Jenkin Lloyd-Jones, editor of the Tulsa *Tribune*); "the standard of perfection is no less than in the likeness of God" (editor of the *West Delaware Tribune*). Highly influential both nationally and internationally (Rosenthal 2008), the word most associated with it is *venerable*. Early on, *CSM* was well received, recognized "as a superior secular paper sponsored by a religious body" (Wolseley 1948, 613). Upon the occasion of *The Christian Science Monitor: The First 80 Years*

Table 1.1
Leaders' Accolades for *The Christian Science Monitor*'s First 80 Years

• **Calvin Coolidge**, during his presidency (1924): "My personal thanks for your fairness and courtesy."

• **Fiorello H. LaGuardia**, mayor of New York: "*The Christian Science Monitor* is the greatest paper in the United States!"

• **Wendell Willkie**, presidential candidate: "*The Christian Science Monitor* is one of the greatest newspapers of the world. I admire and read its editorial page. I know of no newspaper more consistently both wise and right."

• **Thomas E. Dewey**, governor of New York: "I have the warmest regard for *The Christian Science Monitor*, which is truly a great newspaper . . . You have truly earned your high reputation for painstaking accuracy and fairness."

• **Winston Churchill**: "In the United States, *The Christian Science Monitor* [has] a position of singular distinction."

• **Dwight D. Eisenhower**: "True to the highest standards of responsible reporting, the *Monitor* has grown in service to a wide community. With freedom, fairness, and sensitivity, it has recorded the events of our day and written with clarity . . . In its pages are found the facts and opinions upon which intelligent decisions can be firmly based."

• **Lowell Thomas**, commentator: "The *Monitor* is one of the world's great newspapers. I shout that from the housetops at every opportunity."

• **Eleanor Roosevelt**: "*The Christian Science Monitor* seems to me one of the best and most valuable newspapers that we have in this country."

• **Franklin D. Roosevelt**: "The constructive service which *The Christian Science Monitor* has consistently rendered to better understanding between nations is widely appreciated in all parts of the world."

• **Walter Lippmann**, journalist: "There is no more scrupulously objective newspaper dealing with international affairs than the *Monitor*."

• **John F. Kennedy**: "The able and excellent editorial comment and news coverage given this whole problem of Indo-China's independence in the*Monitor* has had an important effect on opinion here in Congress."

(1988), a sampling of accolades from some of the century's most influential national and international leaders and thinkers, listed here in Table 1.1, was included.

John Hughes, who served as editor from 1970 to 1979, winning a Pulitzer Prize during that time and working at the *Monitor* for 24 years, maintains that the newspaper has great credibility wherever he has gone—including bureaus in Africa and Asia. "Mainly, the value of *CSM* is that it gives background and interpretation to a story," he stated (4/28/10), adding that he admires its sense of responsibility.

A Pentagon reporter for the last three years, covering two wars, the military, national security, the FBI, homeland security, the CIA, and more, Gordon Lubold confided that he has easy access to Washington personnel as "everyone knows the brand, and respects it"(2/9/10). He calls them "boutique briefings," an example of access you get to the powers that be in Washington, because people know you and the newspaper you represent. Staff writer Peter Grier describes *CSM* as "an information machine for people who need foreign news for work" (2/19/10).

On July 21, 1999, managing publisher Stephen T. Gray, acknowledging that "this experiment grows out of our dissatisfaction with direct mail," sent out a call to readers to answer the question "How is the *Monitor* different?" Nearly 400 responses, including some from China, Japan, the Netherlands, Sweden, Switzerland, England, and of course the United States supplied some amazing testimonials; here are some examples (7/12/99):

- "Each year it becomes more critical for me as a voting member of a democracy to have a better source of information than the biases of the mainstream media. The *Monitor* provides such a source. I just can't give it up." (Grace Low)
- "Reading the *Monitor* is like being spoken to rather than shouted at." (Kathi Somers)
- "The most bias-free of all news sources." (Th. W. Ruljgrok)
- "[The *Monitor*] is the most outstanding newspaper of social discernment in the world." (Yu-Tang D. Lew)
- "Nonpartisan. Neither left nor right. Inclusive and respectful of competing ideas without being value-neutral. Quirky! Intellectually stimulating! Humorous! Thoughtful! Insightful! Caring!" (William R. Barker)

Bob Garfield (2005), founding contributor to the *Watchdog Blog* of the Nieman Foundation for Journalism at Harvard University, noted in an interview with Marshall Ingwerson that *The Christian Science Monitor* is "more public service than house organ"—to which the managing editor responded, "The *Monitor* has always been a sort of strange beast—a paper with an absolutely sterling journalistic reputation, and yet has this connection with a church." One reporter phrased it this way: "I tell people it's a normal newspaper with a funny name."

Although difficult to document, it has long been said that *Monitor* journalism has had an important, positive role in influencing other media. Elevated to a higher role, many media elites have referred to it as a "newspaperman's [sic] newspaper." Its various editors and staff have been instrumental in founding and serving in professional organizations such as the American Society of Newspaper Editors, the National Conference of Editorial Writers, the American Press Club, Sigma Delta Chi (a journalistic fraternity), the International Federation of Newspaper Editors, the International Press Institute, Overseas Writers, the Women's Press Club, and the Pulitzer Prize Awards Committee. Consistently making Best Newspapers lists in polls, its real influence is apparent in this statement by 60-year veteran Joseph C. Harsch (1993, 218): "My broadcasts on television got me many a flattering glance of recognition on the street and sometimes a sharp word of disapproval from a total stranger, but the opinions I expressed in my columns in the *Monitor* reached the White House and Congress."

"ONLY IN THE *MONITOR*"

This is a refrain I often heard when rhetorically asking where else certain material might be available. It lies at the heart of my purpose in pulling together *CSM* reportage since the 1960s, trying to explain the uniqueness of *Monitor* journalism. What follows is just a sampling, saved to share here: descendants of a Bristol, Rhode Island slave trader confronting the legacy (1/31/08); attending to Cairo's street kids (1/31/08); a book review of Drew Gilpin Faust's *This Republic of Suffering: Death and the American Civil War* and how it still resonates today (1/29/08); lack of safe drinking water globally (3/20/08); whether child-rapists should be executed (4/16/08); justice for African "bush wives" (6/9/08); a Hmong refugee woman's memoir (6/16/08); injured GIs as athletes (6/25/08); self-rehab at San Quentin State Prison (3/5/09); an editorial on helping to stop female circumcision (4/2/08); lexicographer Erin McKean's "Wordnik" online dictionary (3/16/09); "When NYPD blue wears a Muslim topi" (3/19/09), and so much more.

Since then, here are some stories that have appeared in the *Daily News Briefing* that easily fall into my heading of "Only in the *Monitor*": "Who knew that Africa would be involved in the flower industry?" (Ethiopia, *DNB* 5/11/09, 2); Sara Miller Llana's "Mexico's challenge: Street children" (6/2/09, 2); Howard LaFranchi's "China leads student surge in US," an Open Door report on an all-time high of 671,616 foreign students spending $18 billion (11/17/09); Warren Richey's "Court refuses dress code challenge" (1/12/01, 2), about a Texas high schooler barred from wearing a T-shirt emblazoned with "Freedom of Speech" on the front and the text of the First Amendment on the back; or how Egyptian archaeologists' discovery of a new set of tombs from the workers who build the great pyramids more than 4,000 years ago (1/11/01, 3).

Further, although there are numerous examples in the *Weekly Edition* that fit into this category, let me urge you to check these from 2009:

Michael Seaver (4/12), "N. Ireland's full-court press for peace: A basketball team of Catholic and Protestant boys learns how to play together"; Ilene R. Prusher (5/10, West Bank), "New in an Islamic court: Female judge"; Steve Dinnen (5/31), "How a raid changed a town," about a Postville, Iowa immigration sweep; Peter Ford (6/28), "Straight from press to pulp," reporting that a Chinese newspaper (Beijing's *Life Morning News*) was found to be sent directly to recycling centers. It had won awards, but the staff had the sense no one was reading it—and they weren't!

"Why It Matters" is a critical insertion in certain articles explicating matters we readers might not have considered. Here, see Sara Miller Llana (7/26/09, 10), "In Latin America, anti-Semitism spikes," with this explanation: "Jewish leaders say fierce criticism of Israel by leftist leaders such as Venezuela's Hugo Chavez foment anti-Semitism, which spurs attacks. They are concerned that hated and violence against Jews could spread further in the region"; Matthew Clark (8/2/09), "Congo confronts rape": "In this war-torn country, sexual assault is used so frequently as a weapon that some perpetrators don't even consider it wrong"; Gloria Goodale and Daniel B. Wood (9/13/09)'s "All the news that's fit to laugh at": "A cover story on political comedy, interviewing humor experts, reviewing its history, role of *SNL*, Leno and Letterman"; "Behind the veil": Caryle Murphy (12/13/09) answers "Who wears it—and why?" with "It liberates. It represses. It is a prayer. It is a prison. It protects. It obliterates. Rarely in human history has a piece of cloth been assigned so many roles. Been embroiled in so much controversy. Been so misjudged, misunderstood, and manipulated."; or Ursula Lindsey (12/20/09), "Behind a rift in Egypt's Muslim Brotherhood": "The Arab world's oldest, largest Islamist organization, established in 1928, it has 150,000 members and could affect Mubarak's succession plans."

Also, here are a few more examples from early 2010: Ben Arnoldy (2/7), "India skeptical of US pledge" (on carbon emissions): "Climate talk stalemates, Chindia is not being asked to sacrifice, and sees the US as a polluter"; Sibylla Brodzinsky (2/21), "New hub for human trafficking into US": "Colombia uncovers a trail that leads through Moscow, South Africa, and Brazil"; and a book review (2/21) of Kevin and Hannah Salwen's *The Power of Half*: "It began The Hunger Project—influenced by the homeless."

CSM'S ROLE IN THE WORLD OF MEDIA

Contrary to complaints that we hear about how skewed and how screwed up the media is, it seems imperative to address these critiques head on. What follows is a discussion about media bias and media ethics and where *The Christian Science Monitor* fits into polarizing journalistic considerations.

Media Bias

> *When reporters transform the raw stuff of experience into presumed fact and arrange fact into coherent stories, they create a way of seeing individuals and events as well as making sense of politics writ large. Because the success of our democracy depends so heavily on journalists' exercise of their constitutionally protected mission, it is important to understand the ways shifting journalistic perspectives alter the facts that are deemed important, the ways in which fact is framed and frames come to be assumed, and the ways that journalism's facts and frames become the stories we tell each other and other children about the meaning of our times.*
>
> —Jamieson and Waldman, *The Press Effect* (2004, xvii).

Because *The Christian Science Monitor* has been, since its start, economically self-supporting, subsidized as it is by The Mother Church, it has been free to maintain an independent posture in its decision-making. A classic example is its handling of Adolf Hitler. *CSM*'s publication of an October 3, 1923 exclusive interview with Germany's totalitarian leader from 1933 to 1945, responsible for genocides of Jewish, Romani, gays, and others during what became known as the Holocaust, was prescient in its foreboding, the correspondent noting that, "His headquarters resemble a hive of swarming bees . . . Herr Hitler has a potential armed strength which is not to be regarded lightly" (cited in Canham 1958, 229). A month later (November 9, 1923), Hitler appeared on the front page of the *Monitor*, along with another warning tone in a story about his failed attempt at a putsch in Munich. In her study of early Nazi persecution of Jews, Deborah E. Lipstadt (1983) berates *CSM* for not being as outraged as other press in 1933; yet, she tries to explain why, according to its tenets of a "non-sensational and non-alarmist approach," this was difficult. Add to that the knowledge that Christian Scientists were among those singled out for arrest and persecution in Germany and it makes one admire the newspaper's continuing uncompromising coverage of this dark period in the world's history. Still, although steadfastly pro-humanity and liberty, "The *Monitor* was not altogether free from wartime hysteria and susceptibility to propaganda when feelings and events were at their most intense" (Canham 1958, 288).

In answer to the 1949 question, "Is the US press competently doing its job of keeping its readers informed?" then editor Canham, speaking before the National Association of Radio News Directors responded bluntly, "No"—that, in fact, "the failure of the newspapers and the radio to fulfill their responsibilities has caused a 'crisis in confidence,' that the public's mistrust has grown to . . . a degree which is alarming to the integrity and future of our function" (The press 1949). Considering that its circulation at that time was 174,624, it behooves us to review how long these issues have existed. Canham continued:

The press must find a better solution to "the eternal compromise . . . between reader interest and significance. The fact that people are immensely more interested in little girls who fall down wells than in the wheat crop in Italy is a fundamental [news problem] from which we can never hope to escape . . . But we should constantly be aware of the necessity of handing on . . . important and significant news . . . and not simply the easy news which is sensational and violent . . . We [must convert] into terms of human comprehension and human interest the news which is of primary significance to people's lives everywhere.

According to www.honestreporting.com, bias deals with mediated means of influencing public opinion; it lists these as the seven violations of media objectivity: misleading definitions and terminology, imbalanced reporting, opinions disguised as news, lack of context, selective omission, using true facts to draw false conclusions, and distortion of facts. "The *Monitor* reports without bias or blinders and looks beyond the catchphrases and the dogma," we are told.[9]

As to the liberal versus conservative press, it was quite a surprise to some people when Media Matters for America's 2007 study of 1,430 English-language daily newspapers found that 60 percent had more conservative syndicated columnists than liberals (Bauder 2007). As we become more polarized into red/blue allegiances, various media are reacting by reinforcing partisanship. "From the conservative Fox News Channel to the liberal radio startup Air America to political blogs of every stripe, Americans can now pick and choose a news source to fit their ideological bent," Alexandra Marks (2004) has noted, adding, "The rise of opinionated journalism appears to have taken a toll on media credibility."

By way of example, we might examine reportage on the Middle East (e.g., Lavoie 2008). Richard H. Curtiss (1997), executive editor of the *Washington Report*, has singled out the *Monitor* as a news source "with truly objective coverage of the Middle East." "Since the early 20th century, tension between Jewish and Arab communities in the Middle East has been constant, swinging between military clashes, diplomatic efforts, peace talks, terrorism, more clashes, and renewed diplomacy," *DNB Editor's View* outlined (Yemma 5/18/09, 1). "The previous administration tried to reengineer the Middle East through military means, putting diplomacy on the back burner. Obama is taking the opposite approach, seeing an opening with Iran, expressing empathy for Arab and Muslim concerns, and trying to reassure Israel that it still has firm US backing."

"In journalism there are three types of statements: objective facts; obvious opinions; and a third, hazier category that can be called 'judgment terms.' This last category, which appears often (but not exclusively) in Middle East coverage, challenges both readers and reporting by testing the boundaries between fact and opinion," Gilead Ini (2009, 28) has pointed out in "The unseen bias in Middle East reporting." As editor, John Yemma has been told by Yemeni officials that, after Al Jazeera,[10] the Arabic-language news network, *CSM* has provided the most coverage of the country. Maintaining several Middle East reporters in Baghdad and Istanbul, the *Monitor* continues its balanced coverage there.

Media Ethics

Although the term "media ethics" is often jokingly referred to as an oxymoron, in fact it is a well-established and well-engrained topic in the journalistic tradition (Alia 2004; Christians et al. 2008; Friend and Singer 2007; Good and Borden 2010; Patterson and Wilkins 2007; Zelizer and Allan 2002). Media "jump from hype to hype, driven by commercial rather than ethical considerations," Hanusch and Servaes (2010, 47) have argued, and just as many of us worry about business trumping trust, it behooves us to review the *Monitor*'s place in this discussion.

Highly respected journalism professor J. Herbert Altschull (1990, 357) defined ethics as "the study of the formation of moral values and of principles of right and wrong," conceiving of them in media terms as serving humanity rather than the journalist's own ends. Although journalism is mostly self-monitored, without an enforceable code of ethics, its practitioners are expected to operate within those put forth by the Society of Professional Journalists (SPJ), which deal with seeking truth and reporting it, minimizing harm, acting independently, and being accountable. As a means of remaining free of obligation to a person and/or the public, this assumes not taking favors and junkets, not having conflicts of interest, not plagiarizing, protecting confidential sources, and generally upholding concern for the truth. No better description could be drawn of *Monitor* journalists. The Poynter Institute lists seven core values guiding its publishing: accuracy, independence, interdependence, fairness, transparency, professional responsibility, and helpfulness.[11]

Rushworth M. Kidder, president and founder of The Institute for Global Ethics, who wrote a weekly *Perspectives* column on social issues and trends for the *Monitor* from 1983 to 1990, has as his institution's mission "To promote ethical behavior in individuals, and cultures of integrity in institutions and nations through research, public discourse, and practical action."[12] Here is a description of a course called Ethics of Journalism at Columbia University: "Students will deal with ethical issues that often arise in the practice of journalism. Those include verification of information, the relationship between your personal morality and journalistic decisions, issues brought up by competition and the ubiquity of news, and the impact the Internet has on forcing decisions within narrow time frames."

"With its motto of 'To injure no man but to bless all mankind,' the *Monitor* takes readers to the jungles of Southeast Asia as well as the parliaments of Europe, trying to help them understand the world outside their hometowns without the distortion of commercial or political aims," Donald R. Shanor (2003, 112) reminds us. "Its approach is based on the idea that when citizens have access to the truth, they can make the right decisions for themselves and society." From my *Monitor* files come a number of concrete examples: Concerns over journalistic scandals such as when Jason Blair of the *New York Times* was found fraudulent in 2003; "a growing culture of shamelessness" (5/29/03); Abu Ghraib tortures (9/27/04); media coverage of the dead "without offending the living" (1/19/05); ethical investing (1/24/05); manipulation of digital images (2/2/05); the Terri Schiavo right-to-die battle (4/1/05); Congressional corruption (12/12/05); controversial "memoirs" (1/18/06); when "gifts" become bribes (1/25/06); cloning (1/13/06); "virtual" identities (11/29/06); and, more recently, the release of the "Lockerbie bomber" (8/24/09).

"A while ago, I was quoted in *The Christian Science Monitor* about assisted suicide. The story, as originally written, then went on to claim that 84 percent supported the 'right to die' in a Pew Poll. The 84 percent figure actually referred to the right to refuse unwanted medical treatment, which the Pew Poll inaccurately called the right to die. Another, distinct question found that 46 percent supported legalizing assisted suicide, with 45 percent opposed," Wesley J. Smith (2006) reported in his blog, *Secondhand Smoke.* Then, he added, "I complained to the *CSM* about this (and blogged about it). The *CSM* editor investigated my complaint and issued a correction, which now runs with the story. Good for them. That's journalistic integrity."

CSM'S UNIQUENESS

Unique is unique—a stand-alone word that is all too often unnecessarily embellished. It certainly has application to *The Christian Science Monitor.*

"What Makes Us Unique?"

In the reception area of *CSM* headquarters is a sign asking just this question, the answer(s) appearing with the following descriptors:

- Commitment
- Hope
- Context
- Compassion
- Courage

Most amazing of all, of course, is the fact that *The Christian Science Monitor* was founded by Mary Baker Eddy in her 88th year and has lasted, evolving and experimenting, for more than a century. You may already know that it had the first news website to include audio, that it has been an early technological innovator, that it was the first news organization to send a reporter to cover the Iraq war specifically for a website, that Nelson Mandela read the *Monitor* during his years of imprisonment in South Africa and made it his goal, in 1990, to visit the Church that had sustained him, and that, as outlined here, it is the first newspaper to support a multiplatform format (i.e., CSMonitor.com, a 24/7 website; the *Daily New Briefing* via email; and *CSM Weekly*, in print). As demonstrated in Table 1.2, there is much more.

"How we differ" may be best described by editor Richard J. Cattani (1993), as he did when *The Christian Science Monitor* turned 85:

We have been from the start a classical newspaper in what we carry—economic, government, and cultural news, plus opinion and commentary. But our motive separates us: We are dedicated to the service of others; we don't seek power for its own sake. We look for the healing of ignorance, bigotry, injustice, rather than incite the wringing of hands. We affirm that society progresses despite often horrendous learning experiences; we do not fear that civilization is losing its way. We prefer to depict the family of man with our photos and illustrations rather than to reinforce our self-importance by promoting the elite who run things. Behind the commotion of events, we believe, is the stillness of God's creation.

Table 1.2
Uniqueness of *The Christian Science Monitor*

• The *Christian Science Monitor* is the first newspaper with a national audience to shift from a daily print format to a daily online publication that operates 24/7 (*Business Wire* 2008).

• *CSM* has published a "distinctive brand of non-hysterical journalism" on a nonprofit basis since 1908 (Beam 2005).

• *CSM* is "a paper with an absolutely sterling journalistic reputation" (Garfield 2005).

• The *Monitor* is a "longtime oasis of thoughtful, issue oriented, balanced journalism" (Gandleman 2009).

• *CSM* has brought its readers "a compassionate understanding of the world" for more than 100 years.[a]

• "*CSM* is an atypical publication in many ways: church-supported, small but loyal circulation base, minimal reliance on advertising. Add one more anomaly: Seven months after discontinuing its print edition, the *Monitor* is growing and thriving" (Edmonds 2009).

• The *Christian Science Monitor* has exemplary, respected foreign news coverage.

• *CSM* is included, as of March 30, 2010, among the Top 20 "Highest Rated American Newspapers" by *MondoTimes*, the worldwide news media directory.[b]

• The *Monitor* has been labeled the "bloggiest" newspaper online.

• *CSM* is "an essential source of international news and analysis" (Nichols and McChesney 2009).

• The *Christian Science Monitor* is "a global, multimedia news organization that specializes in thoughtful, humane reporting that helps readers understand the world" (Association for Library Collections and Technical Services 2010).

• *CSM*'s commentary section stands out for the wide range of voices it publishes.

• *CSM*, according to *Newsknife* (cited in Jarboe 2009) was one of the top six sources in Google News in February 2009, and Number 1 in terms of most appearances on the home page as a percentage of site total.

• The *Monitor* is the only major secular newspaper owned and operated by a church.

• *CSM* is the "the first major international newspaper to fully embrace that future [the Internet], allowing its reporters to publish news as it happens" (*Business Wire* 2008).

• The *Monitor* is listed as one of the world's most trusted news sources by NewsTrust.[c]

• *CSM*'s Jane Arraf is the longest-serving Western correspondent in Iraq (6/30/09, 1).

• The *Christian Science Monitor* is the only "elite" (among the *Los Angeles Times*, the *New York Times*, the *Wall Street Journal*, the *Washington Post*) nonprofit newspaper.

• The *Christian Science Monitor* is the only news organ that clearly lists its objective: "To injure no man, but to bless all mankind."

---

[a]http://abell.austincollege.edu/Abell/Elinfor/eresources/csm.html.

[b]http://www.mondotimes.com/rating/contentusa.html.

[c]http://newstrust.net/sources.

METHODOLOGY FOR THIS STUDY

As indicated earlier, my interest in this project began in the 1960s, while my desire to write a book about *The Christian Science Monitor*, as outlined in the Preface, dates to the 1980s. During all this time, an assemblage of clippings, samples, folders, and related resources threatened to take over my workspace. Additionally, while most of my material has come from my own original sources, it certainly has been helpful that the *Monitor* was cross-searchable on ProQuest[13] from 1908 to 1996.

Once the contract for this book was signed, cartons and crates and crates and cartons containing all my *Monitor* "stuff" required review and sorting. Working off a tentative table of contents, eventually most of the stacks of books, collections of interesting topics, and miscellany found a home.

Schedule

The date of October 7, 2009 was an important one, as I met with editor John Yemma to discuss my plan and ask a number of questions. From that day onward, he has had an open door policy going above and beyond what a researcher might hope. For issues where he couldn't help, Yemma put me in touch with various staff who could. This access, needless to say, has been invaluable.

Next, it was particularly helpful to be invited to attend several production meetings in November 2009. Working off agendas planning for future issues and topics, in all instances it was especially heartening to observe the participants' teamwork give-and-take. One such meeting, jokingly labeled in my notebook as "Pirates, Palin, Palestine," includes these descriptions about how it went: "collegial, smooth, professional, courteous, open to suggestions, pleased with results but flexible, forward-thinking."

Much preparation went into setting up interviews with *Monitor* staff. Far in advance, they were contacted informing them about my book, including a brief description of the table of contents and my monitoring of the *Monitor*, and inviting them to participate. For those in Boston, that involved offering a number of dates and times; for those elsewhere, a number of time slots were listed. This paragraph was also included: "Let me make it clear that, should we connect, the main purpose is for me to do information-gathering, and that anything you say will be held in confidence. Also, as part of a pattern established when I was my town correspondent to a weekly newspaper, I've found it helpful to let sources see anything about themselves. So, from the start, I have made it clear to John Yemma and others that the publisher will not get the ms. without approval by *Monitor* officials. While typically that might seem like a journalistic quirk, my purpose is to facilitate the telling of your story, so my bias will be clearly laid out."

Responses came back so fast it was like instant messaging. My first thought was that it was because of their profession—news people stay right on top of the news, and are quick to respond. But, as time went on, I realized that this was also part of the general overlay of the *Monitor* newsroom: These folks are organized, yes, but they are also very kind and considerate. Practically everyone agreed, and some who chose not to be interviewed were still polite enough to let me know. It helped, it must be added, to find out that John Yemma had alerted everyone to my project.

The first wave of interviews began in January 2010. As evidenced in Appendix 4, "CSM Interview Schedule," they included 36 in-person interviews, 24 by telephone (indicated by "T"), and one, although we had previously met, by email—allowing 61 conversations in all. Working off an unstructured outline, making it clear that nothing was being tape recorded, the interviews were deliberately conversational and open-ended. Those that took place in the newsroom were in a small conference room, with interviewees sitting by a door that they could close (most did), and the phone calls were mostly without interruptions. Although I had suggested that interviews might take about 15 to 20 minutes, in fact none was that brief and most went at least double that time—there just seemed so much to share. In every instance, at least from my point of view, the discussions were so lively and informative that it was wrenching to quit.

As promised, then, each interview was transcribed and sent on to each person for approval, asking him or her to feel free to make changes. Because so many are professional editors, there were, in fact, a number of tidbits that got maneuvered—such as dates when they joined *CSM*, job titles, maybe misinterpretations on what their job entailed, but fortunately no serious issues were raised. When you hear their narratives throughout this volume, in other words, you will know that they are *real*. Hopefully, their verbatim comments, as *Monitor* staff, add to the credibility of this whole story.

Content Analyses of the *Weekly Edition* and *DNB*

Simultaneously, wanting to be aware of what was being produced during *CSM*'s first year, but knowing that the Web is difficult to deconstruct, my choice was to perform content analyses of both the-*Weekly Edition* and the *Daily News Briefing* (*DNB*). Those results will be apparent throughout this book.

LITERATURE REVIEW

In 1958, highly respected editor Erwin D. Canham published the groundbreaking *Commitment to Freedom: The Story of The Christian Science Monitor*, which, to date, is the most comprehensive, authoritative account of the newspaper's first 50 years. Admittedly "non-neutral," it traces Mary Baker Eddy's decisions and designs for a daily publication, reactions to events ranging from the Great Depression to two world wars and the Cold War—along with the development of standards for coverage from a Christian Science perspective, a review of valuable staff, an accounting of business practices, and a general assessment of its role in field of journalism. You will see it cited frequently here.

To commemorate the *Monitor*'s 75th anniversary, the Christian Science Publishing Society (CSPS) released *Understanding Our Century*. In the introduction, then editor-in-chief Earl W. Foell (Nenneman 1984, ix) declared, "What this paper seeks to give you each day is the writing of *authorities* in all fields who *select* for you what is important to know and understand out of all that morass of news. We aim for results that will be *useful* to each of you." Explaining that its writers undertake "problem-solving journalism," this helps explain its approach: "The *Monitor* refuses to see man as a victim of his environment. We believe that men and women have the mental and spiritual resources to gain dominion over what are portrayed as threats from economic forces, resource shortages, criminal or selfish human nature, and a physically hazardous universe" (p. x). Foell then outlines some fundamental influences in news coverage: "Education—the very bedrock of mankind's progress—the ability to pass on both knowledge and values"; "The role of individual freedom in impelling progress"; "The impact of thought on history—the power of ideas that underlie the actions we perceive as overt news"; and "The spiritual factors that underlie both thought and action" (Ibid.)

Earl W. Foell and Richard A. Nenneman, managing editor of *The Christian Science Monitor,* co-edited a 1986 book, *How Peace Came to the World.* Based on a contest the newspaper ran encouraging readers to think ahead 25 years, it drew on some of the best answers, in 1,300 essays, to these two questions: (1) Is the situation hopeless? (2) Are those behaviorists who say that humans are a warring species whose territorial instincts or aggressive nature is a genetic trait correct? Offering no prize money, just the satisfaction of seeing one's ideas published, entrants came from five continents, numerous different languages, and an incredible range of demographic profiles.

Based on a series of interviews that *The Christian Science Monitor* ran between September, 1986 and April, 1987 with 22 leading thinkers, Rushworth Kidder's *An Agenda for the 21st Century* (1987) addresses what would be the major issues mankind would face. "This is a challenging mandate," then editor Katherine Fanning stated, adding,

Over the years it has led this newspaper not only to report the news of the day but to promote understanding—between races, between nations, between haves and have-nots, between generations, and now between centuries. It has encouraged us to present current events with courage, clarity, and compassion, striving to be as objective as possible and to consider the background surrounding an event, the developing trends, and the implications for the future. And it has cause us to focus on highlighting possible solutions to world problems (p. x).

Not necessarily in order of priority, these items emerged as the most vital: The threat of nuclear annihilation; the danger of overpopulation; degradation of the global environment; the gap between the developing and the industrial worlds; the need for fundamental restructuring of educational systems; and the breakdown of public and private morality (p. 195).

In 1988, CSPS produced *The First 80 Years: The Christian Science Monitor 1908–1988*, which was mainly a collection of headlines. On November 25, 1998, the 90th anniversary edition, reiterated the *Monitor*'s genesis as a non-sensational alternative and included some articles reviewing the past nine decades. Ten years later, the November 25, 2008 issue had a special pull-out section titled "Our First Century," highlighted by a front page article by David T. Cook commenting how, "It is a story rich in courage, devotion, and experimentation," along with "A note from the editor" (John Yemma) focusing on the future, a retrospective on staff (by Roderick Nordell), and photos from the *Monitor* timeline. Otherwise, only a small booklet, "Engaging with *The Christian Science Monitor*," was published for the centenary. Consisting of previous published articles—mostly in the *Christian Science Sentinel* and the *Christian Science Journal*, it was introduced by Mary Metzner Trammell, editor-in-chief of CSPS, with "*The Christian Science Monitor*: An idea that advances humanity." Her inspirational opening includes histories, perspectives, and an explanation for how the motto "First the blade, then the ear, then the full grain in the ear" continues, promising "continually unfolding progress for the *Monitor* as an idea in Mind" (p. 10). Trammell elucidates:

Early on, Mary Baker Eddy proposed this American Standard Bible quote from Mark 4:28 as the *Monitor*'s motto. To her, this parable of Jesus was prophetic of the ultimate prosperity and productivity she expected the newspaper to enjoy, despite all the predictions to the contrary ... The *Monitor*, she knew, was destined to come to full fruition as naturally as seeds sprout—and eventually yield a crop of grain.

Oddly, there have been very few external *Christian Science Monitor*–related publications, these two books from the 1990s being the only ones:

1. Susan Bridge's *Monitoring the News: The Brilliant Launch and Sudden Collapse of* The Monitor *Channel* (1988) reconstructs the creation, in 1991, and demise, in 1992, of *CSM*'s experiment in television. Seeing the medium as a natural, visual extension of what CSPS was producing in print and wanting to reach a wider audience, the producers ensured that the design (a CNN-type global in-depth news and public information channel) and quality were outstanding; yet, when a bitter struggle for control between leaders and administrators ensued, the project became untenable. It is an invaluable case study of media economics and realities—a mission gone awry. Media critic Ken Auletta of the *New Yorker* gave it this review: "This engrossing book is what the *Monitor Channel* promised to be: fair-minded, comprehensive, and scrupulous. In this obituary of a doomed new experiment." "In the aftermath of the *Monitor Channel*'s collapse, a *Rashomon*-like grab-bag of competing explanations were offered," Bridge (p. xvi) noted; "perhaps the problem had been naiveté about the cable fraternity, or wild overspending, or a fatal confusion about corporate mission, or enemies within and without, or bad timing with respect to the economy. Most disheartening were the pronouncements from some sophisticated observers that, given the structure of information markets, the undertaking had been impossible from the outset."

2. Lawrence N. Strout's *Covering McCarthyism: How The Christian Science Monitor Handled Joseph R. McCarthy, 1950–1954* (1999), referring to the senator from Wisconsin who in the late 1940s and early 1950s waged a witch-hunt campaign to disclose Communists, particularly in the State Department, Hollywood (Fuller, 1996), and the media—claiming and reasoning by default that they were unpatriotic, disloyal, subversive, and therefore treasonous—offers a telling insight into the newspaper's internal workings. Focusing on the *Monitor*'s coverage from McCarthy's Lincoln Day speech (February 9, 1950) through his eventual censure by the U.S. Senate (December 2, 1954) through the papers of reporter Richard L. Strout, he credited it as being an early, consistent critic of McCarthy. Despite its conservative leanings, he argues, the newspaper should be credited as "one of the early and consistent critics" of McCarthyism.

Additionally, although they will not identify *CSM* per se, since it is one of many media organizations they are investigating to see changes "as they 'go digital' and confront both the technological and economic challenges that are bound up in that transformation," Riley and Usher (work in progress) have posited these research questions: (1) What were the big decisions—new structures and/or goals—that emerged from the strategic discussions about the transformation of the media environment, and what organizational changes that would be deemed necessary to achieve those goals?; (2) What culture changes are necessary to support these new structures and goals and how are they articulated?; (3) How does collaboration within each organization influence the process of organizational change (e.g., can superior collaboration make it faster?)?; (4) How do digital media get incorporated into the traditional news operation? (Riley, email correspondence 2/23/10).

Over the years, I have had a number of publications (Fuller 1988b, 1991, 2010a) and presentations about how *The Christian Science Monitor* has dealt with a number of issues, including terrorism (Fuller 1988a), Tiananmen (Fuller 1988c), the 1991 Soviet coup (Fuller 1992), the O. J. Simpson trial (Fuller 1997), Islamic perspectives of 9/11 (Fuller 2002), homosexuality (Fuller 2004a), coverage of women (Fuller 2004b), the Beijing Olympic torch (2009), and the tsunami of 2004 (2010b)—many shared with, and acknowledged for cooperation on, staff and writers of the newspaper.

By contrast, there have been a number of books about *The New York Times* (Talese 1969; Tifft and Jones 1999; Frankel 2000; Gelb 2004; Mnookin 2005), and Halberstam's *The Powers That Be* (1979/2000) covered both *The Los Angeles Times* and *The Washington Post*, the latter also part of memoirs by Ben Bradlee (1995) and Katharine Graham (1997). Jerry M. Rosenberg (1982) and Lloyd Wendt's (1984) studies of *The Wall Street Journal*, as well as Allen Neuharth's (1989) description of how he masterminded *USA Today*, are clearly dated.

Other literature reviews that you will see here include media ethics, biographies about Mary Baker Eddy, journalistic problems and proposed solutions, and more.

THE WEB, THE WEEKLY, AND *DNB*

Since they form the essence of *The Christian Science Monitor*'s evolution to date, let me familiarize you with the products that determine the title to this introductory chapter: CSMonitor.com, a 24/7 website; *Daily New Briefing*, via email; and *CSM Weekly*, in print.

CSMonitor.com

The *Monitor* had its website up and running in 1996, one of the first newspapers to do so. This treeless version was very appealing, on many levels. "*Monitor* developing an electronic edition to extend reach" reads an article (10/18/95, 3) signed simply by "A Staff Writer," from my files. With the vocabulary of personal computers, the Internet's World Wide Web, online publishing, text and graphics, and underscoring the notion of opportunity, it is almost worth framing. Ditto for a document titled "A user's guide to the e-Monitor" (Austin 1998), introducing the online version with discussions on how to navigate, join a *Monitor* forum, link to special sites, search archives back to 1980, solve an interactive cross-word puzzle, take a weekly news quiz, "follow breaking news by tapping into wire-service updates," read first chapters of reviewed books, and enjoy columns such as *Web Women, Under the Hood* (about the Web), *Cyberview, Site Reviews,* and *Computers for the Rest of Us.*

Additionally, there was information on what the reader would need to participate in the e-*Monitor*: a personal computer (PC) or Power Mac, a modem with at least 28.8 kilobits per second capability, a Web browser (such as were available free [!] from Netscape or Microsoft), and an Internet account. Rounding it all off was a helpful glossary of e-terms whose definitions have not changed but that have become part of common parlance.

Also almost quaint, just nearly a decade later, is the story of how stories get into the newspaper: Lane Hartill's (2001) account that, to this day, hangs in the reception area of *CSM*'s Boston headquarters. Without repeating all the steps, the idea is pointing out how it got from its origin to your front step. Asking who decides to feature what story in the first place—"gatekeepers"—we see the interplay between various departments: national and international news editors (who fact-check, edit, and write stories, along with deciding headlines and photo captions), photography staff (who select images from archives of more than a million possibilities), art department staff (who focus on creating maps and illustrations), layout department staff (who design and arrange text, photos, arts, and graphics), and copy editors (who double-check everything before it goes to press). Recall: as long as a decade ago, *The Christian Science Monitor* was printed in plants near Boston, Chicago, and San Francisco, who received digital files from the *Monitor*'s pre-press division in four colors that could combine to create hues for what would be printed: blue, magenta red, yellow, and black. When ready, the newspapers were sorted and bagged according to zip codes, trucked to 39 U.S. cities, dropped off at 325 processing centers, then mailed.

How Far the *Monitor*—and Journalism—Have Evolved

Even though research actually took place three years before it began, the decision by CSPS to depend on the website 24/7 did not materialize until April 12, 2009. Already drawing some 1.8 million visitors per month, the change to all-online nevertheless meant the following: original reporting on global news and events seven days a week; continuously updated stories; global conversations between readers and *Monitor* staff; and links to valuable content elsewhere on the Web.

When you log onto CSMonitor.com, you will find the familiar wide range of coverage: World, USA, Commentary, Money, Environment, Innovation, Science, The Culture (Arts, Movies, Music, Family, and Gardening), Books, Photos of the Day, a daily cartoon, *CSM* blogs, and a dazzling enough array to keep you informed and entertained enough to want to return often.

The multimedia Web section[14] is wide ranging, many including audio components, some parts of podcasts, slideshows (e.g., Chile's earthquake, iTunes' top 25 most downloaded songs, the Vancouver Olympic Games), videos (e.g., Bollywood, Arlington Cemetery, rape in the Congo, Apollo 11, Columbian drug submarines, mountain gorillas), and much more. One of the best known and heavily anticipated multimedia sections is the *Monitor Breakfast.* Here is a sampling of some recent postings: A February 23, 2010 *Monitor Books* podcast, including an interview with "Little Bee" by Chris Cleave; "Iran arrests top Sunni militant Abdolmalek Rigi" (Scott Peterson and Pat Murphy); "Obama as campaigner in chief: Will his record improve?" (David Cook and Linda Feldmann); "White House forecast: No roaring economic recovery in 2010" (Mark Trumbull and Pat Murphy); and "Q&A: Why the Marjah offensive matters," by Ben Arnoldy and Pat Murphy.

The Christian Science Monitor Weekly

There had long been discussion about *CSM*'s producing a weekly—perhaps as a supplement—but no one could have predicted the amazing success of what eventually became this 48-page glossy. Maybe part of the reason for its strong reception is that the weekly always sports an eye-catching cover and title article, is printed on high-quality paper, has gorgeous photography and lots of charts and graphs, includes regular and guest contributors, and content-wise has something for everyone.

"A weekly review of global news and ideas," it premiered April 12, 2009, consisting of the following sections: *Dispatches from All Over, World in Brief, People Making a Difference* (PMAD), *Decoder, Monitor Breakfast* interviews, *USA*, *Briefing*, *In Pictures*, *Editorials*, *Readers Write*, *Inklings*, *Opinion/Commentary*, *Money*, *Travel*, *Innovation*, *Environment*, *Culture*, *Home Forum*, *Christian Science Perspective*, *Special Reports and Series*, and *Open Source*. Albeit open to evolving changes, here are brief descriptions of those items:

- *Dispatches from All Over:* Global snapshots
- *World in Brief:* Africa, Americas, Asia, Europe, Latin America, Middle East, United States
- *People Making a Difference:* The idea for PMAD goes back far into *Monitor* history and its goal of presenting solution-oriented journalism, according to Gregory Lamb (email 4/12/10). "Several years ago then-Editor Richard Bergenheim asked the staff to include more stories about people making a difference, though they were not labeled as such." Its columns have included people involved with urban youths; Thai human rights activists; a Finn musician working with special needs students; orphanage builders in South Africa; ecologists at Yellowstone; Pakistani women's rights activists; Sri Lankan soldiers' mothers; a filmmaker and founder of Peace One Day; Haitian student helpers; deforestation fighters in Paraguay; the creator of Scholars at Risk; War Kids Relief; the founder of Create for a Cause (Rwandan clothes); Tibetan exiles helping orphans; Mongolian nomads; a pastor who took homeless men into his church; a UNESCO cultural expert saving museums; a builder of schools and trust in Afghanistan; the starter of a sewing co-op for Rio's poor; a Burmese doctor helping refugees; a former prisoner in North Korea building a university there; the "mother of the street" for the homeless in Kansas City, MO; volunteers for Mentoring Today (juvenile lockups); Interfaith Youth Core; Flow Fund Circle; Friends of the Urban Forest; South Africans bringing food and friendship to refugees; and so many more. Highlighting positive actions by people around the world, PMAD demonstrates what a single person can do to help others.
- *World:* 2009 and 2010 coverage included wide-ranging items such as U.S. outreach to Iran; Northern Ireland's full-court press for peace; the Taliban; South African vote; Japan's "exam hell"; Brazilian stimulus; Ecuadorian leadership; Berlin schools; civility in Iraq; journalists targeted in Russia; Dubai's declining glitz; Nordic biker gangs; Rwanda's rise; the Pope's pilgrimage; African immigrants in Italy; Hamas; Mexico's war on drugs; Syria as a power broker; Sri Lanka's Tamils after Tigers; North Korean threat; Islamist battling for Somalia; Jordan's outsized role; Tiananmen legacy of boldness; Colombia's FARC rebels; Lebanon's titanic vote; tourism in Athens; Cuban embargo; hope for Burundi; India's mandate; Afghans encouraging tourism; Iran's nuclear ambitions; Kenyan exposé; Swedish vice law; new strategies in the Indian Ocean;

Uganda's Rural Development for girls; Kyrgyzstan's opium industry; surfing for brides in Turkey; Honduran coup; Kenyan youths drawn to Jihad; the Tel Aviv "bubble"; Thailand's concerns about blogs; Hezbollah; Argentina's pampas; Peruvian earthquake recovery; lessons on opium in Colombia; a Malawian going to Phillips Exeter; Israeli settlements; France on religion; a Moscow building boom; China's auto industry; unease at the Hungary-Austria border; Palestinian television airing satire; UK youths; Himalayan climate changes; Burma's junta; strongmen in Latin America; Egypt's Muslim Brotherhood; Al Qaeda in West Africa; organic coffee growers piracy; Haiti's earthquake; Japanese whaling; human trafficking; the Greek debt crisis; what Iceland offers; Chile's earthquake; a turning point for Sudan, and many more examples.

- *Cover story*: Beginning April 12, 2009, cover stories included these topics: "The new economy: Ten ways it will look different"; "Galapagos; Obama's mark"; "Quality of life in Iraq"; "Brain boosters: Smart pills?"; "Suburbia: After the mall"; "Staying close to home"; "Pirates, Inc."; "Pakistan: The Taliban"; "Families remix: How recession is reshaping the family"; "Crossfire towns: Drug war violence in Mexico"; "Future of cars"; "American resolve"; "Refugees in America: Mary Wiltenburg, *To be a refugee in America*"; "Lap of luxury" (pets); "China's green revolution"; "Who's shaping the new GOP?"; "Teaching with less"; "Privacy"; "One in 10 million" (social entrepreneurs); "The most trusted faces in news" (political comedy); "Who's moving to the West Bank?"; "Washington's real power brokers"; "The future of war"; "Healthcare: A global survey"; "Berlin Wall"; "Star Trek" (milestones in space); "Risky business: Driving while distracted"; "Point man: Secretary of Defense Robert M. Gates"; "Cities on the rise" (Seattle; Fort Collins, CO; Huntsville, AL; Houston; Boston); "How good is that charity?"; "Iran's waning influence"; "The climate of opinion"; "Behind the veil"; "The e-reader"; "6 ideas that will shape the world"; "Follow the guns"; "The Obama doctrine"; "Africa's continental divide"; "The new cyber spies"; "2010 Winter Olympics"; "Marriage & fidelity"; "Who will switch on American jobs?"; "A new Iraq comes of age"; "United States of anger"; "Finding them homes: Adoption"; "The invisible wars"; "Religion in America"; "Fans or fanatics?"; and "Beyond the bomb."
- *Spotlight*: Highlighted issues
- *Decoder*: by Peter Grier; explains Washington, D.C. (see Chapter 3)
- *Monitor Breakfast*: interviews for this study included this impressive list: Harry Reid, Senate majority leader; Eric Cantor, House Republican whip; Mark Zandi, Economy.com chief economist; Nancy Pelosi, House speaker; Andrew Kohut, director of the Pew Research Center for the People and the Press; Ray Lahood, transportation secretary; Janet Napolitano, homeland security secretary; Haley Barbour, governor of Mississippi; Steny Hoyer, House

majority leader; Arne Duncan, education secretary; Rahm Emanuel, White House chief of staff; Thomas Donohue, U.S. Chamber of Commerce president; John Danforth, UN ambassador; Madeleine Albright, the first U.S. female secretary of state; Andrew Kohut, director of the Global Attitudes Project; John Boehner, House minority leader; Ed Goeas and Celinda Lake, political strategists; Bill McInturff, Republican pollster and strategist; Richard Trumka, AFL-CIO president-elect; Susan Rice, U.S. ambassador to the UN; Karen Ignagni, health insurance industry leader (AHIP); Carl Levin, Senate Armed Services Committee chairman; Nancy Leamond and John Rother, AARP executives; Christina Romer, chair of the President's Council of Economic Advisors; Mike Huckabee; Carter Roberts, president and CEO of the World Wildlife Fund; Mark Zandi, chief economist and co-founder of Economy.com; Duncan McNabb, U.S. Transportation Command; Ed Goeas and Celinda Lake, Battleground Poll; Lee Hamilton, national security expert; Peter Brown, Quinnipiac University Polling Institute; Ray Lahood, transportation secretary; Christina Romer, Obama economic adviser; Stanley Greenberg, CEO of Greenberg Quinlan Rosner Research; Newt Gingrich and Bill McInturff, Republican strategists; Ron Kirk, U.S. trade representative; John Potter, postmaster general; Mitch Daniels, Indiana governor; and James Carville and Stanley Greenberg, Democratic strategists.

- *USA*: Articles have included coverage on "Regular Joe" (Biden); "Obama's plan to 'tax the rich'"; "Columbine: 10 years after"; "Bailout money"; "The $11.3 trillion blueprint for recovery"; "US, Pakistan build military ties"; "New Orleans asks: 'What recession?'"; "A rust belt city strives to shrink its way to success" (Youngstown, Ohio); "Janet Napolitano, master multitasker"; "The culture wars fire up" (e.g., gay marriage, abortion); "Why GED classes are full"; "Who wins, who loses in GM bankruptcy"; "NASA's new breed of astronaut"; "Ranks of atheists grow"; "Healthcare's word cops"; "Can Guantanamo close on time?"; "State of diversity on the courts"; "Why music piracy is cooling off"; "New front in fight against child porn"; "Are higher taxes inevitable?"; "Demand on VA grows" (veterans); "Websites for teen policy wonks"; "Why do cities want the Olympics?"; "How schools aim to handle swine flu"; "What lesson Massachusetts holds for US health reform"; "Long 'to do' list for US parks chief" (Jonathan Jarvis); "Cheat sheet for holiday airfares"; "Is the stimulus doing the job?"; "US Muslims feel new heat"; "Medical pot gains momentum"; "States struggle with foreclosure fraud"; "Is it free speech or a violation?"; "Lessons from 'climategate'"; "Catholics face moral crisis on healthcare" (abortion); "New immigration battle gears up"; "Quiet stories of 2009 that are altering the world"; "Senate vs. House healthcare bills"; "A trillion-dollar political football" (national debt); "GOP and 'tea party'"; "Super Bowl battle"; "Poverty's new face: Suburbs"; "Florida Keys in peril"; "Great Lakes under threat from invader" (Asian carp);

"First lady takes on child obesity"; "Cutting healthcare's costs"; "The candy machine just sold me an iPod"; "For jobless, online friends can be lifelines"; "For religion, against intelligent design" (Francisco Ayala); "Obama's reach for US oil"; "An Internet-service sweepstakes."

- *Briefing*: Background information
- "*In pictures*": photo spreads
- *Editorials*: The *Monitor's* views
- *Readers Write*: Reactions to CSM content, especially editorials
- *Inklings*: Cartoons
- *Opinion/Commentary*: highlighted by regular contributors John Hughes and Walter Rodgers, this section also encourages dichotomous views on open-ended subjects and includes brief biographical data on writers. Op-Ed guidelines for *CSM*[15] are specific: 750 words or less, exclusive to *The Christian Science Monitor*, and completed submissions rather than queries.
- *Money*: In addition to David R. Francis's *Economics Scene*, here are some examples of *CSM's* financial reportage: CEO pay, (un)retirement, financial risk management, green-power premiums, recessionistas (fashion), ethics, the 40-something intern, job creation, career reinvention, solar shakeout, job searches, selling ecoluxe, public service, ethnic malls, world trade, organic products, MBAs, housing, financial innovation, the corner store, charitable giving, learning from crises, smart shoppers, Latinos building credit, aiding the poor, aid to Haiti, globalization, real estate, "Gitmo," corporate money for campaigns, and American workers for Indian firms.
- *Travel*
- *Innovation*: Includes *Horizons: Frontiers of Science and Technology*, and has tackled such subjects as "A wearable web"; "Why 'more pixels!' doesn't mean better pix"; "Segway king's next move"; "Wi-Fi hits the highway"; "What's the carbon footprint of e-mail spam?"; "High hopes for high speed"; "As recession lingers, cellphones take over"; "Motion's future at our fingertips" (Accele-Glove); "Microsoft's Project Natal"; "Sony's motion controller"; "Nintendo's Wii Motion Plus"; "In China, Web censorship"; "In apes' giggles, scientists find important evolutionary clue"; "Computer program can crack your Social Security number"; "Micro-volunteers phone it in"; "The future of file sharing"; "Bike sharing that would create energy, and get you a bus pass"; "A plan to put a Kindle in every backpack"; "Internet use in Asia and Africa set to soar"; "Twitter-only sales on rise"; "US Marines ban popular social-networking websites"; "Rise of the Franken Tablet" (PC screens on outside); "Social media, social impact" ("Twestival" fundraising); "Wikipedia blows past 3 million English articles"; "How smiley faces can save energy"; "Facebook roars past the 3000 million mark"; "Gaming goes Hollywood"; "Taking aim at energy-sucking TVs"; "A refresher on a free calling tool" (Skype); "Why web widgets will invade your TV"; "What's hot on iPhone?

Books, books, books!"; "Oxford's word of the year: 'unfriend'"; "How many words pass your eyes and ears each day?" (34 gigabytes of data and 1000,000 words per day); "E-books: The compatibility conundrum"; and many other techy topics.

- *Environment*: Draws on Earthtalk (ET) from the e-magazine and GreenStuff (GS) eco-news and discoveries and has articles such as "China's green leap forward"; "Guitars: Makers looking for more sustainable woods"; "Zoos aim to help endangered species survive"; "Cheetahs: Conservationists help an endangered cat"; "Gutters: Environmentally friendly replacements"; "Asteroids didn't do in the dinosaurs?"; "Fossil find may be missing link to seal, sea lion, walrus"; "Critical turning point can trigger abrupt climate change"; "Scientists find low-energy ecosystems for carbon dioxide"; "Plastics made by microbes"; "Hybrid cars"; "Bioelectricity versus biofuels"; "Natural pesticides"; "Sunspots' impact on climate change"; "Guilt-free sushi"; "Train travel: High-speed rail will decrease CO2 emissions"; "Sunrise for solar heat power"; "From pest to pesto"; "Renewable energy"; "A major price drop for solar panels"; "National parks face new threats"; "Tuna's plight is a global problem"; "Rain forests: Their future"; "Oil spills poison the Red Sea"; "The secret life of ancient trees" (Vietnam); "Researchers put a price tag on the benefits of coral reefs"; "Outdoor cats are easy prey for coyotes"; "Melting of Mt. Kilimanjaro glaciers is accelerating"; "Fish farms clean up"; "The big cats' best friend" (Ann Van Dyk's Cheetah Centre in DeWildt, South Africa); and "Conservatives embrace God and green."
- *Culture*: Covers arts, movies, music, books, and more and has included a prison drama in Lebanon, WebTV, love poetry, photo exhibits, multimedia, sculptors, Tony and Grammy awards, architectural designs, art galleries, immigrant actors, televised depictions, museum openings, Internet culture, photojournalism, blogs and social networks, star authors, orchestras, role-playing games, videos and video artists, foreign art, folk art, and drama directors along with *Monitor* picks.
- *Home Forum*: Ruth Walker's grammar blog *Verbal Energy* and general ideas
- *Christian Science Perspective*: Religious prayer
- *Special Reports and Series*
- *Open Source*: Beginning September 9, 2009, editor John Yemma included his own column with discussions such as "Great question. Glad you asked" (live town meetings versus those "appropriated by politicians, pitchmen, and business managers to put a gloss of 'we the people' on what is really a spin session,"); "Measuring up online" (his formula: "Metrics + Grain of Salt = Somewhat Useful Information"); "The millennial generation"; "The modern-day myth of fame"; "Politics: Done right, it's a strange sport"; "Bumbling through history"; and, on April 12, 2010, "One year into weekly print, how'd we do?"

In addition, the *Weekly Edition* includes sections on *How the World Press Views America*, a crossword puzzle, *6 Picks by Monitor Staff*, and some advertising. Numerous stories from *CSM* weekly are cited here. From the start, plans for it included the following:

1. Each issue's cover story will feature an in-depth look at a key global issue or trend;
2. Each issue will go beyond the sound bites and superficial analysis to provide clarity and context on crucial issues and will arrive for weekend reading, when readers have more time for thoughtful, longer-form stories;
3. Each issue will be filled with unique stories and perspectives that appear only in the weekly edition, all aiming to live up to the *Monitor*'s mission, articulated by its founder, Mary Baker Eddy: "To injure no man, but to bless all mankind";
4. Each issue will feature a signature *Monitor* article, "People Making a Difference";
5. A hefty four-page editorial and opinion section provides reasoned, positive, unconventional approaches to addressing and solving the issues of the day;
6. The *Monitor* has always been a newspaper for the home, and had a signature feature, "The Home Forum"—a lively collection of essays and other features about life, love, families, and the world that aims to speak directly to the hearts of readers;
7. Sometimes during a crisis or fast-moving global story, it's hard to step back and gain the perspective needed to understand what's really going on. The *Monitor* aims to provide just such a refuge for thoughtful, context-filled reporting and analysis, so readers can truly understand the signs of the times;
8. Each week's best photos from around the world, or a photo essay by a staff photographer or freelancer;
9. The *Monitor*'s coverage of the US begins with a look at the crucial issues and challenges in the nation's capital—and includes highlights of *Monitor*-sponsored breakfast sessions with key Washington players;
10. Many US news organizations are closing foreign bureaus and focusing mostly on local events. But in an ever-more globalizing world, what happens in Beijing and Nairobi increasingly affects people in Boston and Seattle. So, the *Monitor* continues to provide thoughtful, in-depth reporting about the places and people that matter;
11. The *Monitor*'s robust website contains many blogs and Web-only features. The weekly *Web Watch* section highlights the best of the blogs and web packages on the *Monitor*'s site and elsewhere on the Internet;
12. It may be the biggest issue of our time—how mankind interacts with the planet. The *Monitor* covers it with a bias toward hope and an expectation of finding solutions. Also, a regular feature of many *Monitor* stories will be "Why it Matters"—a brief summary of how that story connects to the lives of readers;

13. Big ideas can change the world. The *Monitor* looks at technology and tech trends with an eye toward how these innovations can improve lives around the globe.

Importantly, insightfully, and typically, it is only on the editorial page of the weekly that *The Christian Science Monitor* logo appears, and under it, "Founded in 1908 by Mary Baker Eddy," and under that: "First the blade, then the ear, then the full grain in the ear." Then come personnel listings: "Editor, John Yemma; Managing editor, Marshall Ingwerson; Senior editor, David Cook; Chief editorial writer, Clayton Jones; Managing publisher, Jonathan Wells, and then members of the Christian Science Publishing Society: Mary Trammell, editor in chief; Michael Pabst, Scott Preller, and Judy Wolff, Board of Trustees; and Lyon Osborn, manager. Owen Thomas is deputy editor, Clayton Collins editor of *CSM*'s *Weekly Edition.*"

Daily News Briefing (DNB)

About a month into the *Monitor*'s decision to discontinue its daily print edition—April 27, 2009—it launched a print summary of the day's news. CSPS wanted to give readers a publication they could print out that would be somewhat similar to, if a smaller version of, a traditional newspaper—delivered as a PDF via email. Hence, the *Daily News Briefing* (*DNB*) was born. Featuring abridged versions of timely stories from the *Monitor*'s website, many with notes referencing its web address for more coverage, it debuted May 1, 2009 under the leadership of Ross Atkin at a cost of roughly $70,000 per year. A typical example includes an original column from *Monitor* editors, a handful of condensed top stories, a series of news briefs compiled from wire reports, a "*Monitor*'s View" editorial, and a Christian Science article billed as "a useful tool for prayerfully supporting the world." Delivered by Adobe Acrobat to subscribers paying $5.75 per month (21 issues), it is available weekdays by 5 a.m. EST, with reminders sent by email with appropriate links. Easily printable, the idea behind each three-page *DNB* was to provide a unique service for those wanting highlights of *Monitor* journalism—"an intelligence report for readers who care about the world." But it was an experiment, and no one could have predicted that a year later there would be 3,000 subscribers downloading Monday through Friday issues with an original column by the editors, an abridged capsule of key news stories, a daily prayer, and top headlines. If the idea is to keep in touch with the world, circulation marketing director Patty Collinsworth has noted (2/25/10), "It has morphed beyond its genesis."

As a news organization operated by a trusteeship, then, CSPS at this point is committed to continuing to produce three very different editions—CSMonitor.com, the 24/7 website; the *Daily New Briefing* via email; and *CSM Weekly*, in print. Continuing to work on a formula of explanatory journalism, with a vision, a mission, dedicated people, and built-in safeguards according to its structure, *The Christian Science Monitor* you will soon see is indeed a unique publishing phenomenon.

Chapter 2

"Connecting the Global Dots": Backstory

The object of The Monitor *is to injure no man, but to bless all mankind.*

—Mary Baker Eddy, November 25, 1908

This chapter is titled "Backstory," but it could just as well have been called "Backgrounding," as thorough research has been a signature for *Monitor* correspondents and copyeditors over its 100-plus year history. It begins with a look at journalism in the twenty-first century and then discusses Mary Baker Eddy (MBE) and Christian Science, the Christian Science Publishing Society (CSPS), the Christian Science perspective, and *The Christian Science Monitor* in its latest state of evolution and experiment.

JOURNALISM IN THE TWENTY-FIRST CENTURY

The newspaper is dead. You can read all about it online, blog by blog, where the digital gloom over the death of an industry often veils, if thinly, a pallid glee. The Newspaper Death Watch, a Web site, even has a column titled "R.I.P."

—Jill Lepore (2009, 68)

Journalism is collapsing, and with it comes the more serious threat in our lifetimes to self-government and the rule of law as it has been understood here in the United States.

—Nichols and McChesney (2009)

It's the worst of times for the newspaper industry, and it's not the best time, either, for finding solutions amid a crisis of downsizings, bankruptcies, and closings.

—Alexandra Marks (2009)

Although newspapers—actually newsletters, or news books actually date to the sixteenth century, when the *Boston News-Letter* appeared on April 24, 1704 the role of newspapers as a medium for news began—going through periods of high circulation (peaking in 1988); consolidation; chain ownership; alternative, foreign-language, and minority models; and, more recently, slipping from public favor in print format. In terms of that history, here are some dates:

1847   *The Chicago Tribune* is founded by James Kelly, John E. Wheeler, and Joseph K. C. Forrest

1851   Henry Raymond founds the *New York Times*

1872   *The Boston Globe* is founded by six businessmen, led by Eben Jordan

1877   *The Washington Post* is first published

1881   *The Los Angeles Times* is established

1889   Charles Dow and Edward Jones starts the *Wall Street Journal*

1908   Mary Baker Eddy founds *The Christian Science Monitor*

1919   Joseph Patterson and Robert McCormick start the *New York Daily News*

1955   Various New York literati begin the *Village Voice*

1967   Jim Michaels's *Advocate*, the first gay newspaper, is started

1983   Allen Neuharth founds *USA Today*

Journalism, which involves the business of news in print, broadcast, and various technological forms, also has its roots in America's colonial past, Benjamin Harris's *Publick Occurrences Both Forreign and Domestick* of 1690 being an early example of press independence from governmental control and censorship. The early days of journalism in the United States are marked by four distinct periods: "The colonial era, partisan/Federalist period, penny press (Benjamin Day's *Sun* of 1833), and muckraker/yellow press (the Pulitzer-Hearst circulation wars). With roots in the 1735 colonial jury exoneration of John Peter Zenger for seditious libel, deciding that the press could print what is true, news media developed independently from government censorship and control, with emphasis on First Amendment promises of a free press" (Fuller, work in progress). Throughout, though, individual journalists' personal values—based on truth seeking—have prevailed. But bias about the profession remains, with conservatives claiming that the press—referred to as the "fourth estate"—is too liberal, and liberals that it is too conservative.

More an art than a science, journalism depends on balanced judgments, media ethics asking for anticipations to moral questions and principles. Balancing Aristotle's "Golden Mean," the "Golden Rule" of doing unto others as you would want them to do to you, and any number of maxims and imperatives, the notion of social responsibility has prevailed since the 1947 Hutchins Commission.

We all have heard the bad news, bordering on a death knell, for the fate of newspapers. In what has become something of a mantra, the story revolves around these themes: Newspapers have experienced a decade-long drop in readership; readers and advertising sales have migrated to the Internet, on portal news sites and RSS[1]; corporate turmoil and conglomeration have prevailed; retaining readership with fewer resources plagues the industry; migration of readers and ad sales to the Internet has squeezed newspapers financially; Craigslist.com boasts more than 47 million unique visitors per month; some 200,000 media jobs were lost between 2000 and 2008, and 15,000 newspaper jobs in 2008; the remaining newspapers try to retain readership with fewer resources; and the Committee to Protect Journalists (CPJ) sees increasing risks for reporters.

"The presses stopped forever at no less than 142 daily and weekly newspapers in 2009, a nearly threefold increase over the number of titles succumbing in the prior year," self-proclaimed "Newsosaur" Alan Mutter (2009) has noted in his blog. Some are still carrying on, though, and these are the reasons he thinks they are:

1. *The residual monopoly power of the industry*: While newspaper profits have been bludgeoned by an epic and accelerating downturn in advertising sales since April 2006, most publications continue to make substantial sums of money, owing to their monopoly position in most of the markets they serve.
2. *The magic of the bankruptcy system*: Instead of investing in the creation of new Internet and mobile businesses, publishers took advantage of the cheap interest rates in the middle years of this decade to borrow billions of dollars to either purchase other newspapers or take publishing companies private.

3. *The irrepressible optimism of publishers*: Hope springs eternal among publishers that the woes of the newspaper industry are not a secular shift in their
   business but nothing more than a severe byproduct of the worst economic
   downturn since the 1930s.

By cutting costs, renegotiating debt, or seeking bankruptcy protection,
newspaper executives have done a masterful job of staying afloat (albeit
by throwing tens of thousands of colleagues over the side) during the most
treacherous business conditions most of them have ever seen. They are
counting on an uptick in the economy next year to stop on a dime the
four-year skid in advertising sales that began well before the economy
tanked. If unbridled cost cutting and raw optimism are enough to save
newspapers, they will be just fine. If it takes more than chopping expenses
and praying for the economy to rebound—which seems to be the prevailing
industry strategy—then, unfortunately, we haven't seen the last newspaper
close.

We have read about bankruptcies (e.g., the Tribune Company, which
owns the *Los Angeles Times*, the *Chicago Tribune*, the *Minneapolis Star-
Tribune*, and others), cost cutting (e.g., eliminating certain days, having
smaller versions), staff reductions (e.g., McClatchy Newspapers, which
owns the *Miami Herald*, the *Anchorage Daily News*, and the *Sacramento
Bee*), even putting the newspaper up for sale (Hearst's *San Francisco
Chronicle*). Just think of book titles on the phenomenon: James Squires's
Read All About It!: The Corporate Takeover of America's Newspapers
(1994); Philip Meyer's *The Vanishing Newspaper: Saving Journalism in
the Information Age* (2004); Gene Roberts's *Leaving Readers Behind: The
Age of Corporate Newspapering* (2004); Charles M. Madigan's-*30-: The
Collapse of the Great American Newspaper* (2007); or Kiran Prasad's
e-Journalism: New Media and News Media (2009).

Solutions have ranged from bailouts to tax exemptions to establishing
nonprofit status and/or to developing new business models, including
citizen journalism (Ordonez 2009). If these ideas seem preposterous, Liz
Coville (2009) would have us consider how French president Nicholas
Sarkozy proposed a 600 million euro ($765 million) bailout for newspa-
pers; that Senator Ben Cardin's (D., Maryland) Newspaper Revitalization
Act would grant them 501(c)(3) status—if prohibiting them from making
political endorsements; and that *Pro Publica* already exists as a
Web-based, independent, nonprofit news venture (Regan 2009). *Online
Journalism*, recently started by L. Gordon Crovitz and profiled in the *Uni-
versity of Chicago Magazine* (Mullaney 2009, 33) "provides a technology
infrastructure for a dual revenue-stream platform, letting publishers

devise tailored rate plans for access to newspaper, magazine, and other online content while maintaining traffic to support advertising revenue." There are a number of good resources relative to online journalism, notably Pablo Boczkowski's *Digitizing the News: Innovation in Online Newspapers* (2005), Stuart Allan's *Online News* (2006), Axel Bruns's *Gatewatching* (2005), and Friend and Singer's *Online Journalism Ethics* (2007). "Journalism and press subsidies are the price of civilization," Nichols and McChesney (2010) have argued. "To deliver this public good in sufficient measure to sustain democracy, it must be treated as we treat national security."

Another solution is worth noting: A profile of *Providence Journal* (Rhode Island) executive editor Tom Heslin in *Suffolk Alumni Magazine* (Blanding 2010, 19) pointed out how he "started small, focusing initially on sports . . . tracking traffic to rank what readers wanted—which turned out to be, in order, Red Sox, Patriots, college basketball, high school sports, and, when they got hot, the Celtics." He had designers reformulate the website (Projo.com) to match these priorities, "resulting in a dramatic increase in page views—as much as 300 percent for high school sports coverage."

In his discussion on "The future of journalism," Gerry Storch (2010) discusses "the tradigital way"—when firewalls between the newsroom and interactivity break down. He cites *CSM* editor John Yemma's firsthand experience with a staff whose newspaper has transitioned online while at the same time retaining a weekly print: "While all journalists will have to think multimedia in the future, some will naturally be more skilled at one medium than another," says Yemma,

A photographer may be especially good at web video, for instance. An investigative reporter might excel at databases. A graphic artist may be drawn to mashups and interactive applications such as Flash. And one of the most valuable new skill sets is the hybrid journalist/developer who can build new storytelling tools on the fly. But the core function of the news operation will still be reporters who dig up information and present it to the public.

Storch also cites Chris O'Brien, a business columnist for the *San Jose Mercury News* who also heads the Next Newsroom Project:

One of the early insights we had was that there would NOT be a single ideal newsroom, but rather, that we were entering an era of many next newsrooms [which] would include everything from metro newsrooms to bloggers to nonprofits to citizen journalists platforms. So the next step was to identify a handful of principles we thought should be embraced by any of those newsrooms: 1.) The newsroom should be multi-platform; 2.) The newsroom should be a center of continuous innovation; 3.) The newsroom should place its community at the center of everything it does; 4.) The newsroom should collaborate with other newsrooms in its local ecosystem; 5.) The newsroom should practice transparency to build and maintain trust.

"These problems for the newspaper business stem from a sea change in how consumers get their news, and a stunning lack of foresight displayed by executives in the sector, who marginalized their business by giving content away for free," as Ben Silverman (2009) sees it. "Add in the historically weak economy, continued high newsprint costs, and a longer-than-usual advertising downturn, and you've got a recipe for a wave of newspaper closures. High labor costs are also working against the industry. Many newspaper industry watchers now believe that the days of print newspapers are nearing an end." Ben Parr (2010), writing about "The dire state of the newspaper industry," cited the Newspaper Association of America's advertising revenue estimates as "nothing short of disastrous," a 44.24% fall from grace: "In 2009, newspapers made $27.564 billion in total advertising revenue. As a whole, they generated $24.821 in print revenue, while the rest ($2.743 billion) came from online advertising." Compare these figures to 2008, when newspapers made $37.848 billion—a 27.2 percent drop. Peaking in 2000 at revenues of $48.67 billion, the decline since then has been dramatic (Gunther 2003; Li 2006). Yet, he concludes, "Journalism isn't dead; It's evolving." Imagine the vision of *CSM*, then, realizing it had to move beyond the model and begin its second century on the Web, with a weekly, and still providing daily news reports.

The discipline of journalism, Barbie Zelizer (2004) has argued, has been too insular and self-absorbed and needs to connect more with the many diverse fields it dissects; in other words, its evolution needs to come to terms with new forms of publishing. Elsewhere, explaining "Why journalism's changing faces matter" (2009, 1), she writes:

The changing faces of journalism have been part of the journalistic landscape since the inception of news. From early forms of oral delivery to the most recent online exchanges of information, journalism has always been multiple, multi-dimensional, multi-directional and multiply-faceted, and its multiplicity has become more pronounced as journalism has necessarily mutated across region and locale.

According to the 2010 Pew annual report on journalism, "In 2009 Twitter and other social media emerged as powerful tools for disseminating information and mobilizing citizens such as evading the censors in Iran and communicating from the earthquake disaster zone in Haiti." But all these new tools come with a heightened pace. Ken Auletta (2010, 42) cites White House communications director Anita Dunn: "When journalists call you to discuss a story, it's not because they're interested in having a discussion. They're interested in a response. And the need to file five times a day encourages this." Auletta himself muses: "Instead of seeking context or disputing a claim, reporters often simply get two opposing quotes and file a he said/she said story."

"And so we are about to enter a fractured, chaotic world of news, characterized by superior community conversation but a decidedly diminished level of first-rate journalism," Eric Alterman (2008, 58) has predicted. "The transformation of newspapers from enterprises devoted to objective reporting to a cluster of communities, each engaged in its own kind of 'news'—and each with its own set of 'truths' upon which to base debate and discussion—will mean the loss of a single narrative and agreed-upon set of 'facts' by which to conduct our politics." News is, after all, a $39 billion industry; no wonder so many people are invested in its future.

Leave it to the *Monitor* to offer us an example of where newspapers today mirror our former financial situation. "As the ailing US newspapers industry gasp for air, its counterparts in Asia are breathing in the exhilarating oxygen of success," Simon Montlake (2008) reported from Thailand. "Rising incomes and literacy levels—in an era of growing press freedom, democracy, and private media ownership—have lit a rocket under newsrooms across the region, say newspaper editors, industry analysts, and media executives."

OurBlook blog (cited in Rosan 2010) has called *The Christian Science Monitor* a pioneer in the area of "hyperlocal" journalism, where "users or citizen themselves collect, report, analyze and disseminate news and information for the sites"—even though *CSM* sees itself as global. When OurBlook.com interviewed 24 experts on "The Future of Journalism," the report was dim and discouraging, concurring that, "News organizations are currently facing the same obstacles—a generational shift in media preferences, disruption to their business model because of the Internet, and a worsening economy." The only optimistic voice belonged to *Monitor* editor John Yemma: "I believe this is both a difficult and exciting time in journalism. The old paradigm is dying. The monopoly/oligopoly that news organizations once enjoyed is breaking apart. Amid all the disruption, something new is being born" (cited in "Future of newspapers" 2009). When we met (3/12/10), *CSM* economy editor Laurent

Belsie declared that, "The current upheaval in journalism is the biggest change since the penny press."

Going with Yemma's more positive position, recall that Katharine Graham (1997, 63), decades-long publisher of the *Washington Post*, which her father bought in 1933 at a bankruptcy auction, shared her notion about it: "A newspaper was a public trust, meant to serve the public in a democracy" and that its mission is to tell the truth—as nearly as it may be ascertained. Think, again, about the Society of Professional Journalists (SPJ), which is dedicated to "the public enlightenment (as) the forerunner of justice and the foundation of democracy." "I believe democracy requires 'a sacred contract' between journalists and those who put their trust in us to tell them what we can about how the world really works," Bill Moyers famously said in a speech delivered to SPJ on September 11, 2004.

In a time of e-zines, RSS feeds, Information for Development (i4d), Open Publishing, social media, and any number of software packages that extend literacy and library, we hope that "sacred contract" remains intact.

MARY BAKER EDDY (1821–1910) AND CHRISTIAN SCIENCE

Several biographies of Mrs. Eddy have been written over the years since her passing in 1910—some friendly, some hostile in intent, and some that are essentially inspirational views of her life.

—Richard A. Nenneman (1997, ix)

Mary Baker Eddy (MBE)

The First Church of Christ, Scientist exists to spiritually enlighten, heal, and save. Its purpose is to eliminate spiritual ignorance, heal sickness and disease, overcome sin and death. Designed to reflect the structure of divine reality, this Church proves the understanding of God to be practical in every phase of human existence.

—Arthur P. Wuth (Foreword to Armstrong and Williamson 1980/2009, xi–xii)

Without wanting to be derivative, the essence of the religion known as Christian Science is spiritual healing—physical, mental, and moral. "Discovered" and founded by Mary Baker Eddy[2] in 1866 following a Biblical inspiration she received following what was declared to be a fatal illness, it has since become an established religious movement. A pioneer in mind-body medicine, Eddy's groundbreaking *Science and Health with a Key to the Scriptures* (1875/1994), was recognized in 1992 by the Women's National Book Association as one of the 75 books by women whose words have changed the world; to date, it has sold more than 9 million copies. MBE was prolific, and most of her books have been reprinted and revised (e.g., Eddy 1995, 2002, 2006). And her church, first built in 1892— known as The Mother Church (TMC)—has 3,200 branches in 48 countries.

By any measure, the building of TMC was an enormous project, against all odds. While we know that MBE called it "our prayer in stone," Joseph Armstrong (1980/2009, 5), the first person to detail its story, referred to her as "our teacher and mother. She alone, God's chosen and anointed one, deserves the credit of this mighty victory for Mind's supremacy." He elaborates: "In September 1893, Mary Baker Eddy, Discover and Founder of Christian Science, advised the Directors of The First Church of Christ, Scientist, in Boston, to lay the foundation for a church building the following October" (p. 7). Following issues such as land titles, fund-raising, legal requirements (such as needing to be fireproof), local planning ordinances, choice of building supplies, building permits, engineering inspections, architectural decisions, contractual disputes, a deadlock between builders and firms, discontented masons, material delays, a diminishing building fund, liabilities, choice of materials, and managing the "mechanics of different trades" (p. 36) working together simultaneously, it is a testament to balance. Amazingly, as indicated in an inscription carved in pink granite beneath the windows of the "Mother's Room" on the tower wall, The First Church of Christ, Scientist was erected *Anno Domini* 1894. At the June 1902 annual meeting came the notion of TMC extension. In keeping with a tradition that Christian Science churches are not dedicated until they are paid for, such a ceremony took place on June 10, 1906—costing $2 million, debt-free.

As indicated in the epigraph to this section, Mrs. Eddy was both beloved and reviled. The first and most influential biography published about her appeared in *McClure's Magazine* as a 14-part series between January 1907 and June 1908; although still controversial as to its authorship, since it deviates between admiration and judgment, MBE's reaction to it demonstrates her ability to be above pettiness. The bulk of biographies about her have been laudatory and respectful,[3] with Robert Peel's (1966/1972, 1971/1977, 1977/1982) three-volume biography recognized as the most admiring and comprehensive. At some point, it is helpful to recall MBE biographer Gillian Gill's (1999, 563) caveat that, "Each biography has a tale of its own, and each is shaped by specific circumstances which radically affect the nature and amount of information the word affords. None, not even the 3-volume work by Robert Peel, can be read innocently, without awareness of the publishing history and the political context."

Beginning with the early days that served as a genesis for MBE's "revolutionary interpretation of the scriptures," Peel outlines how she became a healer and organized the church, concluding with how the movement spread around the world and led to the establishment of *The Christian Science Monitor*. "Mrs. Eddy, like many a woman of genius, was no feminist radical," Herbert A. Kenny (1987, 65) has claimed. "She had a wide-ranging knowledge of what was going on in the world and was probably well aware of the numerous suffragette newspapers that came and went." Gillian Gill (1999, 533) contends that "Founding the *Monitor* was an act of affirmation, and its success affirmed Mrs. Eddy's instruction that the way to live is always to strive for the best, meet challenges head-on, and refuse to envision defeat." For John K. Simmons (1991, 108), "Mary Baker Eddy was an authoritarian charismatic religious leader who distrusted the institutionalization of her cause."

Yet, MBE was not without her critics, American humorist Mark Twain (1907/1993) calling her "the queen of frauds and hypocrites" and others slinging epithets such as "Mary Faker Eddy." Cather and Milmine's (1909/1993) book, a rendition from the *McClure's* series, paints a portrait of the founder of Christian Science as having tantrums in childhood, stealing ideas from Shakerism and Phineas Parkhurst Quimby, and being forceful, greedy, vindictive, basking in fame, a "slack" housekeeper and inattentive mother, and shrewd. Sure she was shrewd—how else could she have been such a successful businesswoman? The mean-spirited authors declared that MBE "herself was not always well, was not always happy" (p. 212), and that she was a victim of jealousy. It makes their reader wonder about their own motivations, as even they had to admit the following: "The result of Mrs. Eddy's planning and training and pruning is that she has built up the largest and most powerful organisation ever founded by any woman in America" (p. 480)—and they were referring to the religion, when we must applaud her work in establishing *The Christian Science Monitor*. Recall: Women did not yet have the right to vote, patriarchy prevailed, and a woman challenging the norms of pulpit and press would inevitably come under criticism.

"The nation's press had been preparing for some years to tell the world that Mrs. Eddy was dead, and reporters were thus doubtless gratified to find that Dr. George West (who determined she died of natural causes) prepared a description of the dead woman's face," Robert Peel (1977/1982, 550) gleefully reports:

The entire countenance bore a placid, serene expression, which could not have been sweeter had the woman fallen away in sleep in the midst of pleasant thoughts. I do not recall ever seeing in death before, a face which bore such a beautifully tranquil express.

Tributes from the press (1911/1993), overwhelmingly filled with accolades, focused primarily on MBE's founding of Christian Science, with little mention of the *Monitor*, with one exception: "With the passing of Mrs. Eddy, at the age of ninety, the world has lost one of its remarkable women," declared the *Butte-Tribune Review* (Montana). "Her writings and her teachings will continue to live . . . If Mrs. Eddy had accomplished nothing more, she did a great work when she founded *The Christian Science Monitor*, which in a very short space of time has risen to tremendous proportions in the journalistic field. By this alone her influence for good is difficult to estimate" (pp. 171–172). The *Inland Herald* of Spokane, Washington made a particularly noteworthy comment: "She accomplished in one generation that which followed only centuries after every other great religious leader. No other founder of a great church ever lived to see his work complete. Neither Confucius, Gautama [Buddha], or Saint Augustine ever beheld the fruit of his teachers materialize as Mary Baker Eddy did" (pp. 35–36). A surprisingly large number of the tributes referred to the "cult" of Christian Science, but in contexts that did not seem dismissive or critical.

"How then are we to understand the phenomenon of Mrs. Eddy herself," Julius Silberger (1980, 243) has posited, answering: "Four different kinds of influences could be considered: her endowment of talent and temperament; her psychological development and character structure; the external life events and social changes that affected her and that she mobilized for her own purposes; finally, the role of Divine Inspiration."

Christian Science

Christian Scientists believe in one, infinite God who is All and all-good. They believe that God is not distant and unknowable, but that God is all-encompassing and always present, and that each individual is loved by God, cared for by Him, and made in God's image—spiritual, not material.

http://christianscience.com/beliefs.html

With a theological premise in "the allness of God, who is defined, among other terms, as Spirit and Mind, and the consequent nothingness of the phenomenal world as interpreted by the limited material senses" (Nenneman 1997, 78), Christian Science has healing at its core—the healing power of God's love. In an interview on *Larry King Live* (5/4/01), then head of the Board of Trustees Virginia Harris said simply that Christian Science is a metaphor for prayer—provable, practicable. Prayer, for Christian Scientists, is a process of learning about God's spiritual reality metaphysically, through thought.

TMC has no ordained clergy, depending instead on a global network of practitioners—spiritual healers—and its churches are not used for weddings, funerals, or baptisms. "Following the example of Christ Jesus and his apostles, Mary Baker Eddy saw Christian healing as vital to humanity's situation," von Fettweis and Warneck (1998/2009, 10) have noted. "Her study of the Bible convinced her that this type of healing existed even before the days of Jesus of Nazareth," but she interpreted and brought it to new heights.

These are the tenets of Christian Science, based on *Science and Health with Key to the Scriptures* (Eddy 1875/1994, 497:3–27):

1. "As adherents of Truth, we take the inspired Word of the Bible as our sufficient guide to eternal Life."
2. "We acknowledge and adore one supreme and infinite God. We acknowledge His Son, one Christ; the Holy Ghost or divine Comforter; and man in God's image and likeness."
3. "We acknowledge God's forgiveness of sin in the destruction of sin and the spiritual understanding that casts out evil as unreal. But the belief in sin is punished so long as the belief lasts."
4. "We acknowledge Jesus' atonement as the evidence of divine, efficacious Love, unfolding man's unity with God through Christ Jesus the Way-shower; and we acknowledge that man is saved through Christ, through Truth, Life, and Love as demonstrated by the Galilean Prophet in healing the sick and overcoming sin and death."
5. "We acknowledge that the crucifixion of Jesus and his resurrection served to uplift faith to understand eternal Life, even the allness of Soul, Spirit, and the nothingness of matter."
6. "And we solemnly promise to watch, and pray for that Mind to be in us which was also in Christ Jesus; to do unto others as we would have them do unto us; and to be merciful, just, and pure."

As part of their religious convictions—"to maintain man's freedom from enslavement to any false appetite" (Canham 1958, 68), Christian

Scientists as a rule do not smoke or consume alcoholic stimulants and disapprove of addiction to tea and coffee. Bob Hanna, as advertising sales director, has found it a bit challenging, he shared with me (4/2/10), dealing with *CSM*'s advertising acceptance policy, which forbids tobacco, firearms, caffeine, medicine, argumentative language, and inappropriate graphics. CSPS publications, quite naturally, are disparaging toward topics such as saloons or drunken brawls, psychotropic mood-altering drugs, and even a caffeine buzz—which is why you will not find such subjects therein. In a talk on "Fundamental Christian Science," a special contribution to "Bohemia: A Symposium," Mary Baker Eddy stated the following (cited in *MBE: Prose Works* 2001, 347–348):

Most thinkers concede that Science is the law of God; that matter is not a lawmaker; that man is not the author of Science, and that a phenomenon is chimerical, unless it be the manifestation of a fixed Principle whose noumenon is God and whose phenomenon is Science.

My discovery that mankind is absolutely healed of so-called disease and injuries by other than drugs, surgery, hygiene, electricity, magnetism, or will-power, induced a deep research, which proved conclusively that all effect must be the offspring of a universal cause. I sought this cause, not within but *ab extra*, and I found it was God made manifest in the flesh, and understood through divine Science. Then I was healed, and the greatest of all questions was solved sufficiently to give a reason for the hope that was within me.

Church policy discourages an official membership count, based on the idea that MBE realized Christ Jesus and his few disciplines had an enormous impact on the world not because of their numbers but because of their spirituality and obedience to God. In 1974, Stephen Gottschalk claimed that anywhere from 350,000 to 450,000 people considered themselves Christian Scientists, and in 2001 the American Religious Identification Survey estimated 194,000 Christian Science adults. Also, it is important to note that "Not all members of the staff then or now were Christian Scientists. Mrs. Eddy preferred to have Christian Scientists on the paper whenever possible, but she felt that the first consideration should be that its editors and writers be good newspapermen" (Peel 1977/1982, 497).

What we do know is that there are about 1,500 Christian Science Reading Rooms worldwide—by my count, as listed in the April 2010 *Christian Science Journal*, 489 abroad[4] and 1,068 in the US[5]. The first Reading Room was established in Boston, Massachusetts, in 1888.

Some well-known people who reportedly are members[6] include theatrical stars Carol Channing, Joan Crawford, Doris Day, Colleen Dewhurst, Robert Duvall, Lionel Hampton, Val Kilmer, Ginger Rogers, Jean Stapleton, and Alfre Woodard; political figures John Ehrlichman and H. R. Haldeman of Watergate fame, U.S. Secretary of the Treasury Henry Paulson, former CIA director Stansfield Turner, and CNN political anchor Candy Crowley; artists Fred Babb and Mina Loy (see Vetter 2007); and any number of athletes (e.g., Adin Brown, Doug Jenkins, Nile Kinnick, Shannon Miller George Sisler, Jim Bereolos, and Sid Bream) and scientists—including Alan Shepard, the first American in space. Others you may know who were raised in the faith include Jean Arthur, Hart Crane, Ellen DeGeneres, Daniel Ellsberg, Henry Fonda, Kelsey Grammer, Spalding Gray, Howard Hawks, Ernest Hemingway, Jim Henson, Audrey Hepburn, Bruce Hornsby, Marilyn Monroe, V. S. Pritchett, Danielle Steel, even Elizabeth Taylor.

Two organizations of interest include Principia College, a four-year, private, coeducational liberal arts college located in Elsah, Illinois, that was founded between 1898 and 1906 to "serve the cause of Christian Science" despite having no official affiliation with the church. Adventure Unlimited (A/U), a nonprofit Christian Science camp based in Denver, Colorado, and founded in 1955, runs summer camp ranches.

"It is there, but it is not generally talked about," said reporter Mark Trumbull (4/8/10) about the religion of Christian Science. Many staffers pray about what they are doing so they will do that work better, with the goal of making a unique and valuable contribution to journalism—thus fulfilling the *Monitor*'s mission.

A fourth-generation Christian Scientist, executive assistant Rex Nelles talked about how members don't believe in trying to convert people to the religion but "each person discovers his or her own path and way to salvation." When we talked (3/24/10), he shared what it has meant to him and how relevant it is to those who have it in their lives.

But before leaving this scant and obviously limited description of the religion of Christian Science, it may be helpful to discuss what it is *not*. For starters, it is not Scientology, or mysticism, or a cult. Nor is it antimedicine, as its website[7] makes clear: "There is no biblical or church mandate to forgo medical intervention, nor do Christian Scientists believe that it's God's will that anyone suffer or die.[8] A Christian Scientist's decision to rely on prayer comes from trust, not blind faith, in God, and from a conviction that God's care continues under every circumstance." Do not miss the point that Christian Science is a long-established, globally respected religion, Bible-based, that "starts with God and the conviction that God's goodness embraces each of us, all the time."

THE CHRISTIAN SCIENCE PUBLISHING SOCIETY (CSPS)

Under the auspices of the First Church of Christ, Scientist, which is headquartered in Boston, Massachusetts, the Christian Science Publishing Society was established on January 25, 1898. The church's Board of Directors (the chair rotating annually, today headed by Mary Trammell), determines the overall direction for the church and the Publishing Society, including *The Christian Science Monitor*. The CSPS Board of Trustees—currently chaired by Judy Wolff and joined by Michael Pabst and Scott Preller—is responsible for business operations. It should be underscored that CSPS is run as a business: as per the Deed of Trust, an accurate accounting is due each six months; additionally, as per the Church Manual, the Board of Directors oversees the overall direction of both the church and its publications, and the Board of Trustees is responsible for the business end of publications. Except for an incident involving litigation in the 1920s, which you will read about later in this chapter, the situation has been agreeable and mutually beneficial. "This cooperation works in large part because of the common spiritual dedication underlying the newspaper and earnestly shared by staff," 30-year, highly respected editor Erwin D. Canham (1958, xx) has noted.

In answer to the question, "Why does the Christian Science church own a news organization?" appears this response on *CSM*'s website.[9] It appears here in abbreviated fashion from a story the *Monitor*'s Washington bureau chief, David Cook, related several years ago:

Consider this case. It is 1907. An elderly New England woman finds herself being targeted by Joseph Pulitzer's *New York World*. She is 86 years old and holds some unconventional religious beliefs that she expounds in a book, *Science and Health with Key to the Scriptures*. The book becomes a bestseller, making her wealthy and a well-known public figure.

. . . the next year this woman, Mary Baker Eddy, founds *The Christian Science Monitor*.

Mrs. Eddy had been thinking about a newspaper for a long time before 1907. Way back in 1883 she wrote: "Looking over the newspapers of the day, one naturally reflects that it is dangerous to live, so loaded with disease seems the very air. These descriptions carry fears to many minds, to be depicted in some future time upon the body. A periodical of our own will counteract to some extent this public nuisance; for through our paper we shall be able to reach many homes with healing, purifying thought."

"Long-time church members have described *CSM* as the church's missionary. I like that analogy," science reporter Peter N. Spotts agreeably told me (2/26/10). Provisions from MBE require that any profits from the Publishing Society, which oversees the day-to-day operations of *CSM*, go to the church. But the *Monitor* has been running multimillion-dollar deficits for years. "Over the paper's history, it pioneered a kind of news-relevant, analytical form of news stories that has become a staple of journalism today, and clearly does not want to be a burden," he added.

Mary Baker Eddy described the Publishing Society's major periodicals: "The first was *The Christian Science Journal*, designed to put on record the divine Science of Truth; the second I entitled *Sentinel*, intended to hold guard over Truth, Life and Love; the third, *Der Herold der Christian Science*, to proclaim the universal activity and availability of Truth; the next I named *Monitor*, to spread undivided the Science that operates unspent. The object of The Monitor is to injure no man, but to bless all mankind." Beginning in 1883, then, she was actively involved in writing and editing, and today all of her publications still exist, *Christian Science Quarterly* being a self-study guide for weekly Bible lessons, the *Christian Science Journal* a monthly report of verified healings, and the *Christian Science Sentinel* a weekly about healing in daily life; the *Herald of Christian Science* is published in 13 languages. *Sentinel Radio* provides weekly programs globally, later available on CDs and cassettes. Amazingly, as demonstrated in Table 2.1, CSPS translations are available in some 20 languages.

Publications and Broadcasting

According to a self-produced handout (June 8, 1990) on its critical dates, as early as February 1922 *CSM*'s newly formed American Publishers' Committee on Cable and Radio Communications became active in radio transmissions. By 1919, *The Christian Science Monitor Views the News* AM radio broadcasts began, with shortwave following in 1935 (until 1954), and *News from Everywhere*, a 15-minute cooperation with the Mutual Broadcasting System premiering in 1943. But by 1964 radio was discontinued, and a weekly International Edition of *CSM* was launched in 1974. Short-form radio segments ran from 1977 to 1983, and *Monitor-Radio Weekend Edition* appeared on American Public Radio in 1984. At one point, *MonitorRadio* was broadcast by more than 200 stations in the

Table 2.1
Languages Used for CSPS Translations

بر علا	(Arabic)
中文	(Chinese)
Čeština	(Czech)
Dansk	(Danish)
Nederlands	(Dutch)
سراف	(Farsi)
Suomi	(Finnish)
Français	(French)
Deutsch	(German)
Νεοελληνική	(Greek)
תירבע	(Hebrew)
हिन्दि	(Hindi)
Indonesia	(Indonesian)
Italiano	(Italian)
日本語	(Japanese)
한국어	(Korean)
Norsk	(Norwegian)
Português	(Portuguese)
Русский	(Russian)
Español	(Spanish)
Svensk	(Swedish)
Türkçe	(Turkish)

United States each week to a cumulative audience of about 1.5 million listeners, its shortwave radio network reaching some 11.5 million listeners around the world; *Monitor Month*, an in-house instrument for marketing communication, joined them in being under the auspices of the Christian Science Publishing Society. The *World Service of The Christian Science Monitor*, begun in 1987, reached all corners of the globe, and *World Monitor*, a monthly magazine, began in 1988, lasting until 1993.

CSM's World Edition, a 20-page weekly digest featuring highlights from the daily *Monitor* for readers abroad, was produced until the recent change with the advent of the weekly, and serviced both the United States and international subscribers. Gillian Charters, now copy desk chief, served as editor of its international edition, so when we reminisced about it (2/16/10) she was just as disappointed as I was at its demise, as it was the ideal gift for people serving in the Peace Corps or away from home.

The Monitor Channel, launched on May 1, 1991 as a 24-hour "Television for the Global Citizen," began as award-winning—receiving both a Peabody and a national news Emmy for international news coverage—but soon became the focus of ugly internal squabbles over both direction and cost. It shut down operation just two weeks before celebrating its one-year anniversary (Bridge 1998). The fallout, various *CSM* staff have told me, caused some bad feelings for a number of years.

But there is no question that the publishing society's most visible, most familiar, and most award-winning publication and flagship product is The *Christian Science Monitor*—in all its evolutions.

THE CHRISTIAN SCIENCE PERSPECTIVE

> *Christian Scientists have a deep consciousness of the spiritual nature of man. Their teaching derives from the first chapter of Genesis: that God made all and made it "very good," that He created man in His image and likeness; and that, as Jesus declared, God is spirit. The Christian Scientist thus regards the spiritual or true man as being as incapable of evil as his Maker. Sick, sinning, mortal man is seen as a merely material misconception of the true man. This false conception, the Christian Scientist believes, can be corrected by an increasing understanding of man's spiritual selfhood. Healing and regeneration result.*
>
> *Such an approach explains the attitude of confidence in good which underlies the entire experience of the* Monitor. *The newspaper, like the individual Christian Scientist, does not ignore or dismiss the assertions of evil which confront human experience. It has to deal with them. But it does not believe these evils are the truth about man, and it seeks to replace and correct them with more upright and noble concepts and deeds.*
>
> —Erwin D. Canham (1958, xv)

After 10 years in the newsroom and now serving on the publishing side of *The Christian Science Monitor*, Abe McLaughlin paraphrased a former editor relative to how it covers religion by explaining, "We are not Pollyannas, but we do believe that there is good everywhere and we are dedicated to improving the world by uncovering that good" (cited in Mollmann 2009). Believing this, however, does not preclude the covering of dark and difficult issues: "If we believe there is good everywhere, there might be some bad piled on top, but you are going to dig to the bottom and uncover the good. The approach that I've taken and that fits me in my religion is addressing the tough stuff, transcending the bad and finding hope and light in the situation. That is how I have connected the theology and the reporting."

"It's all about healing—not wallowing in sensation, not looking away, but understanding and looking at what can be done," according to Washington, D.C., staff writer Linda Feldmann. When we spoke (2/23/10), she had been covering the healthcare summit all day, and she said it put Obama in a tough spot. "It's a polarizing time," she noted, with excessive partisanship. Citing how Mary Baker Eddy wanted a global focus, she worries how, since 9/11, we have become more insular.

The question always comes up about how many or what percentage of the staff is of the Christian Science faith. While preference is given to qualified Christian Scientists in hiring, the emphasis is on *qualified*. Many skilled non–Christian Scientists work for the *Monitor* and honor its values and ethics. Long after people have left for other jobs, they still speak fondly of it. For instance, John Yemma has noted that Ned Temko, his predecessor as Middle East correspondent in the late 1970s, went on to become editor of the *Jewish Chronicle*, the oldest and most respected Jewish newspaper in Britain, and always sang the *Monitor*'s praises. "People of all faiths and—perhaps of no faith—have worked for the *Monitor* and cared about what it stands for," Yemma told me in an email (4/29/10), expanding with, "As a 'convert' to Christian Science in the 1970s, one thing that immediately appealed to me as a journalist was that Truth is another word for God."

A devout Christian Scientist himself, David R. Francis, of *Economic Scene* fame, estimated (2/17/10) that, until about 15 years ago or so, perhaps 90 percent of the staff were also. They take Mary Baker Eddy's words seriously: "God is mind, and mind will guide you." Blind fate doesn't govern, he explained. He remains confident that column topics he or an editor chooses will stay in the news, and that a journalist's love of truth can lead him to helpful sources. Think of the individual as reflecting Mind in spiritual reality; the human as mortal can feel guided. Francis maintains that good from God can help him do his professional job. Marshall Ingwerson has reported, "I don't necessarily know who is and who isn't affiliated with the church. Everybody who works for the Monitor has in some way or another signed on to the mission of it, and generally that's just doing what I think journalists regard as good journalism" (Garfield 2005).

CSM

The Monitor's *special method, in its task of serving mankind, is to give proper emphasis to significant news. It does not leave out news just because it is unpleasant, nor seek to throw a rosy glow over a world that is often far from rosy. To describe the* Monitor *as a "clean" newspaper is correct but incomplete. It also strives to expose whatever needs to be uncovered in order to be removed or remedied. It seeks to put the news in a sound perspective, giving greatest emphasis what is important and reducing the merely sensational to its place in an accurate system of values. It seeks also to amuse and entertain, but in wholesome and socially desirable terms.*

In short, the Monitor's *contents must measure up to a system of value judgments which would be agreed upon by thoughtful and intelligent readers as accurate and adequate. Behind these judgments is the paper's purpose to help in uplifting human thinking. It seeks to do this formidable serious task in as bright and readable a manner as possible.*

—Erwin D. Canham (1958, xvi–xvii)

Since its founding, the Monitor *has covered every war, peace, major election, or coup; we're reported on scientific advances from microscope to moon walk, the creative achievements that embellish civilization, and the family and personal arts that bring moral and intellectual stability to households and communities.*

—Richard J. Cattani (1993, 9)

A Brief Historical Review of *The Christian Science Monitor*[10]

The First Church of Christ, Scientist exists to spiritually enlighten, heal, and save. Its purpose is to eliminate spiritual ignorance, heal sickness and disease, overcome sin and death. Designed to reflect the structure of divine reality, this Church proves the understanding of God to be practical in every phase of human existence.

—Armstrong and Williamson (1980/2009, xi–xii)

"The details of the *Monitor*'s start are as remarkable as the building of the original Mother Church edifice," Richard Nenneman (1997, 329) has detailed. "In a little more than three months, apartments had to be torn down, wooden piles driven into the tidal marshland of Back Bay to support printing presses that had not even been ordered, a building constructed to house the operation, and over one hundred employees hired. All this, plus developing an editorial concept for the paper!" At last, after much thought and preparation, as well as innumerable obstacles, MBE was ready to produce *The Christian Science Monitor*, thus named following careful consideration, "to spread undivided the Science that operates unspent." She was insistent on the name, although Nenneman (1997, 329) reminds us that "Many, if not most, of those who were preparing the paper felt it better to leave out the name 'Christian Science.' Many of these same individuals had wanted a paper with the idealism of Christian Science, the absence of sensationalism and over reporting of crime, and an emphasis on those developments that constituted progress in society. But they felt that a paper that bannered the name of their religion would drastically curtail its circulation prospects."

That first issue—November 25, 1908—printed in broadsheet form, included 82,500 copies—was meant to be widely circulated, yet pragmatic thinking saw the printing and circulation of some 38,000 issues for the following day. Stephen Gottschalk (1974, 259) pointed out that it reflected "a significant reorientation of the thought of the movement away from the personal and private to the social and universal," Norman Beasley (1952, 471) said it involved "years of thought, and preparation, and prayer." Typographically attractive, eschewing the popular banner headline, it drew instant raves. For its one-year anniversary, 250,000 copies of a 96-page newspaper were prepared, along with this declaration: "The *Monitor* not only seeks to keep its readers informed of events all over the world, but to interpret those events in a way to show their relation to the great movements that are of service to the human race" (Canham 1958, 113).

Archibald McClennan, the first editor, made it clear from the beginning that "The new publication would not be a church newsletter or a propaganda sheet for the church. Rather the *Monitor* would have its readers as 'its only beneficiaries' and would publish 'all the news it is worth while reading' " (Ibid., 74–75). This principle, along with the notion "To injure no man, but to bless all mankind," Lawrence Strout (1999, xiv) reminds us, has "been referred to repeatedly over the years as major decisions faced those running the day-to-day operations."

What followed next, unfortunately, got a bit nasty, with a power struggle ensuing between the Board of Trustees of the Publishing Society and the Board of Directors of The Mother Church, a 1921 lawsuit eventually having the Massachusetts Supreme Judicial Court decide in favor of TMC's Directors since, according to its *Manual*, they could maintain ultimate authority over publications. To this day, then, the Directors are still the last word. In answer to the question, "Do church leaders determine or influence the *Monitor*'s editorial content?" the *Monitor*'s website replies[11]:

The Board of Directors of the First Church of Christ, Scientist, has oversight over *Monitor* editorials and editorial cartoons, but rarely changes copy. The board selects the *Monitor's* editor, whose staff chooses stories they feel are most appropriate on a daily basis.

It is important to place this history within the context of its day: New England in the nineteenth century, along with the whole country, was in the midst of urban, industrial, scientific, medical, women's rights, and theological transformations. Discussing *The Christian Science Monitor's* founding, managing editor Marshall Ingwerson hones in on that history: "It was the heyday of the Hearst and Pulitzer empires, and what we now call yellow journalism, which was very sensational. And Mrs. Eddy founded the paper with the fairly simple purpose—it's still written by our flag today—our masthead of the paper—To Bless All Mankind—translated, to provide good, sound, quality information with a reader in mind who wants to be a good citizen of the world" (Garfield 2005). Her thoughts on what kind of newspaper the *Monitor* should be were repeated in its September 4, 1934 edition:

The essential function of a newspaper is to print the news. It is the desire and the determination of the *Monitor* today to record and interpret, in true perspective, all of the world's significant news. The test of all *Monitor* news is whether that news is socially important, whether it is news which we all need to know to be informed and alert citizens. It is the goal of the *Monitor* to give to its readers a newspaper which will be vital, realistic, and comprehensive, which will give the good news, to the encouraging news, and to the constructive news the prominence it rightfully deserves. At the same time, the *Monitor* ignores nothing essential to a penetrating understanding of all those aggravated social conditions to which readers of the *Monitor*, particularly, can give healing attention.

Consider: More than a century ago was a press period, in the Gilded Age of the 1890s, synonymous with "sensationalism" (Campbell 2003; Cohen 2000; Kaslow 1995; Kraus 1998; Pelton 1995; Spencer 2007; Winchester 1995). Defined thus by Frank Luther Mott (1941, 539), the crux of sensationalism dealt with circulation battles that got out of control—and all that being based on a cute little comic strip of an Irish immigrant in New York's lower east side: Mickey Dugan, "The Yellow Kid"—and was characterized by

1. Scare headlines in huge print, often of minor news.
2. Lavish use of pictures or imaginary drawings.
3. Use of faked interviews, misleading headlines, pseudoscience, and a parade of false learning from so-called experts.

4. Emphasis on full-color Sunday supplements, usually with comic strips (which is now normal in the United States).
5. Dramatic sympathy with the "underdog" against the system.

"*The Christian Science Monitor*, one of the country's most responsible and enlightened newspaper wrote that responsible journalism had to reject the activities of sensation-seeking newspapers if it were to preserve its good name," Daniel Cohen (2000, 49) has noted. Some people would say that Mary Baker Eddy, fed up with lawsuits and personal attacks in the tawdry press, found her perfect protest tool in founding her own newspaper, with "clean journalism" (Kenney 1987, 64). MBE biographer Gillian Gill (1999, 532), who cites the founding of *The Christian Science Monitor* as "one of Mrs. Eddy's most celebrated, influential, and farsighted achievements," adds some insightful comments about its context:

The treatment she had received from the *New York World* and from *McClure's* magazine had taught Mary Baker Eddy a peculiarly painful lesson about the press's quest for sensationalism and disregard for truth. She felt herself to be in a position to do something about this, not just because her movement had— barely, perhaps, the material resources, but because she felt empowered by God to make changes in the world. And so on July 28 Mrs. Eddy wrote a letter to the directors, and on August 8 a short note to the Trustees of the Publishing Society, instructing them to begin a daily newspaper. The subsequent success of the *Monitor* has masked quite how ambitious Mrs. Eddy's directive was, and how much faith and obedience her officials had to muster as they put her wishes into action. It is true that Mrs. Eddy had always had a profound understanding of the role of what we now call the media in modern society.

Willis Abbot, founder of the American Society of Newspaper Editors (ASNE), was chosen as editor in 1922, and circulation for the *Monitor* rose such that it soon reached the 100,000 figure, and 130,000 in 1930. It dipped a bit, but by the end of World War I the print count went to 123,080.

Throughout its history, *CSM* has not been afraid to experiment with different formats and financial decisions. In 1948, Roland E. Wolseley called it "the most famous experiment in the way of a great religious paper . . . not as a denominational journal, but as a superior secular paper sponsored by a religious body" (p. 613). Learning from what became called the Great Litigation period of 1917 to 1921, when a balance was struck over publishing power between the trustees and the directors, foreign language editions were introduced and foreign bureaus and foreign correspondents were used instead of the paper being wire-service dependent, and it is generally thought that the newspaper peaked in the 1950s.

When rising production costs became untenable, CSPS stepped in with subsidies; but by the mid-1970s, the deficit reached $8 million and staff cutbacks occurred. "Despite critical acclaim, keeping the *Monitor* afloat has required church subsidies for most of its history," Nancy Herther (2008) reminds us. After the *Monitor Channel* fiasco, press reports claimed that TMC had borrowed $41.5 million from an employee pension fund, as well as $5 million from a trustee endowment, for a total of $250 million to date. It was a divisive time, but by 1998 reimbursements were made, *Monitor* circulation rebounded from a low of 75,000 to 90,000, and CSPS committed to a $500,000 national ad campaign and redesign of its newspaper and began investigating other ventures to promote its message. Unfortunately, there were more downs: circulation lows, increased production costs, and advertisers shifting allegiance to the Web.

By 2008, *CSM* was worried about losses of $18.9 million per year when it was only making revenues of $12.5 million—fortunately, making up the difference through an endowment and contributions from church members. It was during this time that *Monitor* editors, publishing staff, and others did a "deep dive," as John Yemma called it, into the future of the publication: analyzing the industry and the *Monitor*'s finances, polling readers, developing prototypes, and bringing in news consultants to help develop a plan for the future. Yemma was hired in the summer of 2008 in the midst of this intense strategic planning period, which kept in mind lessons of the past—especially the overly ambitious spending of the *Monitor Channel* era. Also in 2008 came the announcement of a news- and cost-sharing exchange arrangement with the 153-year old McClatchy Company, a newspaper and Internet publisher, between their bureaus in South Asia, Africa, and Latin America (McClatchy 2008).

"The *Monitor*, alone among American newspapers, has seen the future before," Alex Beam (2008) has noted about the broadcast "experiment-gone-wrong," albeit realizing that the enterprise "instilled a much-needed sense of caution at headquarters." It underwent redesign in 1975, 1983, and 1989, aware throughout that it is "read for the context, perspective, and connections of events—for insight and understanding of the underlying trends—in daily installments" (Nenneman, Cattani, and Hoagland 1989, 15).

Enter the world of the Internet.

The Decision to Go Digital

Situating itself in the center of all the issues plaguing journalism and having done its homework, the next logical step for *The Christian Science Monitor* was to make its move. In 2002, it began promotion of free electronic reproductions of the daily newspaper, following up with subscription offers at half the price of the paper edition. With the realization that the newspaper's circulation had slipped to 80,000 but that CSMonitor.com drew about 600,000 at the beginning, blossoming into about 2 million hits per month after September 11, the future was beckoning.

In an interview on *PBS News Hour* before the transition (Brown 2008), editor John Yemma stated that, "Our plan is to move toward sustainability. And the way that we think we can do that is by having a mix of publications." Deciding not to charge for what had been free online, the idea was that if enough viewers visited CSMonitor.com advertisers would naturally be interested. The math went like this: If the site was already drawing some 3 million viewers per month (according to comScore), continued outstanding *Monitor* journalism might bring that number to 20 or 30 million a month within a few years. While there were some doubters (e.g., Ivan 2008), most people were enthusiastic.

There were other considerations that Yemma explained in another interview, for *Editors Weblog* (Thompson 2008a): Firstly, *CSM*'s publishers "saw the writing on the wall, they knew that the Internet user patterns and reader preferences and so forth were changing the business model of print. Print was becoming increasingly untenable, especially for the *Monitor*, which has an international audience." He continued: "We just don't have enough reach with our print product, but we have great reach with our web product. That's not uncommon in the world of publishing right now to come to that conclusion, but for the *Monitor* we were able to make the change a little faster, because the Christian Science church wanted to move away from subsidizing the *Monitor* within about three to five years."

In preparation, Thompson (2008b) wrote about how "Yemma and his team are restructuring the newsroom, its mindset and the technology powering it." This also meant installing a new content management system, establishing a common editorial pool, training staff for new platforms, and changing mindsets. Thompson concluded: "The media needs newspapers like the *CSM* to pursue these new strategies, as the industry has evolved very little in the last 100 years ... Whether this model will prove successful, time and the market will only tell; but it is undoubtedly a brave and exciting undertaking." Yet more interviews with Patrick

Thornton (2008a, 2008b) discussed increasing traffic, considering how to deal with social media, balancing the many means of storytelling new media offer, expanding podcasting, and, most importantly, maintaining *Monitor* journalism.

"*The Christian Science Monitor* announces shift from print daily to on-line daily and launches weekly print publication," *Business Wire* (2008) announced: "It will produce an enhanced, constantly updated version of its Web site, CSMonitor.com, and launch a weekly print edition and a daily electronic subscription product. In addition, the *Monitor* will discontinue its daily print publication. Consistent with the *Monitor*'s commitment to thoughtful, global news and perspective, its new Web edition will feature original reporting seven days a week, and its new weekly print publication will look behind the headlines and help readers understand global issues."

After careful consideration, checking prototypes and doing financial analyses during several years of preparation, on March 27, 2009 the last daily issue of *The Christian Science Monitor* was published and the paradigm shift was in place. *Newsweek* (Roberts 2008) declared that *CSM* had "simultaneously become the newspaper industry's worst fear and its model for salvation." Table 2.2 includes part of editor John Yemma's (2009a) message about the changes.

While not the first newspaper to go online, since the *Columbus Dispatch* has that distinction dating to 1980, or even the first one to stop print for Web-only circulation (the *Seattle Post-Intelligencer*), according to the Poynter Institute,[12] *The Christian Science Monitor* was the first national newspaper to replace its daily print edition on the Web and, simultaneously, offer weekly and daily email print editions. Throughout, its mission, motives, and approach remained loyal to MBE's master plan: daily news reports, audience interest, and fiscal responsibility.

"The *Monitor*'s decision to go online-only last year was seen by many as a major step in the evolution of newspapers. What was the genesis of that decision?" David Hirschman (2010) of *Media Burst* asked editor John Yemma just about one year after the experiment began. This was the response:

For about two years before they hired me, [the paper] had been involved in a fairly deep-dive [analysis] into the future of print. They looked at their financials, they looked at the future of print, they did prototyping of a weekly in two different forms—a slick weekly and a tabloid weekly—and they'd already made a lot of progress along the lines of moving from daily print to weekly print. It seemed like where they weren't making much progress, and where they were still caught in the old paradigm was "What do we do with print? How do we make it most effective?"—when what we really needed to do was go Web-first. Print should be there, but it shouldn't be the lead dog on the dogsled.

Eoin O'Carroll, online producer, mentioned another canine consideration: "The press as an institution in terms of its historical role as watchdog." He talked openly with me (2/16/10) about the emphasis in journalism on page views, which he likened to "wading into quicksand." Excellent writing is getting compromised; there are no incentives and no particular plaudits to cultivate high-quality prose, he fears. Pressure is on to get stories on Google News and other aggregators, with links and hits.

"What I love most about the *Monitor*'s decision is the courage behind it," Tom Regan, executive director of the Online News Association (2008), declared. Michelle Bearden of *Tampa Bay Online* (2008), anticipating Dan Kennedy of *Common Wealth Magazine* (2009), said it was

Table 2.2
March 27, 2009 Letter to Readers by John Yemma, *CSM* Editor

Dear readers:
The Christian Science Monitor has published its final daily print edition, dated March 27. The key words in that sentence are "daily print." As of today, we are shedding print on a daily basis. But the *Monitor* itself—the century-old journalistic enterprise chronicling the world's challenges and progress—is becoming more daily than ever. And with the launch of our new weekly print edition, the *Monitor* is becoming more vital than ever. No longer inked on wood pulp, no longer trucked from printing plants to your mailbox, no longer published only five days a week, the daily *Monitor* is now a dynamic online newspaper on all days.

The *Monitor* is available everywhere—St. Louis, Johannesburg, Boston, Buenos Aires, Jakarta, Toronto—the instant you go to our website, CSMonitor.com. We've been moving in this direction for more than a decade. Two million individuals now engage with us online each month, about 40 times the number that have been subscribing to the print daily. We are linked deeply and extensively across the Internet. People who never picked up our newspaper read *Christian Science Monitor* articles online, listen to our audiocasts, and view our photo- and video-journalism.

The online *Monitor* responds to events as they unfold. Our website also features timely editorials and commentary, articles on arts, culture, books, *Home Forum* essays, and, as has been the case since its founding, the daily inspirational article. Complementing our 24/7 online *Monitor* is a new print weekly, the first issue of which will be in subscribers' mailboxes in two weeks.

For readers, the daily print *Monitor* has been a friend in the home, a steady and reliable source of information about the world. We are still that friend. You can find us in print weekly and online instantly, with the same commitment to freedom and progress we have always had. We are wearing new clothes, but we remain your *Christian Science Monitor*.
Sincerely,
John Yemma, Editor

"just reinventing itself." While the Web edition would remain free, the weekly costs $3.50 an issue or $89 per year; *DNB*, $219.

The experiment began full-throttle in April 2009. *The Christian Science Monitor* became available 24/7 on the Web, and the weekly premiered April 12, with "A Note to Readers" from the Christian Science Board of Directors and the Trustees of the Christian Science Publishing Society stating, "Now, more than ever, the *Monitor*'s message of hope, courage, and compassion can be woven into the fabric of your day-to-day life." Six months into the experiment, editor John Yemma's *Open Source* column (2009b, 47) used the opportunity for reflection: "We've ranged journalistically from the shape of the post-recession economy to the future of the automobile, from the fight for Afghanistan to the leaking away of privacy in a digital age."

Ideology and Imprint

A longtime staunch supporter of civil liberties and individual freedom, the *Monitor* has clearly bent to the times. Channing Walker (2008) has made the point that, "for Mary Baker Eddy's vision to be realized, *Monitor* readers, at least a portion of them, have to be not only readers they have to be pray-ers. Readers who are actually motivated to pray about the news."

Thinking of itself as performing a public service, its audience being global, the *Monitor* has from the start excelled in reportage of foreign affairs—what Donald R. Shanor (2003, 112) calls "the litmus tests of professional and ethical conduct in journalism." Beginning in 1910, it published a special international edition for its readers in more than 120 countries. "We try to tell stories in human terms, working on both the connections to our readers and the narrative skills that make these topics readable," David Clark Scott, World editor, has explained (cited in Shanor 2003, 111). "People may not understand the chaos in the countries we write about or its causes, but they do recognize the connections to their own lives and families, as, for example, when they read about children in danger." In keeping with MBE's appeal to universality and her aim for healthy, "clean" journalism, that tradition continues.

Although infrequent, *CSM* sticks to a strict journalistic corrections code by pointing out when it has printed something erroneous—perhaps a date, or a statistic, or whatever might have been misleading. Here is a particularly noticeably one (3/22/10, 19): "The story 'Right-to-hunt initiatives rise' (Feb. 21, p. 19) jumped the gun concerning what is happening in North Carolina. The National Rifle Association is still working to get hunting rights on the ballot there, and hopes to do so as a referred constitutional amendment from the state legislature, not as an initiative."

Many correspondents began their careers as "copy kids" or "copy boys," and some of their reminiscences, as you can see in Table 2.3, add to the bigger picture of *CSM*'s history.

Table 2.3
Monitor Memories by Longtime Employees

• "When I joined the *Monitor*, in 1972, we had manual typewriters and Western Union operators for filing," Brad Knickerbocker of the National Bureau recalls. In our phone interview (1/18/10) he elaborated on how reporters got to know various operators' styles and would maneuver their deadlines to be able to work with the speedier ones. "So, I've experienced the full range of technologies and philosophies about daily journalism," he correctly asserts, as today his life with the newspaper exists in real time, with instant messaging (IM) and full-time editing to get pieces Web-ready, with catchy headlines and subheads, appropriate links, photos, and whatever else works.

• Editor and reporter Gregory Lamb, who joined the *Monitor* in 1972, reminisced about working in the wire room with a Telex machine when we met (2/11/10): " I would type out conversations on the Telex keyboard to our foreign correspondents while Overseas News editor Geoffrey Godsell stood over my shoulder dictating. An early form of texting. To send stories to our syndication clients, I would type them out in advance on a long paper punch tape. Then, once I was connected, I would run the tape through a reader at a consistent 60 words per minute, much faster than I could type it 'live.' "

• Rosalie Dunbar, news editor of the Christian Science magazines, recalled for me how, when she came to the *Monitor* in 1978, everything was done on typewriters (2/11/10). Soon thereafter, they learned they were going to be getting desktop computers from a company called Atex, which at the time had one of the leading editorial software programs. Rather than rip up the floor in the newsroom, though, a false floor was built to accommodate all the wires and connections that were needed for the PCs.

• Peter N. Spotts, science editor, who set type by hand in a junior high print-shop class and left the *Miami Herald* for the *Monitor* as the *Herald* was finally giving up linotype machines, is no stranger to technological change in journalism. He had fun telling me (2/26/10) about how, when he joined *CSM* in 1976, stories came in on telex and teletype machines. Even before that story, there was another good one: As a student at the University of Miami, a journalism professor passed around a hat full of slips of paper with names on them. The assignment: Look up the person in *Who's Who*, then draft five questions you'd ask during an interview for a story. Although he had grown up with the *Monitor* in his home, he hadn't paid much attention to bylines or mastheads. When he pulled Erwin Canham's name out of the professor's hat, only after Spotts looked Canham up in *Who's Who* did he learn that Canham was the *Monitor*'s venerable editor. The realization was a kind of epiphany that ultimately led Spotts to apply for a job at the paper (after he'd spent about two years at the *Miami Herald*). He's been there ever since, working in a variety of reporting and editing posts.

(*continued*)

Table 2.3 (Continued)

• Former editor (1970–1979) John Hughes, who still writes a bi-monthly column that appears both in on the Web and the *Weekly*, recalled how deadlines ruled his tenure: "Our problem was delivery," he said (4/28/10). When the newspaper went by mail to a circulation then of about 230,000 households and offices, from five different plants, the big thing was getting into the mail-stream, beating the bulk competition of the *Wall Street Journal*.

Although Mary Baker Eddy only lived to see the *Monitor* for two years, Nenneman (1997, 330) points out that "Her enthusiasm for it demonstrated an almost prophetic foresight that this reaching out to the world through an attempt to report on the entire human condition would be a link to the rest of humanity long before the religion itself would be." While this has been a much-abbreviated historical review of how *The Christian Science Monitor* got its start, what has been left out is mention of the many outstanding journalists who have contributed to it. Pioneers there include a list of Who's Who in the profession: Mallory Browne, Roscoe Drummond, Charles Gratke, Joseph C. Harsch, Joseph Harrison, Harold Hobson, Sisley Huddleston, Peter Lyne, Reuben Henry Markham, John Allan May, Godfrey Sperling, Ronald Maillard Stead, Edmund Stevens, William H. Stringer, Richard L. Strout, and other favorites along the years.

Hopefully this backstory has provided you with insight to understand what is to follow, considering the people and processes behind both its traditional and newest products: An examination *CSM* publishing, case studies, the role of information technology, and predictions for the future.

Chapter 3

Publishing *The Christian Science Monitor*

The Monitor, *unlike many other newspapers, is not a front page publication. It seeks to provide significant information with sufficient background and perspective to increase understanding—and that cannot be accomplished on a front page alone. The paper's identity is realized through all its pages, its photos, its national and international news coverage, its editorials, and its features on the arts, the home, and the whole fabric of the human scene.*

—Katherine W. Fanning, Introduction, *The Christian Science Monitor: The First 80 Years* (1988, xi)

The structure of the *Christian Science Monitor* is such that, although it is headquartered in the United States, the process literally goes on 24/7 around the world. Consisting of eight national bureaus and eight international bureaus as of this writing, production draws on a range of journalists. While *CSM*'s editorial staff accounts for about 83 people, CSPS overall has about 400 employees.

As of mid-2010, the editorial department of *The Christian Science Monitor* is headed by John Yemma as editor, with Marshall Ingwerson as managing editor and Jonathan Wells as managing publisher. Under them come finance, various editors (such as for the weekly magazine and op-ed), national and international news (the former headed by Cheryl Sullivan, the latter by David Scott), copy desk, library, graphics, photography, production, the Web and its online producers, interns, and other administrative positions. Many of these staff members are cited throughout this book, a number working for each of the three news channels; all are key to the process of producing CSMonitor.com (web; 8- to 10-person production crew) *Daily News Briefing* (email; one person), and *CSM Weekly* (print; 12-person editorial crew).

BUREAUS AND THE BUSINESS OF *CSM*

Beginning in Boston, what follows is an introductory organizational look at how the process flows. The best parts are from interviews, of course, but voices from *CSM* personnel appear throughout this book. For example, Beijing correspondent Peter Ford's background is included in Chapter 4, on technology, because it makes for such a good story, and managing publisher Jonathan Wells's wide perspective is reflected in Chapter 5, on findings. What follows here is information on the editors; international news staff (editor Dave C. Scott and deputy editor Amelia Newcomb); and national news staff (editor Cheryl Sullivan, deputy editor Mark Sappenfield, Mark Trumbull, and citations about reporter Peter Spotts and Brad Knickerbocker interspersed).

Editors

John Yemma

When he rejoined the *Monitor* in July 2008 after two decades at the *Boston Globe*, serving in many positions but most recently as deputy managing editor for multimedia, there was loud applause and excited anticipation from trustees and staff alike. "While formats and delivery methods may change, Yemma reaffirmed the *Monitor*'s commitment to unselfish service through daily journalism," former editor David Cook (2008) noted. Upon accepting his new role, with Richard Bergenheim named editor-at-large, Yemma's stated goal was to reposition the *Monitor* as a Web-first, multiplatform news organization specializing in global news, observing that, "Journalism should reflect the variety of life."

Yemma also writes for the *Monitor*'s publications, including the *Weekly* and the *DNB*. His writing style is such that he inserts tidbits such as the derivation of the term "third world" nations (1952, by French demographer Alfred Sauvy, who compared them to the Third Estate of the French Revolution). Or this from his daily column, *Editor's View* (10/26/09, 1): "Historian David Halberstam once suggested that the twentieth century might not be remembered as much for the epic clashes of world war as for the end of colonialism in Asia, Africa, and Latin America. Both are linked, of course, because the defeat of tyranny set the forces of independence and democracy in motion." In another column (11/9/09, 1) Yemma wrote: "News is a function of human activity, ebbing and flowing with the busyness of humans."

In an interview with Leonard Witt (2008), John Yemma underscored that the move to a Web-first model was an innovation, not a last-ditch effort, and how vital journalism is as a watchdog. Seeing the *Monitor* as "serious, thoughtful, and solution-oriented"—beyond spin and celebrity profiles—when he was on NPR's *Fresh Air* with Terry Gross (2009), he underscored his interest in "the human dimension of global news," then outlined how he hoped to move five-fold in five years, with more page views and ad impressions.

Marshall Ingwerson

A 30-year veteran of the *Monitor* and managing editor since 1999, Ingwerson begins his day at 7:40 a.m., meeting with Web and tech people, business staff, news editors, print weekly editors, and others. When we talked (1/19/10) about the *Monitor* perspective of constructive and useful analysis, he pointed out that it is part of "a long, engrained habit" that follows from the earlier days when deadlines were 12 noon for M–F publications. Knowing they would not be first with the news, *Monitor* reporters became used to framing stories that would stand up "when the dust clears." The idea is to qualify and put the facts in context—not too heavy-handedly, but in a way that encourages readers to weigh their own interpretations.

Jonathan Wells

Managing publisher Jonathan Wells has been key to *CSM*'s decision to launch and maintain a Web-first, multiplatform strategy. With a background in law and experience working in the business of media, he was a 2009 Sulzberger fellow at Columbia University's Journalism School. When he joined *The Christian Science Monitor* as director of business development and electronic publishing in 1998, he had the insight to see the Web as pivotal for change. When we talked (2/26/10), Wells provided me with an overall informational overview on the three-pronged multiplatform project: the Web, the print weekly, and *Daily News Briefing* (*DNB*).

The editors knew the *Monitor* needed to be published in new form(s). Media distribution was evolving, and audiences were more frequently finding news on the Web. There was a need to attract new audiences while at the same time maintaining loyal readers, so the research had to be expanded. "The trustees were instrumental in helping to drive change," Wells noted. Wells has worked closely with CSPS board members Judy Wolff, Don Adams, and Walter Jones. The late Richard Bergenheim, a former editor, was also a key player. Chris Urban of Urban Associates and former editor John Hughes proved important for outside consulting.

Realizing that *CSM* distribution is national and international—not local or even regional—and that they didn't like the idea of cutting trees to put out a print product, the team members knew that they needed to go where the audiences were going. More people were online. In terms of developing a strategy, the team considered where the media and journalism were going, and it became clear that the immediate medium of the Web was the answer. This is where John Yemma came in, helping lead the editorial staff into a Web-first delivery while at the same time launching a quality weekly magazine project.

In terms of execution, the Web-centric decision also included producing a weekly for long-time subscribers. As with *DNB*, they determined pricing by "a combination of market studies and competitive analysis" (email 5/5/10). Although current customers didn't represent a huge number, they were a significant and loyal group of supportive, paying subscribers—independent thinkers who are socially responsive and responsible. There was still a role for larger-form journalism, the team realized.

Intensive focus group testing regarding the form of the print publication took place. Multiple layouts and designs were developed and tested, and eventually it was decided that a slightly oversized magazine-like product would work. Each section needed a promise, and readers liked the insertions of "Why it matters" features in certain articles, along with having "People Making a Difference" (*PMAD*) as its own category.

It took about six months to communicate with former subscribers to accept the changes. Consider, too, all the internal transformations that had to occur at the same time: Editorial staff had to learn to write differently for the Web. New production procedures had to be adopted, staff had to be reorganized, and new technology had to be brought in to facilitate Web-first publishing. Both traditional and online producers needed to know more about Web traffic and exposing more people to *Monitor* journalism. The question was: How do you get found? Editors and journalists needed to learn how to encourage readers and visitors to follow internal links, and social networking became an obvious part of that process. Next, you have to retain those readers and visitors, so consumer research continues.

International News

Headed by Dave C. Scott, with Amelia Newcomb as deputy editor, this department currently includes Matt Clark, Carol Huang, Dan Murphy, and Christa Case Bryant in the United States, along with reporters in these foreign bureaus: Ben Arnoldy, New Delhi, India; Scott Baldauf, Johannesburg, South Africa; Peter Ford, Beijing, China; Bob Marquand, Paris, France; Sara Miller Llana, Mexico City; Scott Peterson, Istanbul, Turkey; and Ilene Prusher, Jerusalem, Israel.

After serving as a correspondent covering Wall Street, and later serving as the bureau chief for the *Monitor*'s Latin America and Australasia bureaus, in 1999 David C. Scott was named international news editor. Now, as world editor, Scott says he is happy with the new structure, which enables him to jump on a new story. Yet, as a wish list, he'd like to have more bureaus—for starters in Shanghai, London, Berlin, South America, and Southeast Africa.

Amelia Newcomb, assistant international news editor, had an early stint at the *Monitor* in the 1980s, worked in Washington for a Japanese newspaper, and has reported from China and Japan. A graduate of Harvard with a master's in international relations from the Fletcher School of Law and Diplomacy, she described to me (2/10/10) her typical day: 7:30 a.m., check headlines and emails, see what stories are coming in, and start discussing potential assignments. Editing begins pretty quickly, and plans adjust throughout the day. On most days, editors are working on stories for that day as well as editing pieces for the weekly news magazine. David Scott decides the order of items, which senior editors discuss at 10 a.m.; they operate as a team with four desk editors, overseeing news from the Americas, Africa, Europe, Russia, Asia, Australia, and the Middle East. Being Web-first has changed the daily calculus, as the staff works to respond quickly to the day's news as well as to offer more in-depth stories.

National News

Under the direction of Cheryl Sullivan, the staff is spread around the country. As of this writing, Mark Sappenfield, Judy Douglass, Stacy Teicher Khadaroo, Peter Spotts, and Mark Trumbull are in Boston; Patrik Jonsson reports from Atlanta, Georgia, Mike Farrell from San Francisco; Mark Guarino from Chicago; Brad Knickerbocker from Ashland, Oregon; Amanda Paulson from Chicago; Ron Scherer from New York; and Dan Wood from Los Angeles. In addition to general reporting, some have specialties, as you will see.

National news editor Cheryl Sullivan, like many other *Monitor* employees, has had an interrupted career, with time out to have children, but she sees herself as news-oriented and now straddles two worlds: news and managing a large department (a staff of 22) that keeps moving forward. "A big part of my job has to do with personnel and logistics," she confided (3/25/10). It's an incredible position; working with Mark Sappenfield, Judy Douglass, Brad Knickerbocker, and Andrew Heining, the challenge is "keeping all the balls in the air without dropping them—or at least not very many," she wrote in an email (4/20/10)—and, for her, "disconnecting" on the weekends. No wonder: Her day begins at 6 a.m., and involves getting kids off, reading the daily Christian Science Lesson Sermon, checking news (NPR, WBZ, *Boston Globe*, *USA Today*, *Wall Street Journal*, *New York Times*, CNN, and more) and email, talking to correspondents around the country, handing out assignments, and lining up coverage for what seem like top news items, for a classic example of how the *Monitor* approaches a subject, with concern for individual decision and spiritual growth. I loved her philosophy: "Believe it. Believe in it."

What Mark Sappenfield does as deputy national news editor is help to edit the stories that come in from reporters and decide what topics the *Monitor* should be covering. But he is most interested in the *craft* of writing; so, as part of the organization's goal to drive traffic to the website seven days a week, he also works as a blogger on Sundays. On these days, he checks out what's out there, synthesizing it and looking for connections and meaning, the goal being to add original, fresh analysis to his "derivative reporting." Mark told me (1/19/10) that he knew he wanted to work at the *Monitor*, so majored in journalism and in 1996 joined as a subeditor.

With 16 years experience writing and editing, Mark Guarino is prolific—online every day, producing anywhere from five to seven stories per week. Working in the Chicago bureau, he reflected in our phone conversation (2/9/10) that he finds it less regional and more about getting the pulse of the Midwest.

Washington

Bureau chief of Washington, D.C., *CSM*'s largest national bureau after its headquarters in Boston, is David Cook—who previously has served as editor of *Monitor Broadcasting* (1991 to 1994), as managing editor of the Emmy Award–winning nightly television news program *World Monitor*, and as editor of the *Monitor* (1994 to 2001), when CSMonitor.com was launched and when the newspaper was awarded a 1996 Pulitzer Prize for international reporting. As such, he has great credibility in terms of a wide perspective, and it was certainly impressive to talk with him (2/13/10). The *Monitor's* foundation, he reiterated, comes from statements made 100 years ago by Mary Baker Eddy. Host of *CSM's Monitor Breakfast* interviews, a staple since February 1966, which have included four presidents and nearly every other key political figure you could name, he alerts several dozen news organizations each week so they can participate. The challenge, though, is that public officials today care less about newspapers and are more aware of the risks of live television. In discussing policies, Cook pointed out that there are certain standards of conduct that are understood, and ethics are followed carefully—such as being concerned about effects on families and free trips. Cook was a champion of having the breakfast interviews videotaped and placed on the Web so the public can participate.

Linda Feldmann has extensive experience covering Washington, D.C., and for the past few presidencies she has covered the White House. A mainstay of the *Monitor*, appearing frequently in the *Weekly Edition* and on the Web, she can be seen from time to time on C-SPAN and other Washington news programs. Part of the White House pool, trafficking with the president in a rotation, Feldmann claims that "We learn by osmosis" (2/23/10). Married to *CSM* reporter Warren Richey, who covers the Supreme Court, she shared what it was like being part of the D.C. bureau and told a funny story about when the Dalai Lama visited Washington: He was supposed to use a back exit, but when he did he ran right into some bags of trash. Feldman immediately pulled out her Blackberry, took a photo, and posted it, labeled "Trashgate," on her Facebook blog. Then she posted it on the *Monitor* website with an extended caption.

Weekly Edition

For *CSM* weekly, deputy editor Owen Thomas helps to make decisions upon, among other things, cover stories on topics ranging from "a sports-mad America or progress toward a nuclear-free world," he explained to me (3/12/10). He has enjoyed being able to employ all his talents in his work. In 1977 he became a summer copy kid at the *Monitor*, having also worked for his college newspaper at Principia, and he substituted on *News in Brief*, which, at the time, he considered quite a bit of responsibility for a summer worker. Yes, he attends a number of meetings, declaring, "but they can't survive if they aren't urgent." Mondays, he has a cover topic meeting at 2 p.m.; Tuesday, a news-gathering at 11 a.m.; and Thursday, a feature "sketch" meeting at 2 p.m. for the following week's production. Thomas has been features editor and likes managerial issues, especially working in teams: "Helping me, and helping my church."

Clayton Collins, *Weekly Edition* editor, served as a staff editor on *World Monitor: The Christian Science Monitor Monthly* for its entire run. It premiered in October 1988 as a full-color magazine, with an eventual subscriber base of 250,000, but only lasted until 1993. "So I'm probably the only editor here who's worked directly on production of the *Monitor* in three print frequencies (daily, weekly, monthly)," he mused in an email (4/12/10) about his 20 years and roles with *CSM*, including being deputy foreign editor and features writer and editor.

Editorials

> *Understanding the history and purpose behind the creation of the* Monitor *is important when evaluating its editorial policies and practices.*
>
> —Lawrence N. Strout (1999, p. xiii)

Starting with its first issue, editorials in the *Monitor* have set the bar high. Originally, they took up the entire last page, which called for lots of copy, but by 1934 the two-column format was established. Canham (1958, 370) boasts that the editorial section has "carried forward the paper's interest in awakening people." As you might imagine, these editorials have expressed the *Monitor*'s objectivity, including—for the 2009–2010 year of study—opinions on bullet trains, extending foster care to age 21, "sexting" overreach, South Africa's continental legacy, Obama's education goals, the burka revolution, downsizing the prom, legalizing marijuana, e-colleges, cyber-defense, China's green tech, electric cars, prison cuts, child-sex tourists, vets on campus, coerced healthcare insurance, the decarboned electric bill, abortion and healthcare, the postal service, the death penalty, cybercrime, donor fatigue in Haiti, nuclear power, foreign adoptions, and global warming.

Clayton Jones, chief editorial writer, oversees the op-ed (opinion, editorial), and "Commentary" section, working with Francine Kiefer, Josh Burek, and Jenna Fisher. He began in 1969, recalling for me (2/10/10) that the printing presses were in the basement then, and he has had his current post since 1999. While he and his staff jump on hot stories, looking for links to other writings, they are mainly concerned about having an "ideological balance." Discussing his role in a January 7, 2010 *Talk to the*

Editor,[1] Jones pointed out how important it is to have commentary along with objective news, encouraging readers to think about their own opinions. *Monitor* editorials, he emphasizes, include the opinions of the publisher by a team of people, without a byline, expressing hope or compassion and pointing toward solutions and trends. They are particularly unique in that they don't endorse candidates and are not ideologically driven but enjoy stimulating, sound debate.

Space requirements limit my reportage on opinion and commentary for 2009–2010, from a wide range of contributors representing a wide range of opinion, but here is a sampling: Atticus Finch, retiring the "war on terror," diversity in the Supreme Court, consumers and carbon, legalized gambling, Congress, the tyranny of taxing "sin," Shanghai's expo, America in 2050, needing music, Facebook's shadow culture, Cezanne's legacy, Obama's best link to the Muslim world: Turkey, Build America bonds, women in finance, blacks getting reparations, Iran's upheaval, Burma, the Darfur genocide, charter schools, healthcare reform, sushi without bluefin tuna, racism, Somalia, closing Gitmo, Middle East reporting, neoconservatism, our flag, a Muslim solution for Afghanistan, India's unborn girls, child abuse, family courts, Facebook, Palin's populism, master cheese-makers, energy subsidies, Ayn Rand, women's rights in Honduras, public housing, African leaders, bullet trains, Palestinian resistance, "tea partyers," layoffs, Northern Ireland peace, Iraqi voters, the Senate filibuster, China's bubble, gerrymandering, partisan agendas, and much more.

Once the Commentary section of the *Weekly* hit its new stride, feedback came in. Responses to these editorial opinions, from letters@ CSMonitor.com or *Readers Write*, concerned issues such as child abuse and the court, transatlantic love, Muslims' rich heritage, Iran's *realpolitik*, right-wing rhetoric, U.S. mail and jobs, building schools not bombs, restoring sanity to Wall Street, separation of church and hospital, moral consistency, community first, Obama's realist idealism, the death penalty, battlefield robots, high-speed rail, illegal aliens, the media's role in an angry United States, sea horses, private money for nuclear power, and the United States' attitude to war. Over the years, *CSM* editors report, they have received everything from adoration to scathing rebukes.

Inklings

With cartoons ranging from "Will the last person to flee Congress please turn off the lights?" (3/1/10) to Peanuts, at an empty mailbox, screaming, "RATS! I'm switching to Facebook" (3/15/10), a daily laugh is a necessity. "We like cartoons that challenge your thinking but don't break it," Clayton Jones, chief editorial writer and *Inklings* overseer, has said.[2] He adds: "Bring a little levity to your day. Humor is important to journalism, because it brings us together."

Beginning with "wholesome" comics such as Paul R. Carmack's *The Diary of Snubs, Our Dog, The Adventures of Waddles* (yes, a duck!), and Guernsey Le Pelley's *Tubby and Buddy*, the newspaper began a shift to political cartoons with in-house cartoonists Gene Langley and Brian Barling, as well as Jeff Danziger (1988) from 1987 to 1997, and Clay Bennett[3]—winner of the Pulitzer Prize for Editorial Cartooning in 2002—from 1997 to 2007. Editorial cartoons relative to McCarthyism cited by Strout (1999, 11) are particularly revealing, including this one: "A jockey riding 'Headlined Disloyalty Charges' streaked ahead of another jockey riding, 'Less Heralded Exonerations,' obviously referring to the claim that McCarthy's charges received more prominent attention than did rebuttals or the evidence" ("Unfairly matched," March 18, 1950, 18).

Commentary and Columnists

How fortunate it is that John Hughes, a Pulitzer Prize winner and former editor of the *Monitor* (1970–1979) contributes a bimonthly column to the *Weekly Edition*. Having also served as assistant secretary of state for public affairs, U.S. State Department spokesman, director of the Voice of America, CEO of the *Deseret Morning News*, and currently as a professor of communications at Brigham Young University, his wide-ranging experiences and expertise are invaluable. Best of all, he maintains a keen sense of humor—as evidenced in "A trip down the *Monitor*'s memory lane" (3/26/09), recounting high jinx amongst colleagues. It was a highpoint of this research to talk to Hughes (4/28/10), much as it has been to read his columns over time. This last year, he has written about the following: "Obama's real target should be the culture of greed"; "Where democracy and Islam coexist"; "Hillary: Dutiful diplomat, or 2012 candidate?"; "North Korea's defiance puts Obama in a corner"; "A nuclear-free world? Not yet"; "Faith in America lifts the public mood"; "Iranian exiles in Iraq pose tough dilemma for Obama"; "EU presidency would be bully pulpit for Blair"; "Indonesia gets love. Pakistan gets tough love"; "Female cops in Iraq? Arab women seize freedom"; "From Cheney to Dobbs, resolutions to swear by"; "In the war of ideas, Uncle Sam's voice must be heard"; "Haiti-type disasters require a UN rapid-response unit"; "Cuba's growing clout in Venezuela spells trouble"; and "Can South Africa live up to Mandela's legacy?"

"In 1973 I was between jobs and went to see Godfrey Sperling, Jr., then the *Monitor*'s [news manager of the Washington bureau]," now-veteran columnist Walter Rodgers recalled (2/24/10). "I needed a job. He never said he did not have a vacancy, but from questions I asked at news conferences, he knew my politics were slightly left of center. I strongly sensed in our brief interview that he did not think me *Monitor* material. That ended my brief flirtation with *The Christian Science Monitor*." Soon afterward, the Associated Press hired Rodgers as their White House radio correspondent in the post-Watergate Ford and Carter years and for first year of Ronald Reagan's presidency. In late 1981, ABC News hired him, within two years naming him their Moscow bureau chief for five years—including the first four years of Mikhail Gorbachev's tenure. From there, he went on to be ABC's Justice Department correspondent, then joined CNN to become their Jerusalem bureau chief and senior international correspondent. When, upon retirement, *CSM* approached him to write a column, Rodgers then mused, "I remembered the elegant *Monitor* journalists of my youth: Erwin Canham, Joseph Harsch, Richard Strout, and Roscoe Drummond, and I said to myself, 'That is fine company,' so I said 'yes' to the column idea." And how happy we readers are that he agreed. Here are some of his recent titles: "America: A superpower no more"; "The danger of an Israeli strike on Iran"; "Religious bullying happens here, too"; "Republicans need fresh ideas, not a savior"; "If Nigeria turns a corner, women will be steering"; "Caveats for journalists in combat zones"; "Sarah Palin: Can she be more than a political celebrity?"; "Forget Afghanistan. Let's nation-build at home first"; "There's a reason France is one of the best places to live"; "Pacifying Afghanistan: A dangerous dream"; "Oprah's rise, and the fall of network news"; "Terror trials will pose tough questions about Islam"; "A year into Obama's presidency, is America postracial?"; "Struggle over Arctic riches: A new (very) cold war"; and "Illegal immigration undermines America's character."

Josh Burek runs the *Monitor*'s opinion section, making sure published pieces cover a wide range of both newsworthy topics and points of view. Not magnetized by beltway issues, he aims at diversity in terms of contributors ranging from recognized experts to regular moms and students. "On the Web, where there's an overabundance of information, the idea is to present content that's scarce—that's not seen as a mere commodity," he asserted (2/17/10). While the *Monitor* recently stopped paying for opinion essays from freelancers, that decision hasn't stopped writers from submitting insightful essays. Burek says he receives well over 100 essays a week, from which he publishes about 10. Aside from two veteran voices that appear biweekly in the print edition, the *Monitor*'s opinion section doesn't feature regular columnists—a rarity in the news industry. Burek says that can be a strength: "Every day people compete to get published in the *Monitor*, helping make it the most diverse page possible."

Would you be able to answer this question on *Jeopardy?*: Her commentary and opinions appear without her byline and she is the reporter who made George Bush get teary on 9/11. Answer:*Monitor* editorial writer Francine Kiefer. She joined the *Monitor* in 1980, then went to the San Jose *Mercury News* for a while before returning to serve at the White House for *CSM*, did various jobs, then became the *Monitor*'s German correspondent in 1989—the year the wall came down—and in 1998 she was in Washington, covering the White House for *CSM*. She has done lots of research on Hans Vogel, a political opponent of Hitler, and is half done writing a book about him, she told me (2/25/10). And, as to the second part of the *Jeopardy* question, White House correspondent Richard Keil (2004) reported how, on September 13, 2001, Kiefer asked a key question that other reporters later declared wishing they had thought to pose: "How is this affecting you personally, sir, and what are you praying for?" He continues:

Bush, standing behind the desk that Franklin Roosevelt used as president, suddenly turned his head away, toward the South Lawn, his palms still planted firmly on the desk blotter.

He turned back to face us a few moments later, his eyes brimming.

"I'm not thinking of myself. I'm thinking of the families, all those children," he said, pausing to maintain his composure. "I think of myself as a loving guy, but I have a job to do."

I glanced around the room and noticed that everyone—Karen Hughes, his closest advisor; [Gordon] Johndroe; even the other reporters—had tears in their eyes.

Specialty Editors

Within the *Monitor* are a number of specialty areas, each with its own editor(s). What follows are descriptions of *Decoder*; the Education, Science, Money, Innovation, Environment, and Culture sections; film and book reviews; the *Home Forum*; the copy desk; and online editorials.

Decoder

As the sole writer for *Decoder*, ever since the *Weekly Edition* began Peter Grier has submitted his column under the logo that design director John Kehe created; then, it is up to him to come up with an idea. His self-set goal, he explained (2/19/10), is having something "based on serious stories, explanatory and educational," such as how the president had to buy his own food. He plays off the news and likes variety, such as his article about Valentine's Day and Supreme Court judges.

Here are some of Grier's subjects during the time of my study: "Michelle's garden secret"; "Yo, tourists: See capitol, skip the White House"; "Everyone's a critic of presidential speeches"; "Take your protest home"; "So you wanna be a Supreme Court justice?"; "When Washington does math, be very skeptical"; "Washington is not funny. Except Joe Biden"; "The public grilling" (Sonia Sotomayor); "It takes a reporter to know a reporter"; "July 4 trivia test"; "Only one president can claim a sport of his own" (Hooverball); "Bitten by their own words" (presidents and tape recorders); "How the US knows that's no Wal-Mart in the desert" (spy satellites); "Tale of Teddy Roosevelt's Nobel Peace Prize"; "The Sarah Palin stamp of approval" (tweets for candidates); "First lesson of Diplomatic Protocol 101: The bow"; "Which president was the best football player?"; "fil'i.bus.ter: Monumental hints" (labels for Washington, D.C. memorials); "Hail to the . . . postmaster general" (losing $7 billion this year); "First ladies vs. 'fashionistas'"; "The power of a few choice words" (Ted Sorensen); and "A face only a $50 bill could love."

Education

Although there is not a specific section on education in *CSM*'s weekly, there have been a range of relevant articles, such as about free education in Russia, Obama encouraging education in China and India, South Africa's education gap, China boosting rural education, a Newsmaker Breakfast with education secretary Arne Duncan, colleges that offer no-frills education, the role of education in Women's History Month, and *Monitor* editorials on testing Obama's education goals and zapping the education gap. Amanda Paulson and Stacy Teicher Khadaroo are education co-reporters, Amanda working the first part of the week and Stacy taking over midway. For now, both are new mothers working out of their homes. Their three-part series on teaching, "What makes teachers good," which ran in March 2009, recently won an Education Writers Association (EWA) award.

Paulson also serves as midwest bureau chief—which she (jokingly?) described as "anything between coasts" (2/23/10). She began with *CSM* as a junior editorial assistant (JEDA), having graduated from Dartmouth and serving as an intern in 2000. Although she speaks both French and Spanish, she has only used these skills occasionally on the job. What she has loved the most about working with the *Monitor*, she wanted me to know, was the people, whom she respects as very smart and genuinely nice. "They create a family-friendly work environment, which is rare," she said.

Stacy Teicher Khadaroo, education reporter, told me by telephone how she has worn lots of hats during her 14-year stint with the *Monitor* (2/12/10). For her, education has been her main focus, incorporating a variety of subjects; basically, she keeps up by following education research, publications, and government policies and still reports on the "No Child Left Behind" campaign, testing, disadvantaged students, and much more.

Science

Responding to reader concern about climate change, *The Christian Science Monitor* launched a long-term initiative in April 2007,[4] intending to be a key source for those wishing to better understand and respond to scientific research on the topic. Whether "green" or general, the subject of science has long been a staple of *Monitor* reportage.

It's been fun pulling out his "geek stuff," science editor Peter N. Spotts shared with me (2/26/10). Specializing in the many aspects of science, contributing to national and international news, writing *Horizons*, and writing articles such as "Eureka! Water is found on the moon" (*DNB* 11/16/09, 2), part of his email signature includes a quotation from a paleontology email list: "I just bought a 12-pound theropod for Thanksgiving dinner."

Money

"Money Man" Laurent Belsie has been a long-time part of *CSM*, "reinventing" himself, as he told me (3/12/10), along the way. He began in 1981, after graduating from Northwestern University with a degree in journalism. Born in Paris, his family moved to Indiana, where his father worked in the travel industry. After marriage, Belsie moved to Chicago, where he wrote about city politics, agriculture, and manufacturing while his wife earned a Ph.D. When they moved to the Pittsburgh area in 1989, he switched focus to concentrate on technology, launching the *Monitor*'s "Computers for the Rest of Us" column. In St. Louis, he became a business page reporter and later, in Boston, the economy editor.

Introduced to the *Monitor* by an older brother, David R. Francis, columnist of *Economic Scene*, decided at the age of 12 that he wanted to be a *Monitor* journalist. Despite being a Canadian, he faced the likelihood of being drafted into the U.S. Army if he immigrated to the United States when he was first offered a job at the *Monitor*, after graduating from college in Ottawa with a journalism degree in 1954. So he worked for the *Winnipeg Free Press*, the *Victoria Daily Colonist*, and the *Financial Post* in Toronto for several years until he was past draft age. Then he was finally able to join *CSM*—in Boston briefly, then in the New York bureau in 1961. After that came stints in Washington and Bonn, and in 1974 he was back to Boston as business editor. Francis's interest in financial journalism obviously continues, as he regularly keeps up with reading reports from the Center on Budget and Policy Priorities, the Economic Policy Institute, the Peterson Institute for International Economics, Citizens for Tax Justice, the CATO Institute, the American Heritage Foundation, the Brookings Institution, and other think tanks. All this research comes together for his column, which he has written since the 1960s. Because he has such a large list of contacts (anywhere between 200 to 300 economists alone), most of Francis's reportage is based on interviews, he told me during our interview (2/17/10).

Here are some examples of what Francis has contributed from April 2009 to April 2010: "Economic slump provides tinder for global markets"; "Tax the heirs of the rich"; "Can the world cope with $1.5 quadrillion in derivatives?"; "Why IMF should lighten up on world's poorest nations"; "Can the US manage China's economic comeback?"; "Healthcare reform would cut pay of many professionals"; "Fed's stimulus runs risk of inflation, devalued dollar"; "Recession has changed the immigration debate"; "Sanction on Iran and Israel could defuse Middle East"; "US is slipping toward plutocracy"; "China's investments pose new global challenge"; "More spending on Afghan war could hurt the dollar"; "On US deficits, the worries are bipartisan"; "If Obama needs revenue, why not tax corporations?"; "Does the Federal Reserve need an audit?"; "New ways to tax Wall Street's rich"; "Big banks are too big—and unproductive"; "Workers' share of America's pie is shrinking"; and "An 800-year history lesson: Big debts, long recovery."

Francis considers himself a moderate liberal, as he supports a redistribution of income away from the rich, more regulation for banks, and a check on bank and CEO bonuses and would prefer a single payer healthcare. "I know whom I respect and whom I want to read," he stated. He gets about 100 emails per day, which he reads along with several newspapers out of his home office, and comes into the *Monitor* newsroom to do his column on Thursdays. The *Monitor* maintains an archive of his columns on its Website.

Innovation

Beginning around 1930, scientific journalism began to be taken seriously, and *The Christian Science Monitor*, Robert C. Cowen (1984, 88–89) reminds us, was an early leader in that process:

This newspaper, published by a church, has striven to keep theology out of its news columns. It endeavors to make its coverage of science news unbiased, factual, and reasonably complete. But when the occasion demands, it has not hesitated to nail its colors to the masthead. Thus, it has taken stands on the moral, ethical, and social issues raised by the sciences.

Editorially, it has supported free inquiry and the dissemination of scientific knowledge. It has urged wider public participation in the oversight and regulation of socially important research, such as in genetic engineering. It has welcomed the larger view of mankind, of our place in the cosmos, and of our responsibilities to our home planet that the sciences are developing. It has endorsed the principle of separation of church and state in the classroom and decried efforts to debase science teaching to please certain fundamentalist interpretations of the Bible . . . This newspaper has given editorial support to the progress of the sciences in the hope that the insights gained by free exploration of the natural world will help humanity choose life.

As innovation editor, Chris Gaylord told me (2/10/10) that he jumped at the chance to practice what he had learned as a history major, then as an intern at *CSM*. His work involves preparing a biweekly section for print, putting articles online after they have appeared in the weekly, coblogging on the *Horizons* blog with Matthew Shaer, and editing Peter N. Spotts's science blog, *Discoveries*. Whether writing about the world's cheapest car (India's Tata Nano, costing $2,500), the Doomsday Clock, Google's "superphone" Nexus One, the carbon footprint of email spam, pixels, Twitter-only sales, biodegradable phones, blocking online ads, warranties, e-books, or 3-D glasses, his well-researched reportage helps geeks, Green folks, and everyday consumers stay on top of what's new in technology. *Horizons* got 128,000 hits in May, 2009; 279,000 in July, 2009; and 2 million in October; optimistically, the editors hope to get 10 million per month in the future. After all, *CSM* hit the 14.5 million mark in March, 2010, and *Horizons* continues to be popular. So far, its most popular topics have been about Punxatawny Phil, YouTube's addition of 1080p HD video, looking into the Bloom Box fuel cells, and Gaylord's column titled "Got a new computer? Install these nine programs right away."

Environment

Judy Lowe, environment editor, alternates her section with *Innovation*. When we met (1/20/10), she confessed that gardening is really her passion—as seen in her blog *Diggin' It*. "We say we want to be *green*—to reduce carbon emissions and our carbon footprints, use our resources wisely, and architecturally to design and build efficiently, but obviously that is a major commitment."

Culture

> The best, the most profound modern artists have understood, in the words of one Monitor *reviewer, that, "freedom as freedom-free has not proved sufficient; to be out of prison is an adequate aim in life only for a man behind bars." The best, the most profound modern artists have come to view their mission as a search for order—an organization of the new "facts," no longer ruling out continuity with our past.*
>
> —Melvin Maddocks (1984, 103)

Under the direction of Susan Leach, culture editor, this section typically begins with an article of general cultural interest, then has a film review, "6 Picks: Recommendations from the *Monitor* Staff" (including music, books, television shows, albums, CDs, DVDs, and other media choices), poetry, and the *Home Forum*, which usually contains one or two timeless contributions and Ruth Walker's *Verbal Energy* column. A long-time *Monitor* staple, Walker writes about topics such as a word-a-day website, words retaining "a certain roguish appeal," the dance of language, ethics and borrowed words, "noodle-hanging idioms," verbal turn signals, communication and eye contact, the word of the year ("unfriend"), apostrophes, equal-opportunity nouns, lost illusions, and many other linguistic plays.

Each issue of the weekly also contains the *Monitor Crossword* (yes, with the solution also available!), handled by copyeditor Gillian Charters; Clare Turner of CSPS is responsible for the *Monitor*'s religious article, "A Christian Science Perspective." Film and book reviews also appear in the Culture section, but operate autonomously.

Film Reviews

> It was not the best of years; it was not the worst of years. But 2009 reaffirmed a truism about popular culture: One way or the other, whatever

*is going on in the zeitgeist will somehow seep into the movies. Some of
the year's more interesting films, as well as some of the least defensible,
mirrored in often equal measure the world around them.*

—Peter Rainer, *Ten best films of 2009* (12/27/09–1/3/10, 48).

Following in the footsteps of David Sterritt, who held the job of film
reviewer for 35 years, Peter Rainer joined the *Monitor* in 2005—headquartered in Los Angeles instead of his predecessor's New York City. "The
movie business is bi-coastal," he pointed out (2/22/10). The schedule that
works best for him is seeing movies in the evening, even though it admittedly "isn't very helpful for a social life." Screenings usually include a mix
of critics and peripheral audience; good at gut feelings, he doesn't like to
talk to other critics. Mostly, Rainer reported enjoying being a film critic,
except he admitted he has been known to walk out of screenings at film fes-
tivals when the movies were insufferable, and he clearly does not like for-
mulaic styles. Catch this for credibility: he sees some 250 to 300 films per
year! Though far from exclusively so, his emphasis for the *CSM* weekly, as
opposed to online, is international, independent, and documentary fare.[5]

Book Reviews

The section operates independently, in its own right. One or more
books are reviewed each week, along with a sidebar called "What are
you reading? *Monitor* readers share their favorite titles," and *Short Takes*
includes brief reviews ranging from literature to memoirs. Declaring that
she has the greatest job at the *Monitor*, Marjorie Kehe, book editor, began
working in *CSM*'s New York office on education. She loves to talk about
books, especially fiction, which are reviewed year-round, with double
issues and a special summer reading guide. When we met (2/10/10),
I teased her about being the most popular person on staff, but she
deflected the praise by pointing out that staff know they can have access
to the many books publishers send her for review. One of her favorite
perks is being able to interview many people in the book world. In an online *Talk to the Editor*[6] conversation with John Yemma, hosted by Pat
Murphy, Kehe said that "the book market tends to reflect who we are,
and where our mentality is." They discussed the December 20, 2009 *CSM*
weekly issue on "The Future of Reading," and encouraged her to share
her current favorite books, so the self-described "child of two English
teachers" suggested Michael Lewis's *The Big Short: Inside the Doomsday*

Machine (Norton, 2010), on the U.S. economy. Noting a dark side in fiction in general (such as Stieg Larsson's trilogy), along with young people's reaction to Stephanie Meyer's *Twilight* series, she nevertheless reported that most *Monitor* readers prefer nonfiction, especially Greg Mortenson's *Three Cups of Tea* (2007) and its follow-up *Stones into Schools* (2009). As suggestions for summer reading, she told about Stephen King's baseball novella, a thriller by Scott Turow, Jonathan Alter's review of Obama's first year, Laura Bush's memoir, and enough others to keep us on Kindles.[7]

Home Forum

As prescribed specifically by Mary Baker Eddy, this column, ostensibly containing a light essay, sometimes some art or poems, and maybe an excerpt from a literary work, is meant to serve high cultural interests. It also includes the religious article—often with a translation in a foreign language—the only explicit instance of Christian Science being employed in the paper. Here are some examples from the 2009–2010 Web-first year: "Keeping up with the Obamas"; "The boss" (a Rwandan silverback gorilla); "Sahara called" (a Tuareg tribesman with cell phone); "My mother, my 'friend' " (on Facebook); "Commuter, converted"; "In Audubon's steps"; "A wild life" (Bhutan classroom); "Jobless in Maine"; "Pigskin passion, handed off"; "Not strangers for long" (friendly Ghanaians); "Reading Gogol in Wyoming"; "Zimbabwe's language of hope"; "Adventures in eBayland"; "Timbuktu tech"; "Visible relief" (Port-au-Prince, Haiti); "Crossing lines at the Olympics"; "When night falls" (migrating geese); and "Mrs. Mugabe, I presume?"

John Gould (1992, 17) looked back at his 50 years writing for *Home Forum*—which at first was called "Dispatches from the Farm," with subjects such as gathering eggs, dew on morning buttercups, mince pies, and platitudes about bucolic life before the editors requested that it become more "literary." He recounted:

I once wrote about the flag, and four readers sent me four flags—one of them a Jolly Roger. I mentioned peddling ice, and a lady sang "The Ice Man's Song" into a cassette for me. When I dwelt on the old three-tine kitchen fork, over 400 readers mailed me three-tine forks—the most active topic in the half century. We spent the winter on thank-you notes, and then several months mailing forks to readers who said they didn't have one, but would like one if we got too many.

Rosalie Dunbar, news editor of the Christian Science magazines, actually works for the *Journal*, *Sentinel*, and *Herald* (JSH) editorial department. She and Clare Turner, editor of the *Christian Science Perspective*, sometimes solicit entries—especially those related to breaking events such as a oil spill on the Gulf coast—and they also get unsolicited manuscripts. Being a church member is a requirement for authors, so it is natural to want to support and cultivate contributors. Some of their writers can produce newsworthy articles spontaneously; some can quickly elucidate on a particular subject, such as their country's elections; and occasionally the editors reprint something from the *Christian Science Sentinel*, adapted to the *Monitor* audience. For much of its early history, the religious article ran without a byline, but with the move to the Web the decision was made to include author names. This last year they have covered events such as the World Economic Forum in Davos, Pakistan's refugees, the Berlin Wall 20 years later, help for Haiti, hope in Iraq, orphans of the world, prayer for Poland, and much more.

The Daily Religious Article: Christian Science Perspective

To produce an international daily newspaper with a Christian con- science and a balanced judgment of the world scene might be a vital part of the total contribution that a young church designed to "reinstate primitive Christianity and its lost element of healing" could make toward the healing of the nations.

The Monitor *was never designed to be merely a house organ for the church that publishes it, nor even to be a "religious" newspaper in the ordinary sense of the word.*

—Robert Peel (1984, 110)

This solitary explicit reference to Mary Baker Eddy's denomination is said to be of interest to many non–Christian Scientist readers also. For example, in discussing an attack on Washington's Holocaust Museum, "Helping put an end to hate crimes" (*DNB* 6/18/09, 3), Rosalie E. Dunbar cites the Southern Poverty Law Center's report about 926 hate groups in the United States, then considers, "Instead of feeling helpless in the face of violence, we can respond right now through prayer." Matt Schmidt's "When evil feels powerful" (*DNB* 6/22/09, 3) reports: "My morning news- paper recently had a front-page photograph of a building in Pakistan that had been bombed by militants. This was in such contrast to the good, lov- ing acts that I knew were going on there . . . Trying to find inspiration, I thought about this Bible verse: 'Do not fret because of evil men or be envious of those who do wrong'"(Ps. 37:1).

"I think of it as a beacon of hope—here is this paragraph that can speak to someone lost, or dark," said Clare Turner (2/26/10), editor of the daily *Monitor* religious article, adding that, "The *Monitor* is solution-oriented, with an underlying expectation of (spiritual) healing." It is inspirational writing, so staff looks for spiritual insight, particularly as it relates to Christian Science. They keep in touch with the various *CSM* editors for tie-ins and aim to be responsive to news and needs. A number of contributors are Christian Science practitioners who offer insight on how they are praying about some of the issues facing our world. Contributors can submit headlines, but, as that is part of the editing process, they are often changed. There is not much feedback, but if so it is usually positive. Turner has been editing the religious article since 2000, having come from the *Christian Science Sentinel* in the late 1990s. *DNB* uses a shortened version of *A Christian Science Perspective*, so she has a new challenge: reducing a submission from 700 to 325 words.

The daily *Christian Science Perspective* article appears on spirituality .com and on christianscience.com. "There are three versions," Rosalie Dunbar explained in an email (4/29/10), and all can be considered an agenda for prayer. The print article, at about 525 words in length, runs first in the *Weekly Edition*—hopefully, with a connection to the cover story. For example, the spiritual view of the first magazine's theme of the new economy reported, "Central to rebuilding the economy is knowing who the real builder is." Other themes have included helping endangered species, praying for the homeless, Pakistan's refugees, Haitians, healing hurtful memories, humor's healing effect, keeping healthcare choices broad, daily philanthropy, solutions to climate change, blessings of fidelity, and peace on earth.

Oftentimes, the print article is posted on the Web, expanded to 675 to 750 words. There are also standard articles addressing topics such as "finding a home, a job, a purpose in life, or dealing with anger, fear, grief, loss, loneliness." Since its history had *Christian Science Perspective* running on the *Home Forum* page, the staff likes to retain the spirit of "home" in the mix. Lastly is the *Daily New Briefing* edition, a reduced version of about 250 words giving a summary of the article's key metaphysical points.

Copyeditors

The editorial-page staff has the difficult task of translating general policy directives and positions into explicit editorials which will be the voice of the paper. Their work is based on long experience. Each has had a

wide background. Unlike staff correspondents and columnists, their
work perforce but undeservedly must be done anonymously.

—Erwin D. Canham (1958, 371)

Having started in the *Monitor*'s London bureau for three years in the
1960s and spending another three years in Boston as a reporter on New
England news and the editorial page, then 26 years as director of publications for Harvard's School of Education, Gillian Charters returned in
2001, editing *Monitor World* and then becoming copy desk chief. She
described her schedule to me when we met (2/16/10): Early in the week
she checks the Web, as everything gets busier at the end of the week, when
reporters are meeting deadlines "by the skin of our teeth" and things get
bottlenecked. Realizing how much pressure desk editors with the overseas
news and national news departments have working 24/7, she noted how
editing has changed tremendously over the years. Her job—which used
to be shared by 8 to 10 people, but now is just her and Heather Ehmke—
is to read everything, correct typos, fact-check, and make suggestions for
changes. "Editors have too much to do—they need to produce for the
Web and so have much more work," Charters realizes under the current
system. What happens, then, is that some things go straight to the Web
and retroactively get fixed up.

Online Editors

Brought on 2-1/2 years ago as an online editor, Jimmy Orr works on
Web journalism, trying to signal to the reader *The Christian Science Monitor*'s
presence. Having run the White House website during George W. Bush's
first term, he now manages a team of people whose focus is to add value
to stories and blogs. Consistently, they ask: How do we best present the
content? What strategies do we take to get our content noticed? Further,
recognizing that their main charge is working with the newsroom on
change, they keep a constant eye on frequency and networking. "Change
is the hardest thing in the world. As an organization, don't look inward.
Mindset is critical," Orr mused during our interview (1/20/10). "We can't
just rely on our current audience to grow a new audience," he emailed me
later (3/12/10), "It's about broadening our focus and getting to know
influencers who can drive traffic to our site." He meets each morning at
10 a.m. with John Yemma and Marshall Ingwerson, analyzing traffic; right
now, 85 to 90 percent is in the United States, with about 10 million hits

per month. The goal is 25 million. Being social is part of the process, along with embracing the new paradigm: "You can't just throw a story out there and hope people will read it. It's also finding the audience," Orr cautions, noting that, "It's changing the way we do business."

"The written story takes precedence," deputy online editor Pat Murphy declared when we met (3/12/10). Other accoutrements should be complimentary, so he tries to come up with interesting titles for videos, photographs, and such. As you can see, this involves multimedia. "We're all online now," he contends. He is in charge of the *Monitor Daily Podcast* (digital media files distributed over the Internet), whereby *CSM* conducts conversations with a reporter or staff member; audio only, they take place on the second floor of the building. Murphy also is the conduit for "Talk to the Editor," a live video webcast hosted online on the *Editor's Blog* at CSMonitor.com that began in May 2009 and airs each Thursday from 1 to 1:30 p.m. with interviews of various editors and *CSM* staff. So far, he and John Yemma have talked to more than 30 staff writers, correspondents, and guests about news events.

FINANCES AND FINANCIAL STAFF

> From its inception, the Monitor *has had a keen interest in global economic progress. It has seen such progress as evidence that the human spirit was freeing itself from the limiting belief that mankind must live "by the sweat of its brow." Thus, economic growth has been deemed important as evidence of greater human freedom than for the accumulation of material goods.*
>
> —Richard A. Nenneman (1984, 43)

Owing to its economic independence, which has liberated the *Monitor* from having to make political and/or industrial commitments, its investments have consistently been kept quite private. Consistent with the Christian Scientific, generally positive approach to life—expecting good as part of God's harmonious plan—it has nevertheless remained rational and pragmatic when it comes to fiscal planning and accountability. Learning a lesson when it warned readers about what eventually became the stock market crash of 1929, its *Money* section remains widely respected and read.

In 1916, operating costs for *The Christian Science Monitor* were $920,112; in 1919, $1,726,313; and in 1945 the figure was $4,350,177. At the time of its 50th anniversary, its budget was reported as $6,593,000, expended thus: editorial, $1,259,000; advertising, $1,431,000; circulation $623,000; production, $2,065,000; and $1,215,000 for other technical operations. When one considers its unique product, with highly qualified staff and numerous foreign bureaus, it is amazing that it has been able to hang in there.

Advertisers in the *Monitor* have always been varied—current ones being the following: www.TEACH12.com/8*CSM*, Armored Safe, Audubon, Axios Press, Baylor University Press, Bose, the Bradford Exchange, Century One Books, Citrix (MyPC), Concernusa.org, DirecTV, Dish Network, EdenPURE, Endless Pools, First Street, Guaranteed Consumer Funding, Hawthorne Village, Hammacher Schlemmer, Heat Surge, The-HistoryShirt, The Holy Bible in its Original Order, Institute of Analytical Reading, International Currency, Investment Rarities Incorporated, Jump-Sport, LifeLock, Mellen Investment Company, Neuton mowers, Newmarket Press, Newsmax, Omaha Steaks, Oomingmak, Oxfam, Paramount Rare Coin and Currency, Paul Frederick, PBS, ProFlowers, Recreation Equipment, Red Envelope, Sea Eagle, Sears, Simplicity Sofas, Smucker's, Sophisticated Shirts, Stamps.com, Strang-Tradex Group, TAAC, US Rare Coin and Bullion Reserve, Van Guard Tours and Cruises, Vonage, and YMT Vacations. Portraying a pattern similar to other dailies, the *Monitor*'s income has traditionally been 40 percent from subscribers, 60 percent from advertisers.

Finances at the *Monitor*, as at all news organizations, are a continuing concern (Passantino 2004). Staff salaries at *CSM* certainly are modest. The Web currently draws about $1/2 million annually in revenue. Some of its sponsored links include a booking agency (Grabow Entertainment), business resources (business cards and checks), computers (Memory Upgrade), charitable donations (car and boat), graphic design (LogoBee), real estate (international shipping, mortgage calculator, moving companies), speakers bureaus (Christian, motivational, and sports), and Web services (dedicated servers and Web hosting).

Senior marketing director Susan Hackney comes to the role well prepared to manage change, having 20 years in senior management roles in marketing and through ongoing executive leadership training; she was selected to attend Aramark Corporation's executive leadership program at Penn State and as a Sulzberger fellow at Columbia's Journalism School. Responsible for development and vision of the *Monitor*'s shift from a daily print publication to a Web-first format, she continually balances notions of audience, brand distinction, circulation, and public relations during the transition. "This is more than just a job," she said (4/9/10). "*The Christian Science Monitor* matters—personally. It's nice that we are approaching tough problems in a similar way. We're a team, and it feels comfortable that everyone has the best intentions."

Advertising sales director Bob Hanna is the ideal person in this role at a critical juncture when *CSM* is deciding who its target niche is and how to best attract and keep him or her. He came on as a consultant in 2007, having worked at Burst Media for a dozen years and at both newspapers and magazines before that. So far, he finds, people either love the *Monitor* or say they don't want to advertise in a religious publication. He lists the following as a profile of the *Monitor*'s audience: affluent, educated, and not necessarily Christian Scientist. For him, the experience has been finding a very tolerant organization with lots of room for different points of view. "They are a generous group of people—period. Always thoughtful, always courteous," he told me when we talked on the phone (4/2/10). *Wired* magazine (Keane 2008) quotes him as saying that "ad revenue has been growing at a healthy clip: September was the strongest month by far, despite the stalled economy. The magazine was conceived to maintain some subscription revenue and to appeal to readers who are committed to print." *CSM* uses the James G. Elliott Company, an independent advertising sales rep firm, to oversee *Monitor* advertising. On the Web it uses various third-party online ad networks to fill unsold ad space on *CSM* onitor.com. "Most major publishers rely on these services to fill the space they are unable to sell through their own efforts," he wrote in an email (4/30/10), adding that, "The goal, of course, is to minimize our reliance on them."

Donal Toole was brought in 5-1/2 years ago as part of an experienced finance and strategy team under a new church treasurer who was driving to improve the financial operations of TMC. Although there was no thought at this time of doing away with the M–F format, it was apparent to most finance professionals that the daily was not sustainable. After several initiatives to figure out the future of the *Monitor* had not yet yielded a viable plan, an outside consultant was brought in, initially meeting with just the Board of Trustees. Then the discussion was expanded to finance to model out the alternatives. When introduced to *Monitor* management, finance worked initially with the consultant, then as a team to build out a four-year flight path to break even without betraying *Monitor* values. Toole's role, as finance and strategy director, changed at this point, and he was brought into the team to work on and be part of the implementation. "It's not enough to produce good *Monitor* journalism—it must be read as it is valued, and it will make money," he asserted (2/26/10). He said he admires Mary Baker Eddy's considerable flexibility and business acumen, and likes being part of a change movement.

Abe McLaughlin, product manager, has as his goal bringing reader feedback into the loop. He pointed out that *The Christian Science Monitor* weekly has grown from a 48-page magazine with a circulation of 43,000 when it was launched in April, 2009 to complement the *Monitor* on the Web, and how, by the time of our interview (1/20/10), it had grown to 65,000. Check out this link: http://www.digitaleditiononline.com/publi cation/?=27986&pre=1. Additionally, free newsletters are provided to 50,000 e-subscribers, and currently CSMonitor.com draws some four million visitors per month.

Hired to help them convert to being Web-first, Patty Collinsworth, circulation marketing director, brought 10 years of marketing experience with her, and it showed: circulation soared from 40,000 at the beginning to 75,000 for the weekly, *DNB* from zero to 3,000 subscribers. "The challenge was to convert daily subscribers. They had hoped for 85 percent, but were thrilled to get 93 percent," she revealed when we met (2/25/10). Realizing that people were price- and time-sensitive and that the organization wanted to maintain *Monitor* quality journalism, they went all out. "We knew we wanted to grow," she recalled. Still committed to daily journalism, Collinsworth and her colleagues looked at it financially as an opportunity to do the deeper dive. Calling it a classic example of teamwork, she said, "It is a wonderful group of people—dedicated and invested, making a difference." They had to sell the product, and it helped that the price would be less for the weekly than for the M–F newspaper. The business plan was changed to adapt to the Web, but they realized they still needed the revenues coming from print. Wanting to be thoughtful in the process, they took the best of what they had, and the results a year later confirm those efforts.

Direct marketing manager Haide Bolanos, whose area of expertise is international relations, performs a range of jobs as she plans and implements direct mail campaigns to increase new subscriptions. Deadline-driven, she knows her contribution makes a difference: "At this organization, it's not just a job. I am grateful to be part of the change—it's a gift," she shared (2/25/10).

SUPPORT STAFF

Photography and Multimedia

There is a long and distinguished history of outstanding illustrations in the *Monitor*. Early credit goes to Dwight G. Sturges, who etched many a masterpiece over a quarter century, along with portrait artist Frank Saddler, cartographer Russell Lenz, illustrator Gene Langley, and many more.

The first issue (4/12/09) of the *Weekly* featured as its centerfold a photographic extravaganza titled "Earth in transition: Spring and fall"; from there have come other eye-catching treats such as "Stages of sport," "Global moments," "Water world," "Motherhood's pride and joy," "Don't try this at home," "Sandlot summer," "Water, water everywhere," "Lives in limbo," "The steeplechase of bicycle racing," "Berlin wall legacy," "Images of Asia," "Panoply of patterns," "South Africa's tenuous transit," "The little-seen side of Kabul," "Haiti's charcoal trade," "In far Patagonia," and "Street treats, worldwide." As noted in that last example of award-winning *CSM* visual coverage, emphasis is on global images—such as a sunflower garden in northern India, a coal miner in central China, a D-Day memorial, the Cuban military, Obama boarding Air Force One, all-girl teen Iraqi rappers, a Palestinian boy at the Jerusalem barrier, an Indian cyclone, Filipino policeman, Mexican customs, children playing in Jakarta, turmoil in Honduras, Turkmen soldiers, Chinese farmers, Spanish flamenco dancers, and many more.

Director of photography and multimedia Alfredo Sosa came on loan from another newspaper 13 years ago and became permanent staff as features editor in 1997. Since then, the department has undergone some staffing cuts due to immense changes in digital technology and market realities of the field. "Today, our department is made of two photographers, two editors, and an intern position," he explained (2/17/10), and they also use other photographers on limited contracts to cover other areas. In relation to how he approaches photography and responsibility to his subjects, he said: "There is an ethical standard in journalism in general, and at the *Monitor* in particular, that is understood. We deal in trust. That's our currency." The department includes Sosa as director, Melanie Stetson-Freeman as photographer, Joanne Ciccarello as picture editor, and Mary Knox Merrill as photographer and editor.

As a photographer, Melanie Stetson Freedman discussed with me (1/20/10) how she represents visually what other staff put into words. A long-time employee of the *Monitor*, her work has taken her to many amazing parts of the world.

Called in as a consultant for redesign of the newspaper in 1998, having worked in the entertainment industry in California—on retail design, posters, advertising, movies, and more—John Kehe has stayed on to be become design director. "It's nice to have a job helping to disseminate information to the world. This job is a privilege," he told me (2/19/10). "My whole career has been based on noticing visual things," he shared. Every page of the weekly goes under his watchful eyes, and he and his graphic artists have created an archive of world maps that are customized for news and feature stories every day. Kehe and the weekly staff are always trying to improve the *Monitor*'s content and design—utilizing focus groups, surveys, and reader feedback to make the *Monitor* a better and more vital visual reading experience.

Libraries

CSM has clippings dating to its founding in 1908; in addition, the *Monitor* library includes a print and magazine collection, reference books, a collection of "compassionate photography," and some 40 subscriptions to journals. Its librarian, Leigh Montgomery, likes to stay ahead of the curve and loves to share knowledge—particularly along the lines of electronic resource management. "Don't sit and wait for questions," she told me, is her motto (2/16/10). The *CSM* library has been archiving photos digitally since 1996, the vision being to sell photos to readers as part of its editorial obligation. Although that never quite materialized, the library has had a few relationships with photo vendors, most recently Pictopia. "As content is our most important asset, selling it in other markets is getting more attention these days," Montgomery noted in an email (4/12/10).

Judith A. Huenneke, senior research archivist of the Mary Baker Eddy Library for the Betterment of Humanity, began as a proofreader at the Christian Science Publishing Society nearly three decades ago and now oversees historical research into the collection of items related to the founder of both the Christian Science faith and, along with a number of faith-related journals, *The Christian Science Monitor*. She celebrates the direction the organization is taking, she told me when we met (3/23/10). Ask any researcher and they will laud her help (several Eddy biographies in these references cite Judy). In addition, Huenneke also enjoys writing about her subject, and she contributes to the *Christian Science Sentinel* and the *Christian Science Journal*. For example, her article "To enlighten mankind: 100 years of *The Christian Science Monitor*" (2008) was included in the centennial celebration.

Interns

By any measure, staff all agree that interns the *Monitor* draws are first rate. They are hired four times per year: summertime, September until the end of the year, winter and spring, and January to May. Most want to do international news and cover stories. They get paid and are given short-term housing, and—most amazingly—many are hired. The website (http://www.*CSM*onitor.com/About/Careers) has a write-up for newspaper and website internships.

Administrative Staff

In her role as manager of planning and administration, Cindy Anderson works with the many businesses within the single organization. Particularly in her role with managing publisher Jonathan Wells, she sees how they all interact, using an ocean liner analogy to describe it to me (3/23/10): "At times of change it takes some people longer than others to adjust. There might be lots of currents, so you need to take precautions from going aground." But she is very pleased with how this first year has gone—even if "course corrections" are still being made.

His title of executive assistant hardly describes all that Rex Nelles does around *CSM*. Working both for editor John Yemma, who oversees the *Monitor* news staff, and managing publisher Jonathan Wells, who is in charge of the whole publishing society, he has his hands full, floating between them and trying to be one step ahead of information management. Nelles began at CSPS in 2006, working with the Committee on Publications—which was very helpful, he told me (3/24/10), for seeing the wider picture of how the *Monitor* fits in administratively.

Ed Blomquist joined the Christian Science Publishing Society as copyright administrator in 2000. Responsible for licensing *Monitor* and other Publishing Society content to third parties who want to repurpose it for textbooks, websites, and other uses, he also serves as part of the *Monitor*'s syndication team and works closely with the Office of the General Counsel to assist internal clients regarding rights issues.

MONITOR JOURNALISM

Overwhelmingly, as you can see from the many stories cited here, the *Monitor*'s stance aims to be analytical. Add to that the adjectives *sensitive*, *sensible*, and *solution-oriented*. Often, it emphasizes anniversaries and remembrances, such as the 40th anniversary of our putting a man on the moon (July 20, 1969) or the Woodstock music festival, or the 20th anniversary of the Pan-European Picnic that set the stage for tearing down the Berlin Wall.

CSM styles

In writing, there are *speeders* (people who can just sit down and crank text out right then and there) and *bleeders*, for whom it's a much tougher, longer process—usually with lots of revisions along the way. Adam Gopnick, author of *Angels and Ages* (2010), which draws on the fact that

Darwin and Lincoln were born within a few hours of each other on February 12, 1809, points out how Darwin's eloquence rested on "the slow crawl of fact," just as Lincoln opted for legal minutiae over grandiose oratory.

"As writing styles evolve, we wear a lot of hats," Los Angeles reporter Gloria Goodale realizes (4/11/10). It was especially fun to talk about the recent Oscar coverage as an example that has to begin the moment the event concludes. The telecast was over at 9 p.m., and Goodale was on the phone with a producer leaving the event moments later—the story was filed within an hour or so. "This is in contrast to the longer time frame for magazine stories, which can take a few days or even more if they involve travel," she said, glad that women directors (i.e., Kathryn Bigelow for *Hurt Locker*) are being recognized. She cited the notion of "necklace reporting"—different beads, more frequent and smaller, linked and connected.

"Writing is still work," long-time science reporter Peter N. Spotts has noted (2/26/10), citing colleague Mark Sappenfield and former and current editors Dick Cattani and John Yemma as writers who appear more adept at the craft.

Her work is more than just a job, according to Amelia Newcomb of World News, who told me (2/10/10) that "*The Christian Science Monitor* tries to look at the world is a constructive way." She appreciates being part of the news process, adding: "The *Monitor* is a *kind* paper." Its goal is to help the reader understand.

People Making a Difference (PMAD) editor Gregory Lamb claims that "Think links" are at the heart of his work today in adjusting to the Web. When we met (2/11/10), he spoke highly of Richard Bergenheim's notion of codifying a story so it exemplifies *Monitor* quality. His own work is wide-ranging, with articles on brain boosters, privacy, media overload, climate change, the Segway, AcceleGlove, recycling computers, higher education's virtual future, smart phones, robot warriors, and much more.

CSM Perspectives

World War II was the turning point for *CSM*, according to Howard La Franchi, diplomatic correspondent. The paper had a sustainable bureau in London, foreign bureaus and reporters elsewhere, and a good reputation and the brand was established as a result of respected wartime reporting ("The story of CS wartime activities, 1947," in Schuette 2008). "But the TV era ushered in new challenges for the *Monitor*, as the demand for faster electronic news also encouraged other traditional print news sources to adopt something closer to the *Monitor* style of journalism," he said (4/2/10). He worries about the *Monitor*'s message for people who do not want analytic reportage, the kind of value-added journalism the *CSM* is known for. "The *Monitor*'s gift to the world is different in its vision of humankind," he reported. When La Franchi was recently in Haiti, seeing people organizing themselves and their fellow Haitians, he found himself focusing on individuals and their efforts in the face of huge adversity. He was intrigued to find a restaurateur in Port-au-Prince who turned his establishment into a soup kitchen—and thrilled to make contact with a Boston Haitian-American who was so moved upon reading the story that she wanted to help the restaurateur stay open. "We see things differently," he mused—the human spirit coming through, especially in adversity. As staff, they are protective of and sensitive to the "brand," realizing that MBE wanted *CSM* journalists to keep abreast of the times while preserving the mission. "The trick," he posited, "is to preserve what we do differently."

"The challenge," says Peter Ford, Beijing bureau chief, "is maintaining *Monitor* journalism while boosting readership and providing content." Since its history has prevented it from being the first with breaking news, reporters have long learned the value of providing the story-behind-the-story, with considerations of historical, social, and principled perspectives. Articles about events around the world might include, for example, geographic, cultural, political, economic, and broad-based research and/or interviews about individual citizens.

"There were a number of factors," Jonathan Wells, managing publisher, pointed out (2/26/10) about the *Monitor*'s transition from print to its Web-first launch, "but maintaining the lens of Christian Science, with its emphasis on reducing fear and identifying solutions, was prime." It was a three-year process that began early in 2007, working with the trustees, instilling a commitment to keep clarity, context, and perspective. As per the Christian Science notion of Mind and evolution in thinking, the organization realized it needed to adapt to moving audiences. "It was a conceptual journey," Wells stressed. Mary Trammell, editor-in-chief for all CSPS publications, "was a strong partner with the Board of Trustees in guiding the *Monitor*'s transition," Wells said in an email (5/5/10). The team needed to be very clear about their distinct product, dedicated to public service as part of the *CSM*'s century-old tradition. Continuing the founder's mission, "To injure no man, but to bless all mankind," this new *CSM* adopted what is known as a "unique value proposition," or UVP—explaining world news to thoughtful people who care about solutions. It speaks to a global community, aided by its many foreign bureaus.

The audience is independent thinkers who are socially responsive and responsible. "This was an illumination of a path forward. Progress was possible." They looked at other publications and realized how important it was to keep its unique purpose and style.

Overall, Francine Kiefer says, they are "still using *Monitor* journalism/ values, but choice for the daily Web *CSM* is mostly, but not always, dictated by what is on Google that day" (2/25/10). She writes her own headlines and thinks that editorial writing is one of the scariest jobs at the *Monitor*, as "you feel a certain pressure to solve the world's problems— until you remember that what you're really trying to do is shed a light and contribute something useful to a debate," she added in an email (4/ 18/10). Editorial writers need to be familiar with a wide range of topics, and if they don't know about something they at least need to know where to go for a quick education in it.

Deputy editor of the *CSM* weekly Owen Thomas talked to me (3/12/10) about the standard for *Monitor* journalism: he feels obligations to other members, saying, "There is not a lot of ego involved here—we are all invested in what's going to work." Thomas works intensely with a small group of people, then might move to another assignment where he works with a different group, equally intensely. He may not interact with his previous colleagues on a day-to-day basis, but he notes that "a residue of goodwill remains to knit together the staff." If a staff member doesn't like it, they will fall away, and there are few firings.

"I love the *Monitor*," eco-renovation blogger Alexandra Marks exclaimed when we talked (4/27/10). "It is distinguished by thoughtful, stepped back, in-depth journalism. Plus, it is the kinds of audience I like writing for, who appreciate reporterly balanced spin, interviews with people of varying opinions, and context."

TOPICS RELATED TO *CSM* PUBLISHING

Philosophically, *The Christian Science Monitor* has first and foremost been committed to the notion of freedom—a stance that helped editors form humanitarian opinions on foreign affairs topics. In Mary Baker Eddy's footsteps, it has taken "its stand on the side of those who exposed and denounced evils, who demanded that the social order should be improved, but always within the framework of the Constitution, and above all reflecting the Golden Rule" (Canham 1958, 91). As with any organization, it has had its share of external and internal issues, which have all been part of its evolution.

Obituaries and Tributes

Erwin D. Canham (1958, 123) reminds us that "Christian Scientists wish to turn the attention of people to the thought of immortality, toward man's eternal, spiritual birthright of life." Back in 1942, Eric W. Allen queried, "Is *The Christian Science Monitor* unethical in its attitude toward death and despair? Or are the other papers wrong in the way they handle catastrophes?" (p. 147) While in its early days the *Monitor* had quirky taboos about reporting on medicine or accidents, that was largely over by the second half of twentieth century. While the *Monitor* doesn't follow every new FDA drug approval or health claim, it has no problem covering issues like swine flu, SARS, AIDS, the product recalls of drugs like Tylenol, national healthcare, and many other medical topics.

While the *Monitor* might call obituaries "tributes," the type of story is the same, as Washington bureau chief Dave Cook told me (2/13/10): the *Monitor* tends to run an appreciation or retrospective. Examples might be John Hughes's (6/17/98) recollection of reporter Joe Harsch as a supreme chronicler—with "superb journalistic skills (and) a sweeping sense of history—or calling former editors Earl Foell "the incomparable Earl . . . a man of quality" (7/12/99), or Richard J. Cattani "a *Monitor* hero . . . a passionate believer in the mission of unselfish service through journalism" (12/29/99). Robert S. McNamara was remembered as "the cerebral secretary of defense who was vilified for prosecuting the Vietnam War, then devoted himself to helping the world's poorest nations" (7/7/09); Walter Cronkite, "a reporter first and foremost" (7/20/09, 1); Eunice Kennedy Shriver "carried on the family's public service tradition by founding the Special Olympics and championing the rights of the mentally disabled" (8/12/09). Senator Edward "Ted" Kennedy's passing got special notice as the end of the Kennedy era, Gail Russell Chaddock writing that he "ended the third longest career in US Senate history in a way few indicated when he began it—out of the shadow of two larger-than-life brothers and with a run of legislative achievements second to none" (8/27/09, 1). The editorial that day read: "Ted Kennedy persevered. Through family tragedy. Through personal recklessness. Through a long Senate career of fighting for liberal (but not only) causes: healthcare, social justice, education. The world needs more of his resilience in individuals who seek to help others, whether of the left or right."

In a column noting the death of Michael Jackson, editor John Yemma (*DNB* 6/29/09, 1) remarked that he was undoubtedly the most influential pop artist of our time: "As musicologists have pointed out since his passing last week, his vocal and dance skills and his mysterious and ultimately tragic personal life synched up with the rise of the music video and MTV in the early 1980s to make him as popular in Senegal and central China as in Topeka and South America." Daniel B. Wood had an article titled "Outpouring over MJ," subtitled "His music trumps other aspects of his life for many" (p. 3), and for the *Christian Science Perspective* (6/30/09, 3), Jenny Roemer Nelles detailed, in "Superstars—and what stays with us":

The unexpected death last week of Michael Jackson, an international pop super-star, prompted emotional responses from people around the world. Despite his life being mired in controversies, and speculation about his oddities, Jackson's music managed to connect people consistently on a global level. What can the spiritual thinker do to honor the lives of people who have made creative contri-butions to society? What's helped me is first knowing that each individual, in public spotlight or not, has a direct connection to God, who is Life.

Taboos and Tribulations

At the start, decisions on taboo topics fell to Mrs. Eddy, but when she passed on—a *Monitor* preference to the word "died," as per Canham (1958, 121)—those policies perforce were determined according to tradi-tional Christian Science thinking in case-by-case journalistic fashion. Upholding high standards against the trivial, the weird, as well as the sen-sational, it is easy to see why sexy, scandalous, and tawdry items such as kidnappings, murders, rape, and other inhumanities are absent.

One young reporter found out about *Monitor* taboos the hard way. Covering a number of animal deaths at a local zoo and wondering about poor conditions, she included the zoo's defense in the face of attacks from animal rights activists: "Animals get sick. They die. It's just a coincidence." *CSM* wasn't interested.

There are some stories that have morphed into urban legends about *Monitor* taboos—most dating from decades ago and deriving not from outright rules but because an editor or reporter made assumptions about what was not prohibited and then self-censored. Take coffee. It was said that staff were prohibited from mentioning it, and one reporter told me about how someone had written a book review about a coffee table book that was changed to "hot beverage book." Long ago, another outlined, she had a hot story about Uganda, but was discouraged from writing it, as the country was known for its coffee plantations. Needless to say, there is no wine column in the *Monitor,* and references to recreational drinking and smoking are rare, but, like other media outlets, it covered the famous "beer summit" that President Obama held in the summer of 2009 with Harvard scholar Henry Louis Gates and the Cambridge, Massachusetts, police officer who arrested him. You can see the variety of subjects the *Monitor* pursues in the following: Ron Scherer's "Regulation looms for e-cigarettes" (10/19/09, 2), Nick Squires's "Binge drinking spreads to Italy" (10/2/09, 2), or Mark Rice-Oxley's "Britain reconsiders assisted suicide" (9/24/09, 1). To its credit, *CSM*'s *Top Headlines* (*DNB* 5/20/09, 2) recently reported on child abuse in the Roman Catholic Church, an anti-abortionist killing a Kansas abortion doctor (8/13/09), Mexico's drug war (3/25/10), and the killing of an Arizona rancher by an illegal immigrant (4/1/10).

Still, *Monitor* journalists are wary of veering too far into the current fascination with celebrity and pop culture. "Like everyone, we've had hits and misses," editor John Yemma (2010b) self-disclosed:

There are two types of misses: the spinach that goes uneaten and the junk food that makes you sorry afterwards. We do almost all original content, but we were experimenting the other day by posting AP stories. One that went up with too little consideration was on the marital woes of Sandra Bullock. It shot to the top of our most-viewed list. The problem is, we don't do celebrity gossip.

Reviewing the kind of content that *The Christian Science Monitor* had while Mary Baker Eddy was still available for consultation, Canham (1958, 118) points out how its candid, outspoken journalism was "combined with a good deal of experimentation, pioneering, and learning by trial." Obviously, that attitude and approach remain.

Chapter 4

"To Proclaim the Universal Activity and Availability of Truth": Case Studies

When you were introduced to the notion of *CSM*'s unique role in journalism, in Chapter 1, the argument was posited that this is because the *Monitor* operates in a manner contrary to Hollywood portrayals of newspapers and newspeople; that it is consistently aware of its mission ("To injure no man, but to bless all mankind"); that it has long been respected; that its reportage is characterized by analytical, objective, constructive, public-service, solution-oriented writing; that it is nonpartisan; that it is secular; that its emphasis is global in design; that it values excellence and integrity; and that is has evolved, through experimentation, for more than 100 years. This chapter provides examples of the kinds of coverage the *Monitor* has included in selected case studies on disaster communication, gender and gender orientation, health, homeless(ness), international events, religion, and sports.

DISASTER COMMUNICATION

> *The complications that face humankind are vast and puzzling. Information and interpretation, today more than ever, are required to avoid the greatest of disasters.*
>
> —Erwin D. Canham (1958, xxiii)

The newly evolving field of disaster communication has, as its numerous aspects, sociocultural, economic, psychological, political, medical, institutional, managerial, and other concerns. Variously incorporating personal, interpersonal, and intercultural communication, mass media, technology, philanthropic reactions, ethical considerations, and implications for development communication, disasters might be natural (e.g., hurricanes, tsunamis, earthquakes, volcano eruptions, floods, fires, typhoons, tornadoes, cyclones, climatic issues ranging from heat waves to freezes, landslides), manmade (e.g., mining accidents, nuclear bombings or meltdowns, oil spills, traffic control errors, drug abuse, hiking or climbing challenges, stampedes, explosions, economic upheavals, even war), or, as airlines label them, "acts of God." Sometimes, disasters, such as HIV/AIDS, fires, gas leaks, and even terrorism such as that witnessed on 9/11, are combinations or confluences of nature, natural selection, and/or governmental action or inaction.

Keeping in mind that the whole reason for interest in disasters is their effects on populations and policies, it is helpful to have longitudinal studies, such as of survivors of Hurricane Katrina, which might offer insights into demographic vulnerabilities such as age, race, religion, and gender and sexism—lessons that will hopefully help prevention and political action. Always, we search for inspirations of the human spirit.

Entire genres abound in this field, the most popular being disaster and apocalyptic movies (both mainstream and documentary) and books. While there is a growing literature on this topic (e.g., Bankoff, Frerks, and Hilhorst 2004; Birkland 2006; de Villiers 2008; Hoffman and Oliver-Smith 2002; McEntire 2008; Sylves 2008), Rebecca Solnit (2009, 2) makes a most cogent comment: "In the wake of an earthquake, a bombing, or a major storm, most people are altruistic, urgently engaged in caring for themselves and those around them, strangers and neighbors as well as friends and loved ones. The image of the selfish, panicky, or regressively savage human beings in times of disaster has little truth to it."

There had been some misperceptions about whether the *Monitor* would even cover disaster—debunked by John Yemma's *Editor's Blog* of March 12, 2010, "Paying attention to the obvious," which includes this classic journalistic lesson:

A great story about the obvious is told by Everett Martin. a retired journalist, summer 1954. "It was a quiet day, and late in the afternoon I put in a call to Ed Mills at the State House to see if he was sending in any copy," Martin recalls. "He told me that it was very quiet there—just a lot of trees down in the Commons and he heard that the steeple of the Old North Church had blown off. I was astounded. Sitting in our fortress building (*Monitor* headquarters), we didn't even know that one of the worst hurricanes ever to hit Boston had roared through." . . . There was a common assumption that the *Monitor* didn't cover natural disasters—though it had done a bang-up job covering the Great Depression, World War II, Korea, and plenty of other disasters. Martin and photographer Gordon Converse went after the story, and they did it in a *Monitor* way. Among the headlines: "Buzzards Bay Cottagers Act as a Team in Meeting Post-Storm Challenge," and "Radar Proves Accuracy in Tracing Storm Course."

If you ignore the obvious, you miss stories of human resilience and ingenuity. It's the way we've covered the Haiti earthquake, the east Asian tsunami, and many other disasters since then. Two weeks after Martin and Converse hit the road, another big hurricane was approaching. This time, Martin recalled, "The newsroom was filled with dedicated hurricane hunters."

While the *Monitor* certainly has heavily covered Katrina, the 2008 earthquake in China's Sichuan Province and the 2010 earthquake in Chile, what follows is a discussion particularly of the Indian Ocean tsunami of 2004 and the 2009 earthquake in Haiti.

Tsunami 2004

> *If they hadn't been pulverized by an earthquake, the Spartans of ancient Greece might have defeated the Athenians, changing the course of Western culture. But for a volcano, the Panama Canal would be in Nicaragua. And if the modern Greeks and Turks had not helped each other after their own earthquakes five years ago, they might well still be mortal enemies instead of friendly neighbors.*
>
> *As Asian nations reel from the tsunamis that struck two weeks ago, history suggests that the tragedy could engender political fallout—both good and bad—that will reshape the region as surely as the giant waves redrew its coastlines.*
>
> —Peter Ford, *The Christian Science Monitor* (1/11/2005, 1)

From a wide range of perspectives, *CSM* covered Tsunami 2004, continuing throughout the next years, and still monitors events, people, and processes. That coverage has included a number of different areas, notably economics, technology, philanthropy, religion, global aid efforts, historical significance, media involvement, access issues, and most importantly personal stories.

My own interest in the topic of disaster communication began when, on December 26, 2004 ("Boxing Day" for some countries), "the world's worst recorded natural disaster," a tsunami caused by "the largest earthquake in 40 years," galvanized the largest global relief effort in history.

My *Monitor*, typically, provided the most comprehensive and compassionate coverage—moving from statistics and scenarios to a wider perspective of the occurrence. Additionally, contrary to other mainstream media, that coverage—some 133 articles in the content-analyzed year, along with photos, cartoons, editorials, and more (Fuller 2010a)—continued well beyond its breaking date. More than 225,000 people were killed, another 1.7 million displaced, and untold others injured and made homeless. Lives were linked from Asia to Africa, at the same time touching those of many more around the world to the point where some $13.6 billion in aid was pledged.

Because this was such an amazing response, and because both the media and the public became so enraptured and enmeshed in the story of the tsunami, I invited several scholars to a panel at the Union for Democratic Communication (UDC)'s international conference[1] at Boca Raton, Florida, in November 2005. Ironically, our panel never materialized because of Hurricane Katrina. Since interest had been so high, my next decision was to put together a book, *Tsunami Communication*, with contributors from Argentina, India, Canada, New Zealand, Malaysia, Finland, Singapore, Australia, Sri Lanka, Thailand, and the United States. Reportage on it was presented at the 2010 International Communications Association annual conference in Singapore (Fuller 2010b).

The *Monitor*'s 133 citations on Tsunami 2004 included 36 front-page articles, four editorials (how tsunamis need not take lives, the quality of mercy, Indonesia taking the challenge, a "tsunami" of private giving), eight opinion articles (lessons learned, vital technology as a human right, foreign aid, helping kids understand tsunamis, disaster relief, media convergence, attention to the tsunami zone, the role of Arab media), some responses in terms of *Readers Write* (advice on tsunami planning, American generosity, and natural barriers to tsunamis), and some columns labeled "Spiritual Perspective" (comforting the world, contributions, adopting tsunami orphans). Additionally, there were stories involving suggestions of aid agencies, ripple effects, teaching the tsunami to youngsters, advertisements for the UN World Food Programme and the International Service Society, a chart on how the region was (re)building, a cartoon by Clay Bennett of two soldiers tossing "Tsunami Aid" packages out of an airplane, emphases on peace agreements, Asian adoptions, comparisons among worldwide disasters, book reviews, and some incredibly touching photographs.

Citing specific agencies, emphasis was on relief—who was doing what, when, and where, and how *you*, as reader, could help. As it had done before, the First Church of Christ, Scientist itself established a fund—this time called Tsunami Relief—and the philanthropic outpouring of humanitarian groups and individuals became a story in and of itself. An editorial (1/24/05) stated, "Stand up, America, and take a deep bow for yourself. You have crossed a remarkable threshold in compassion." There was also "the positive subject of rebuilding, a push for tsunami-alert systems, stories of various connections to the tragedy, research in tsunami science, calls for commitment to infrastructures in developing countries" (Fuller 2010a, 108), a three-part, multipage series titled "In its wake: Rebuilding after the tsunami" (Wood 2/1/05, 2/4/05, and 2/7/05), and reportage on recovery efforts many months later—one of my favorites being an article about how some story lines in Indian soap operas included health information such as oral rehydration salts for diarrhea along with appeals for tsunami victims (6/10/05). John Hughes, who won a 1967 Pulitzer prize for his coverage of Indonesia, had this perspective: "Beyond their humanitarian instincts, American taxpayers have well-founded political reasons to support continuing aid to a country that may play a significant role in the war against terrorism. In the wake of the tsunami, humanitarian aid without strings is perhaps the best kind of public diplomacy—doing good deeds and letting people make of it what they will" (2/9/05). "Rebirth in Aceh," a progress report two years after Tsunami 2004 (12/1/06), suggested positive news relative to redevelopment in Indonesia—Simon Montlake's "New Foundations," focusing on jobs, homes, families, and "building peace amid building pains." At the three-year mark, though (Montlake 12/26/07, 4), it was clear that "unprecedented aid boosted rebuilding, but political and economic challenges remain."

Haiti's Earthquake

According to what Dave Scott, *World* editor, told me (1/19/10), when a devastating earthquake hit Haiti on January 12, 2010 the *Monitor* had it on the Web within 1-1/2 hours, and within 24 hours—coordinating reports with Sara Miller Llana, staff reporter headquartered in Mexico City—they had 15 to 20 stories and items posted. Matt Clark pulled on a number of blogs for his *DNB* opener on January 14, "Relief effort ramps up in Haiti," reading: "As Haitians pick through rubble in the wake of Tuesday's magnitude-7.0 earthquake, aid groups around the world are mobilizing at a breakneck pace to help the Western Hemisphere's poorest nation recover." Dan Murphy lead the January 15, 2010 *DNB* with "Disaster aid starts to pour into Haiti," pointing out how the chaos complicated matters, and Marshall Ingwerson's *Editor's View* provided a classic case of *Monitor* journalism:

"The poorest country in the Western hemisphere." That identifying phrase has followed Haiti through the decades. It's a nation that began as a slave rebellion, throwing off French masters, that was met with economic isolation as slave-owning neighbor countries sought to punish Haitians for their impunity.

Poverty did not bring on the earthquake, but what it's doing is devastating to Haitians.

The US military has made a couple of attempts in the 20th century—once near the beginning and once near the end—to create stability in the forlorn nation. Each time, the US has taken a lighter touch, kept a more respectful distance from Haiti's fragile political institutions.

This earthquake opens the door, perhaps even the moral demand, for another intervention that extends past the emergency aid of coming weeks. No one would call it an invasion this time. If that happens, have we learned enough about how to help to make, this time, a more lasting progress?

Sara Miller Llana and staff photographer Mary Knox Merrill were dispatched right away to Haiti to cover the quake. They drove in from the Dominican Republic, where they rented a van, loaded it with food and water, and lived out of it for the next two weeks. Gordon Lubold volunteered to go because, as Pentagon and National Security correspondent, his editors were keen on including the military angle. It was a crude set-up, he told me by phone (2/9/10), but he was able to send stories by Blackberry while the other *Monitor* reporter, Howard LaFranchi, used a portable satellite. Mark Glaser, executive editor of *Media Shift*, reviewed the best online resources for following Haiti news[2] and recommended coverage from the *Monitor*, pointing out how a reporter and photographer were already there and that the *Monitor* had launched a "Haiti earthquake diary"[3] by a correspondent who had covered the country for many years.

Back in Boston, a *CSM* intern went to a Haitian community center to talk to many people who count the country as their own. John Hughes had a column entitled "Haiti-type disasters require a UN rapid-response unit" (2/7/10), and the weekly included articles on the geology of the quake, forms of aid, and the U.S. missionaries, as well as an editorial on donor fatigue; Rosalie E. Dunbar's "Prayers of love for Haiti's people" (1/16/2010) was particularly striking, as she was struck with how often the word "catastrophe" was used in news reports. Realizing that, "This small island nation, the poorest country in the Western Hemisphere, needs our prayers," she urged readers to remember God as refuge and strength: "The people of Haiti deserve this because they are dearly loved by their Father-Mother God."[4] "Envisioning a new Haiti" was a special series by Stephanie Hanes and Sara Miller Llana (1/31/10) outlining how hope emerged but encouraging experts to think outside the box. By January 28, 2010 it was encouraging to read Howard LaFranchi's report that "Haiti's economy shows signs of life." Dan Kennedy (2010), writing about "Chile and earthquake fatigue" in *Media Nation*, cited how well the *Monitor*, "a leading non-profit source of international news," did in its coverage.

GENDER AND GENDER ORIENTATION

Gender

Women make up almost half the world's population, and around the world they are struggling to raise the standard of social and political equality with men. Yet, whether it's gaining the right to own property in African countries, equal pay for work that men do too, or learning to read (out of the world's 960 million illiterates, two-thirds are women), there is progress every day.

—Editorial, *The Christian Science Monitor*[5]

Founded by a woman (MBE), the *Monitor* mentored a journalistic pioneer: Cora Rigby, the first woman to head a Washington bureau and charter member of what became known as the Washington Press Club, in 1919. Margaret Ramsey served as editor of *Home Forum* when it premiered in 1922, and CSM's first art editor of the magazine section was Frances Davis, in 1934. The *Monitor* was early having a female editor (Katherine Fanning, 1983 to 1988), and today about one-third of its publishing staff is made up of women, including some at senior roles. Traditionally, it has had gender-neutral, even pro-woman coverage—such as framing the O. J. Simpson case as dealing with domestic violence (Fuller 1997), not just a racial divide. A simple Google search of *The Christian Science Monitor* and "women" garners more than 9 million citations. A mini-site called "Women Making History Today," about women making a difference, existed for quite a while on CSMonitor.com—including articles on women's rights, women and work, histories of women, sportswomen, women's education, and women's lives around the world (Fuller 2004 a).

By way of showing my long-time interest in this topic, let me share a sampling of articles from my file labeled "*CSM*/Women": an editorial (3/9/92) titled "Sexual Abuse of Power," on Anita Hill, rape charges

against William Kennedy Smith and Mike Tyson, and sexual impropri-
eties of Senator Brock Adams, pointed out problems of sexual harassment
and coerciveness by powerful men; Women's History Month is usually
highlighted, as is Women's Day (March 8); reportage has included stories
about an ex-call girl trying to legalize prostitution and the post-Beijing
Report Card on Women (1995); women's sports stories, whether about
the WNBA, Texas Latinas foiling WPGA plans, or a partially blind female
Olympic shooter, are balanced and insightful; gender workplace issues are
covered, including clergy and the military; international issues—such as
female genital mutilation (FGM), the killing of women in the name of
family honor, battered women in Eastern Europe, women's rights in
Morocco, Mexican wives left behind as men cross the border into the
United States, even activist women in the West Bank—provide stories
we might never know otherwise; coverage of "girl on girl" violence
includes statistics and suggestions; and men's roles, as caregivers for elderly parents or on leave from the war, are also included. "Climate change
and role of women" (11/25/09, 2), from South Africa, reports: "It is often
asserted that climate change will affect women the most in the developing
world. That's because most women will have to walk farther for drinking
water, work harder to grow food, pull daughters out of school to help
with family chores, and fuss more about family hygiene as the world
becomes a hotter, drier, place to live." Coverage has also included global
artists, such as Tunisia's female filmmakers; Mexico's pink "ladies-only"
buses to counter harassment; religious articles, such as an evangelical
group's challenge to a biblical basis for male leadership or Muslim women
fitting into European society; and technological abilities and achievements of women.

Oftentimes, feminism is equated with notions of culture devaluing
women, positioning them as second-class citizens in a society where
men have both written and controlled the dominant dialogue. Both
physically and emotionally, gender differences manifest themselves in
our languages, our worldviews, our interpersonal interactions, and our
general approaches to life and living. Let us consider how the *Monitor*
views women biologically, politically, and economically.

Biological Perspective

Based on the notion of women controlling their own bodies, especially
their reproductive systems, *CSM*'s discussions have ranged from the conse-
quences of sex-selective abortions (7/15/04) to two Iranian women conquer-
ing Mount Everest (6/1/05, 7) to "gendercide" (4/4/06) and much more.

Political Perspective

Seeking change from within the system, the *Monitor*'s liberal application of feminism seeks equality through many means. Articles on Title 1X (Richey 6/14/04, 1+), women-centered books, Melanie Stetson Freeman's "Photographer's Journey" (8/20/04, 12–14), the world of Afghan war widows, sportswomen, female leaders such as Nobel Laureate Wangari Maathai of Kenya or Prime Minister Benazir Bhutto of Pakistan, India's United Women Front (12/11/07, 7), Kashmiri mothers searching for lost husbands and sons (2/1/08, 7), or the fact that women gained 25 percent of Iraqi seats in provincial elections and that two Palestinian women in the West Bank are the Middle East's first female *Sharia* judges (editorial *DNB* 5/12/09, 3)— all are unique coverage. Before the selection of Sonia Sotomayor, Linda Feldmann's (*DNB* 5/19/09, 1) "Another woman on Supreme Court?" pointed out that, "For advocates of women's rights, adding another female justice is not about diversity for diversity's sake. It's about bringing women's perspectives and life experiences into interpretations of law, and about helping the male justices see things through their eyes."

Sticky subjects, such as the Kobe Bryant rape accusation case, tend to be dealt with from a wide perspective—there, in terms of celebrity, shield laws, and "deeper issues about gender" and women's sexuality (Miller and Paulson 9/3/04, 3). Judith Matloff's "Rwanda copes with babies of mass rape" (3/27/95, 1) was reportedly the first outing of genocidal mass rapes. Then, consider this reportage on the woman whose conviction brought both division and derision:

When lifestyle doyenne Martha Stewart arrives at the Alderson Federal Prison Camp, the multimillionaire businesswoman won't just be joining other storied names such as Billie Holiday, "Tokyo Rose," and Lynette (Squeaky) Fromme who have done time at the campus-like collection of cottages in the West Virginia mountains. She will also be stepping into a piece of feminist history. Alderson was the nation's first federal women's prison. It opened as part of a reform movement in the 1920s as a place where "fallen" women could reclaim dignity as well as learn skills. (Marks, 10/8/04, 1+)

Economic Perspective

Rooted in a view of oppression, oftentimes determined by class and underscored in popular culture, financial issues deal clearly with exploitation, and many of us worry about the feminization of poverty (Fuller 2008a). In the *Monitor*, we get everything from an Asian pirated bicycle headgear favored by women in Beijing (Marquand 8/18/04, 7) to discussion of a WIC (Women, Infants, and Children)-only store in Washington, D.C. (Harman 9/8/2004, 16), a "spouse tax" on military wives (2/22/08, 9), female pilots (3/7/06), women hit by the troubled economy (7/2/08: 2), and Alexandra Kosteniuk, women's world chess champion (2/23/09).

Gender Orientation

What is the Christian Science view of homosexuality? Christian Science sets out a high moral ideal when it comes to human relationships and sex. It accepts the Ten Commandments and teachings of Christ Jesus on these subjects. The book that explains Christian Science says that sex should be limited to marriage, and that marriage is "the legal and moral provision for generation among humankind."

At the same time, Christian Science acknowledges that all of us have a lot of growing to do to reach the standard of pure spiritual love that Christ Jesus taught and lived. It encourages us to be as free as possible from judging each other, while still supporting each individual's moral and spiritual progress. Christian Science affirms the spiritual identity that we all have from God. We believe this can bring healing to individuals and to society as a whole.

—http://christianscience.com/questions-christian-science-faq.html

It struck me that, after having monitored the *Monitor* for so long, I'd hardly seen the word "homosexual," never mind "gay" or "lesbian," and certainly not "bisexual"; so it came as a pleasant surprise to find *CSM* providing some of the best, unbiased reportage on issues such as gay bishops, gay marriages, and even gay rights (Fuller 2004b).

In response to my query on their stance, this is what a representative wrote me: "The First Church of Christ, Scientist, takes no official position on homosexuality or other social or personal issues. Everyone is encouraged to find their own perspective on these issues through their own spiritual searching and discovery" (email 9/29/03). Why had *CSM's* gay-related reportage been so limited, then? Even openly gays like Barney Frank, Martina Navratilova, or Melissa Etheridge were cited without the moniker so many other media consider necessary. Christian Science practitioners with whom I have discussed homosexuality have called it everything from a disease to a tragedy to a moral lapse. Other practitioners, none being "official" voices of the church—especially younger members—have a more modern view. In this, Christian Scientists mirror the range of attitudes in American society, which recently has evolved from disapproval to acceptance of members of the gay community and concern for their civil rights.

When *CSM* covered the issue of gay bishops, it took wide perspectives, discussing different attitudes—generational, political, and religious. "For today's teenagers, homosexuality has never been a taboo topic," Amanda Paulson (2/27/03, 1) pointed out:

They've grown up with positive gay characters on MTV's the *Real World*, and on network shows like *Will and Grace*. Many have "gay-straight-alliances" at their high schools. And it's a safe bet that they know someone who's gay. All of which helps explain why for many young people, their reaction to today's debates over gay rights from marriage to anti-sodomy laws is simply: What's the big deal? In fact, the biggest divide over gay rights in America today may not be along political parties or religious factions, but among generations.

Jane Lampman (7/28/03, 1), *CSM* religion and ethics correspondent, said about the Episcopalians: "Their choices threaten to split the U.S. church and the worldwide Anglican Communion to which it belongs." Whether relative to welcoming gays into its ranks, blessing same-sex unions, or even ordaining gay clergy, what seems to concern *CSM* most is divisiveness over sticking with scripture and/or interpreting morality.

Beyond these specific cases, the *Monitor* has also chosen to tackle gay rights in general. Based simply on my own content analysis, a number of articles have appeared dealing with issues such as gay-rights activism (Knickerbocker 8/12/93, 8/8/94, 11/2/09), Supreme Court cases (Marquand 10/10/95), media (Spaid 4/30/97; Campbell 4//6/01), education (Baldauf 9/29/97), gay rights (Marks 7/23/98), gay adoptions (Baldauf 9/29/97), legal protections for gays following the murder of gay student Matthew Shepard (Baldauf 9/29/98; Hughes 10/31/98), gays in the military (Moniz 7/13/99; Lubold 2/3/10; Knickerbocker 3/8/10), pedophilia in the Catholic Church (Lampman 3/22/04), New Jersey Governor James McGreevey's self-outing as gay (Scherer and Baldwin 8/16/04), even gay tourism in Israel (Harman 8/13/08) and legalizing gay marriage in Mexico (Llana 12/23/09). Giving front-page coverage of the U.S. Supreme Court decision in *Lawrence v. Texas* recognizing that "consenting adults have a constitutional right to engage privately in homosexual conduct without government interference," it pointed out how lower courts have held back gay and lesbian civil rights (Richey 2/9/04). Basically, it paints the picture as both political (Paul and Miller 3/11/04) and human(e).

Stepping back from this reportage, it is important to note that this religious newspaper has tackled lesbian, gay, bisexual, and transgender (LGBT) subjects at all. As we stand in such divisive times, it behooves us to follow issues relative to the separation of church and state. Gay clergy as an issue forces followers to come to terms with their compassion. Gay marriage, "the most contentious issue to face the country since abortion" (Lampman 11/21/03, 13), brings to the fore our definitions of marriage (Sappenfield 3/5/04; Farrell and Wood 5/27/09), as well as our determinations of religious liberties (Lampman 3/1/04). Stem cell research stirs socioemotional and, by default, political reactions.

Let me also share a bit of the results of what happened during this research. Plugging in "Christian Science" and "homosexuality" gave 249,000 hits on Google; then searching with "gay" (1,840,000 hits!) not only yielded good material: I got a cookie. It turns out there is a group of gay, lesbian, bisexual, and transgender Christian Scientists who have formed a group called Emergence International (EI), founded in 1979. Walter of EI Publications invited my participation. Best of all, he alerted me to their monthly newsletter, where I learned about their conferences and Bruce Stores's *Christian Science: Its Encounter With Lesbian/Gay America* (2004). A life-long gay practitioner of Christian Science, once married and the father of a son who is now an activist for gay rights, Stores has been a journalist for *Seattle Gay News*. He outlines a history of "the change from blatant discrimination of sexual minorities to a degree of acceptance by Christian Science Church officials" (p. xv)—quietly. So quietly, in fact, that many members are still unaware of that evolution from what has traditionally been classic ecclesiastical authoritarianism.

HEALTH AND DISEASE

What do you do in the case of communicable disease? Christian Scientists care about their neighbors and fellow community members and gladly abide by city and state laws or mandates regarding quarantines, vaccinations, and the like. The Christian Science Journal, Christian Science Sentinel, *and* The Herald of Christian Science *also contain documented healings of communicable diseases and show the role prayer can play, not just in protecting and healing individuals, but in helping communities as well.*

—http://christianscience.com/questions-christian-science-faq.html

Respectful of the medical profession, although individually committed to spiritual healing, Christian Scientist newspeople are open to publishing societal, legal, and/or economic-political news about the health field. Its photographs generally do not feature people smoking or drinking—a famous exception being one of Winston Churchill with a cigar at FDR's White House in 1942. Yet, it should be noted, Christian Scientists prefer not to interfere with other peoples' lifestyle choices. On its editorial pages, though, the *Monitor* has continually crusaded on behalf of medical freedom and a person's right to choose therapy.

An editorial titled "What Is Christian Science treatment?" appeared August 3, 1990 in *CSM,* revealing that it is not simply "positive thinking" or "mind over matter": "Christian Scientists understand their healing method to be based solely on the healing power of *God*, not of the human mind. Christian Science treatment relies on the regenerative power of Spirit, God, and is wholly Biblical and Christian in its approach to the healing of disease" (p. 17). My long-collected files include a range of health-related articles, such as on Norman Cousins's 1979 *Anatomy of an Illness* (7/5/94), an editorial on the abortion divide (11/27/95) stating "We agree with Roe v. Wade, not because we favor abortion, but because we strongly believe that governments have no business interfering in private health-care decisions, including choice of treatment," a conference sponsored by Harvard Medical School on "Spirituality and Healing" (12/18/96), how a voluntary smallpox program best serves us (12/13/02), the stem-cell debate (9/16/04), an overmedicated America (5/9/05), hypnotism (6/9/08), flu-shot resistance as an ethics issue (10/9/09), and many more, as seen below. Dave Cook told me (2/13/10) that diseases might be mentioned, but not their symptoms; still, you can see that the *Monitor* has used great integrity here.

HIV/AIDS

There was an early response to acquired immune deficiency syndrome: "What about AIDS?" (5/5/89) positioned it as "One issue that touches something either controversial or personal, moral or political, in almost everyone's point of view." Seeing it as a disease threatening human life and recognizing that "Sexual ambiguities, societal strife, economic inequities, drug addiction, loneliness, desperation, anger, and sin make harsh and sometimes deadly attacks upon people's moral judgments," the idea is to look (more) deeply into our relationship with God.

In my own research of this pandemic (Fuller 2003, 2008a), the *Monitor* has been invaluable, whether with articles dealing with myths and superstitions, problems with street children, traditional healers, and/or mediated images. Prevention is key to Nicole Itano's analysis of multiple partnerships (12/1/08); *World in Brief* has reported on the United States lifting of a 22-year-old ban on individuals diagnosed with HIV/AIDS from entering the country (12/13/09); and "AIDS and the deep realism of spirit" was the theme of a *Christian Science Perspective* (8/3/09, 3) reviewing the statistics (25 million people have died, with 11.6 orphans in Africa), then reading: "While AIDS may seem to render one vulnerable, Christ, the spiritual impetus of Jesus' healing mission, is well able to open our eyes to Love's healing and restorative power for all who desire to be free." After we talked about this topic (2/11/10), Rosalie Dunbar, news editor of Christian Science magazines, was so sweet as to get me some copies of how the *Christian Science Sentinel* has featured it. "AIDS: A healing response" was the cover story for February 22, 2010, her emphasis being against fear and (self-)condemnation and on helping or saving children.

H1N1

More recently, with worries about the H1N1 swine flu virus, John Yemma's *Editor's View* (*DNB* 5/1/09, 1) discussed how global reaction to its outbreak was treading the line between caution and overreaction. "Considering two other big events—Hurricane Katrina's delayed aid and Y2K's overdone preparation, and knowing that the Centers for Disease Control and Prevention (CDC) estimate some 36,000 Americans die each year from flu complications," he concludes, "In uncertain times, a big response appears to be the safest response."

Mexico, the country hit hardest by H1N1, including a five-day economic shutdown estimated to have cost $2.2 billion and a reduction of .03 in its GDP, had further implications, as Sara Miller Llana (5/7/09, 1) reminds us in "Mexico City returns to normal": "But while business will bounce back for many, Mexico still will contend with stigmas and diplomatic rifts that may take much longer to resolve."

When the World Health Organization (WHO) announced difficulties stopping H1N1 from circling the globe, *Christian Science Perspective* (*DNB* 6/12/09, 3)'s "Combating the threat of swine flu" included Jeremy Carper's comment: "I'm grateful to health service providers for their alertness in announcing the spread of this potential scourge, because it is also an alert to all who pray. They have a mission as first responders, too." "Swine flu: A plan, not a prediction" (8/31/09, 3) was an editorial after the fear subsided, declaring that "The federal government seems to be strik-ing the right balance—steering the public away from alarm, while trying to plan and prepare." Later, Patrik Jonsson's "Flu-shot resistance an ethics issue" (10/9/09, 2) asked whose rights should be considered as to having vaccines—individuals' or the government's.

Health Concerns Covered by the *Monitor*

Among *Top Headlines* in *DNB* (5/6/09, 2) came an announcement that the White House wanted $63 billion set aside to fight global diseases over the next six years. Based on an initiative under the Bush administration to fight HIV/AIDS, tuberculosis, and malaria, Obama's budget specified more money for prenatal and postnatal care, children's health, and fighting tropi-cal diseases. Healthcare, which represents 17 percent of our GNP—the U.S. government spending an average of $7,681 per person, or $2.3 trillion last year—is already heavily covered. Recognizing that "Nothing in the US federal budget, and little in the private economy, is as expensive and fast-growing as healthcare costs," Marshall Ingwerson's DNB *Editor's View* (5/12/09, 1) cites how this issue has "the greatest direct impact on the most people."

Mental health is a common refrain—whether for posttraumatic stress by soldiers facing "multiple deployments and extended tours" (*DNB* 3/13/09) or general malaise. Gordon Lubold, Pentagon reporter, has seen this close-up in his concerns about public policies for veterans. Routinely confronting stories about mental health as he covers the Department of Veterans Affairs, he wrote me in an email (4/18/10) that sometimes it can be chal-lenging to write about such topics and at the same time fall in line with *Monitor* "sensibilities and sensitivities."

Discussing legal drugs used as a "brain boost" for the mentally ill, the editorial "Eroding the essence of Humanness" (5/18/09, 3) opines that "The bigger danger in this new 'mind hacking' is that it furthers the idea that people are material machines that can be altered like robots to perform ever-greater mental feats and that they are dependent on their medicine cabinets." Gregory M. Lamb's cover story "Smart pills?" (5/10/09) asks, as more people take stimulants to boost memory and job performance, are we becoming "too dependent on our medicine cabinets . . . [and are we] the sum of our experiences or the sum of our pills?"

The marijuana topic has drawn quite a bit of ink. In response to an article on the website (5/21/09) about legalization—weighing economic, political, physiological, and psychological effects—the *Monitor* ques-tioned adding it to tobacco and alcohol "When the US had such a poor record in dealing with the two big 'licits.' " Readers responded in *Commentary* (6/21/09): the deputy director of the National Organization for the Reform of Marijuana Laws (NORML) reported that, "The continued criminalization of cannabis had led to the arrest of more than 20 million Americans since 1965, empowered and enriched criminals, and alienated millions of otherwise law-abiding citizens while creating disrespect for the rule of law." For balance, check this from the director of communications for the Marijuana Policy Project: "In 2003, the American Academy of HIV Medicine said that, 'When appropriately prescribed and monitored, marijuana/cannabis can provide immeasurable benefits for the health and well-being of our patients.' "

HOMELESS(NESS)

> *Hobo, vagrant, tramp, panhandler, bum, Sad Sack, vagabond, drifter, street urchin, down-and-out, the displaced, beggar, runaway, panhandler—think of all the epithets we have used over the years for the homeless. Review, also, places we were told where they might be found: Skid Row, soup kitchens, tenements, the Bowery, or slums.*
>
> —Linda K. Fuller (1999, 159)

Having researched and reported on mediated images of the homeless (Fuller 1999, 2007), it was natural for me to monitor the *Monitor*'s coverage of a problem where, worldwide, more than 100 million homeless people now live, 42 percent of them in the United States being children and families. While causes can vary—disabilities, substance abuse, job loss, lack of affordable healthcare and health services, lack of affordable housing, wartime experiences, or combinations of these—all are a byproduct of poverty.

Not surprisingly, there has been extensive coverage of homelessness and the homeless. While my files do not include anything about the Reagan-era notion of "They're happy that way," or more recent media interest in "bum fights," where homeless people are pitted against one another, there are stories on street papers sold by homeless around the country (11/17/03); homeless female veterans (7/18/07); an art show staged by Moscow's homeless (1/8/08); *BackStory*'s profile of a formerly homeless man (2/26/08); a book club in Cleveland that serves as a shelter for the homeless (2/28/08); a "Seldom Seen Actors" theater (3/2/09); *Home Forum*'s inspirational story of a homeless girl who is now an actress (3/23/09); book reviews (11/4/08; 2/21/10); *People Making a Difference*'s Richard Berry, who took homeless men into his church (11/22/09); Marcia Merrick, "mother of the street" for homeless in Kansas City, Missouri (3/8/10); a religious article, "A prayer for the homeless," suggesting: "Refuse to accept the view that they are useless, without value . . . " (4/26/10); Peter Ford's reportage on the problem of rising homelessness in Japan (9/4/09:2); and Amanda Paulson's report "After foster care, road can be rocky" (2/8/10), about how many young people from the system face homelessness.

Teresa Heinz (2004) performed a critical discourse analysis on "the homeless as criminals or consumers," comparing how *The Christian Science Monitor* and the *Washington Post* covered the topic, not surprisingly finding *CSM* taking a "more analytical, features-oriented approach" (p. 10). One of her favorite examples was a Jeff Danziger cartoon (12/1/86) depicting homeless people sitting outside of the American "horn of plenty, wealth, surplus, and excess."

INTERNATIONAL EVENTS

> The *Monitor*'s interest in world affairs has long been regarded as its chief distinction. From its first issue, it received analytical dispatches covering the chief problem areas of the world. At the same time it recorded progressive human achievement.
>
> —Erwin D. Canham (1958, xviii)

As has been repeatedly pointed out here, the *Monitor* has always been global in its interest and reach. Here is just a sampling of some of those topics: Communism and Russia, and terrorism (the David Rohde and Jill Carroll stories).

Communism and Russia

As evidenced in Lawrence N. Strout's book about how *The Christian Science Monitor* covered McCarthyism in the early 1950s, its stance against Communism has been consistently evident. Analyzing the papers of Richard L. Strout, who, we learn, was incorrectly suspected of being a Communist sympathizer but who *World Monitor* editor Earl W. Foell (1990, 19) called "the preeminent chronicler of the American scene—indeed of the American civilization," the scary divide between paranoia and right thinking becomes clear. "An extensive review of the *Monitor's* editorials, columns, and news articles about McCarthy suggests that had all media outlets have been as thorough and fair in reporting, and as outspoken yet responsible in criticism," Strout (1999, 147) suggests, "perhaps the public would have been better informed about McCarthy, and therefore better able to judge McCarthy's actions earlier." In retrospect, he adds, "The *Monitor*, though always critical of the junior senator's actions, never stooped to name-calling, never intentionally distorted McCarthy's positions, and never sought to make 'enemies' with McCarthy or anyone else" (p. 154).

But it was quite a bombshell when David E. Walker (1957), who worked for the *Monitor* from 1942 to 1944, revealed in an autobiography his identity as a Communist. Recruited for British Intelligence, he wrote for a series of newspapers, planting rumors along the way. Additionally, news has recently been revealed about acclaimed journalist Edmund Stevens (1910–1992), who covered Russia for the *Monitor*—including Stalin's Great Purge, the Russo-Finnish war, and more; never accused of being a "fellow traveler," his recently unearthed, unpublished memoirs reveal that he was, in fact, a Communist who worked as a translator and writer to help the Bolshevik cause. Cheryl Heckler (2007, 7–8) provides this background:

While Marx used his "overlapping skills" to trigger a social revolution and an entirely new Russia, Stevens would use his to explain and analyze social revolution as it unfolded before his own eyes. He would thrive as a journalist during World War II, solidify *The Christian Science Monitor*'s reputation as an international leader in reporting and interpreting Russian culture, win a Pulitzer for his analyses of postwar Russia, and stand in journalism history as the only American-born reporter to work out of the Soviet Union for nearly half of the twentieth century.

In 1991, the CSPS released *Communism: Its rise and fall in the 20th century* (Ralston), "Dedicated to the journalists and all others who have labored every day to maintain the pose and perspective on events which have distinguished *The Christian Science Monitor* since 1908." Explicitly not a history of either the movement or the Soviet Union, it details the perspective the newspaper brought to bear on "events which threatened the entire world with tyranny, terror, and destruction" (p. xi). Between photographs and reprints of *Monitor* articles, as well as Edmund Stevens's award-winning "This is Russia—uncensored" series, the reader is privy to a critical view of why freedom is to vital to our world. Then fast forward to the present, and here are two representative articles in the *Monitor* relative to Communism: Michael J. Jordan (11/9/09), "After the Berlin Wall, nostalgia for Communism creeps back," and Daniel A. Bell (2/24/2010), "China's alternative to Communism and democracy" (Confucianism).

My interest in what we now call the former Soviet Union dates from the fact that, 10 days after my visit to Russia in August 1991, came news of its attempted coup. People asked me if there had been any indications, but the answer was emphatically "No." When "experts" on so many sides had misjudged the intensity of what was brewing in the country, there was a single exception: *The Christian Science Monitor*. Fortunately, during my absence, a backlog of issues awaited my attention (Fuller 1992). While the major news story had been the U.S.-Soviet summit on nuclear arms, the newspaper also included an editorial on Mikhail Gorbachev's waning popularity, front-page discussions about incentives for Soviet businessmen, concentration on domestic reforms, and most-favored nation status. No fewer than 327 articles about events in Russia ran in the next eight months, along with 28 front-page photographs, eight political cartoons by staff artist Jeff Danziger, and relevant book and Russian film reviews. The *Monitor* appropriately won an Emmy Award for its predictions about and coverage of the Soviet Union as well as an excellence award from the Society of Newspaper Design (SND) for its coverage of "democracy in the USSR." It helped to have had a Moscow bureau for decades, extensive contacts among government officials and private citizens, and, most of all, the *Monitor*'s trademark historical, developmental approach to news.

Coup leaders thought they had only to crack down on the press, but they had not accounted for the power of information, communication, and technology. A combination of cable television, electronic mail, telephones, and fax technologies helped keep up a constant flow during the crisis. Boris Yeltsin, the *Monitor* reported, took phone calls from President Bush and Britain's John Major and faxed a friend in Washington, D.C., who in turn made Yeltsin's messages available to the worldwide media. Computer bulletin boards were left free to operate, and two electronic mail services—the Internet and SovAm Teleport—were kept quite busy. Wire services flowed in both directions, and the British Broadcasting Corporation (BBC) and Voice of America (VOA) shortwave broadcasts went uninterrupted. CNN, typically limited to hotels in the Soviet Union, was regularly picked up by Muscovite broadcasting buffs who aimed their antennas at the central transmission tower.

Monitor staffer John Hughes (8/29/91) wrote about how VOA correspondents used Finnish-made cell phones to call in their reports to their Moscow bureau, which transmitted them live to headquarters in Washington, then back almost instantly via shortwave to listeners across the USSR. Radio Liberty and Radio Free Europe, meanwhile, kept up their beaming broadcasts—the former in Russian and 11 other languages, the latter to the Baltic republics, Eastern European countries, and Poland, where 115,000 Soviet citizens remained trapped. Gorbachev, who we were told was ill and out of town, we later discovered depended greatly on these many shortwave broadcasts; in addition, he used videotape to smuggle out proof that he was clearly in fine health. "What they failed to realize is that the world is undergoing an information revolution," Hughes reflected (p. 19). George Gerbner (1993, 185) labeled the Moscow coup a case of "instant history," occurring "when control of video-satellite-computer technologies makes it possible to blanket the world in real time with selected images, provoke reactions that feed back into the event, speed its revolution, and quick-freeze the outcome into received history."

While it may seem dated, the argument can be made that *Monitor* coverage of the 1991 Soviet coup cuts into the fabric of deeper historical, social, economic, political, and psychological issues both in the former USSR and worldwide. David Hoffman (1993, 19), president of Internews, has noted, "The first line of defense for democracy in Russia is its media . . . Press and broadcast freedom is a political right that must be raised to the same level of concern by the West as any other human right. Political, economic, and moral support for Russia's news media will be aid well spent."

On March 4, 2010, on the *Monitor's* Global News Blog, dateline Phnom Penh, Cambodia, correspondent Julie Masis had "Why some Cambodians speak Russian"—detailing how, in post–Khmer Rouge 1982, the USSR had established a scholarship program there. Huma Yusuf's "Russia suspends Iran arms sale following Israeli PM's visit to Moscow" (2/17/10) paints a more strained picture that, unfortunately, has become a contentious norm in terms of America's concerns over the Putin-Medvedev government. Ariel Cohen, senior research fellow in Russian and Eurasian Studies and International Energy Policy at the Katherine and Shelby Cullom Davis Institute for International Policy at the Heritage Foundation, contributed, "What Russia needs most: Civil society engagement, not appeasement" (2/10/10), stressing a need for engagement. Much as we had hoped Russia would move toward a liberal democracy once the other Soviet-controlled territories (Armenia, Azerbaijan, Belarus, Estonia, Georgia, Kazakhstan, Kyrgyzstan, Latvia, Lithuania, Moldova, Tajikistan, Turkmenistan, Ukraine, Uzbekistan) were broken off, the Obama-Biden administration's recent experiences can be described as tense at best. Most recently, Fred Weir's "Russian history: Version 1.0 or 2.0?" (*DNB* 5/22/09, 1) tells about a bitter joke from the Soviet era: Russia is the world's only country with an unpredictable past.

Terrorism

In what now looks mild by comparison, the 1980s were marked by a climate of global fear over terrorism. When invited to participate in the Terrorism and News Media Research Project, quite naturally my first reaction was to wonder how *The Christian Science Monitor* had dealt with the topic. Checking the *CSM Index*, no entries were found for 1975 through 1978, with the researcher directed to check the term "violence." All too soon, unfortunately, everything changed, and within a decade events, and reportage, increased dramatically (Fuller 1988a). Wanting to sensitize my students to this turn of events—including stereotyping of who were most likely terrorists—it was most instructive to have them perform a terrorism simulation that involved those stereotypes, their perceptions of how media operate, and the elusive definition of human behavioral response.

By the time Tiananmen occurred—the 1989 prodemocracy, anticorruption protests in the People's Republic of China (PRC)—*CSM* was committed to covering this kind of news crisis; in this case, 185 articles in the *Monitor* and eight in *World Monitor* (Fuller 1991). On the 20th anniversary of the events in Tiananmen Square, Peter Ford ("Tiananmen: A strained anniversary," 6/5/09, 2) quoted one of the protestors as explicating who made up that group: "The ones who made the big sacrifice in 1989 were not the students or the intellectuals, but the workers and other citizens."

Terrorism takes many forms, evolving with the times. For *CSM*, it has taken on very personal dimensions. Elizabeth Pond was held captive in Cambodia while covering the Vietnam war, nevertheless saying that, "I think that as a reporter the only way you can get the story is to take risks" (cited in Marks 1995). In 1996, when correspondent David Rohde was taken prisoner in Bosnia for 10 days, the *Monitor* was one of the first newspapers publishing content online, and it used that medium to help release him. When freelancer Jill Carroll was kidnapped in 2006 in Baghdad and held hostage for three months, she described her ordeal in an 11-part series. Of course these incidents account for much of my files, but let me update you: Elizabeth Pond is currently a correspondent for the *Washington Quarterly*, based out of Berlin; David Rohde, who won the

1996 Pulitzer Prize for International Reporting for his coverage of the Srebrenica massacre, is now an investigative journalist for the *New York Times*; and Jill Carroll, whose ordeal brought unprecedented attention to the *Monitor*, has had her story captured in *Hostage* (CSPS 2006), was named a fellow at Harvard's Joan Shorenstein Center on the Press, Politics and Public Policy, was recipient of a Courage in Journalism Award in 2006 by the International Women's Media Foundation (IWMF), and was honored with the Chicago Journalists Association's Daniel Pearl Award for courage and integrity in journalism, but she subsequently left the profession to become a firefighter in Fairfax, Virginia.

Foreign policy has been a staple at the *Monitor*. While there are obviously thousands of examples, several are worth noting:

- An editorial (*DNB* 5/7/10, 3) saying that, when leaders of Pakistan, Afghanistan, and Israel—labeled as "pivotal and US-friendly nations"—came to the White House "soon after the new president made warm overtures to Iran, Syria, China, Cuba, and Venezuela," "The Obama foreign policy doctrine" reported that they seemed to fit into a pattern of squeezing friends into changing their ways while disarming enemies and ignoring friends.
- Stating that Pakistan's weak government's resistance to Taliban militia is "arguably the world's most serious security question," Matthew Clark's *Editor's View* (*DNB* 5/11/09, 1) details concerns over the country's nuclear arsenal and the institution of strict Islamic laws, but we are relieved to know that the *Monitor* is deeply imbedded there, providing "penetrating analysis you'd be hard-pressed to find anywhere else."
- John Yemma's *Editor's View* (6/25/09, 1) sees examples of "central governments silencing dissent. Iran is using truncheons, tear gas, and bullets. China uses detention. Both are also trying to control opponents by clamping down on Internet use."
- Also, Yemma's *Editor's View* (10/23/09, 1) states: "China and India account for 35 percent of the world's population. Less than 50 years ago, both were impoverished. In recent years, both have become economic powers—China, on the strength of industrial exports; India, as a hub of outsourced services. Despite the rise of a wealthy class in both countries, millions still live hand-to-mouth."

RELIGION

Following the example of Mary Baker Eddy's Christian Scientist attitude toward other religions—which is to say, love and respect—the *Monitor* has only broken that stance when it saw churches trying to intervene in political issues or to dominate governments. Opposed to all such aggressions, and holding firmly for the separation of church and state, it supports public education, by way of example, but does not question the right of a religious group to provide its own form(s) of instruction—at its own costs.

To its credit, *CSM* has consistently—and positively—covered and included other religions in its reportage, its "Matters of Faith: Monitoring World Religion" a staple for many years. In 1999 (Lampman 12/16/99), it had a pull-out section titled "A thousand years of religion"—"the light—and shadow—it has cast on the world." Amongst its topics were the age-old quest for religious freedom; (architectural) places to pray; the changing nature of science, theology, and medicine; holy wars, from the Crusades to the Balkans; women in church leadership; and 10 major religious events in the West (the Great Schism of 1054, when Christianity split into Eastern Orthodox and Roman Catholic branches; the Crusades of 1095; the spread of Islam in the thirteenth century; the Gutenberg Bible in 1456; church support of art, music and intellectual life, such as the Vatican commission of Michelangelo to paint the ceiling of the Sistine Chapel; Martin Luther's 95 theses, 1517; missionary movements beginning in the sixteenth century; religious liberty in the New World; challenges to religious ideas in the nineteenth century, such as Darwin's theory of evolution, Freud's statement that religion is an illusion, and Marx's materialistic world view; and the Holocaust). Lampman has also had articles such as "Mixing prophecy and politics" (7/4/04), about the founding of the Christian Friends of Israel; "Property rights: Not a given for churches" (2/16/05); "For evangelicals, a bid to 'reclaim America'" (3/16/05); "Women clergy bring a new sensibility to an old calling" (7/19/06), about the Episcopal Church; and "Women take on the Torah" (2/21/08, 15), as only men have interpreted Hebrew scriptures.

"Charting America's religious landscape" (10/10/02) included a map of the United States with designations of who lived where, along with a graph of growing religions (led by the Church of Jesus Christ of Latter-day Saints, Christian churches and churches of Christ, Assemblies of God, independent charismatic churches, and the Catholic church). In September 2004 came a major review of "350 years of Jewish history in America," with perspectives on its impact, assimilation, influence, and wondering how future generations will define "Jewish."

Religious articles might also deal with church and state (8/4/97); legalities (2/18/96, 3/21/05, 6/1/05, 6/28/05, on the Supreme Court), art (4/17/03), leaders (7/1/96, the Dalai Lama; 4/4/05, John Paul II; 6/24/05, Billy Graham; 12/11/07, Mitt Romney), churches involved in healthcare (4/25/05), religious laws (3/2/05, on Pakistan); faith-based schools (9/24/04); books, including *The Monitor's Guide to Religion Bestsellers*, plus specific reviews (3/21/05, Rick Warren's *Purpose-Driven Life*), life-or-death care choices (lots in 2005 over the Terri Schiavo case, the *Monitor* consensus and concern being that judges and lawmakers take caution), megachurches (9/25/03), physician-assisted suicide (1/18/06), and even fashion (5/4/05, T-shirts with religious slogans).

Typically nonjudgmental, mostly bordering on superlatives, the *Monitor* nevertheless has not shied away from controversial subjects. An example is Michael Spencer's "The coming evangelical collapse" (3/11/09), predicting the "deterioration of the mainline Protestant world ... [that] will fundamentally alter the religious and cultural environment in the West. Within two generations, evangelicalism will be a house deserted of half its occupants." Why? The errors of identifying their movement as a culture war and with political conservatism, failing to pass on an orthodox faith to young people, having megachurches that are consumer driven, providing education unable to withstand secularism, abandoning efforts to "do good," and having an inability to pass on "a vital evangelical confidence in the Bible and the importance of the faith." As is so often the case, we need to learn from history.

The *Monitor* and Islam

Following the terrorist attacks in the United States on September 11, 2001, the *Monitor* focused on Islam. Its headline read, "The nation reels," the feature article describing terrorist attacks against the World Trade Center and the Pentagon, then admonishing how it all would "challenge aspects of America's core identity"; an editorial was titled "Resilience and restraint: Strength of character needed after Tuesday's plane attacks" (9/12/01, 8).

My analysis of *CSM* and Islam was presented to the Media, Religion, and Culture Working Group of the International Association of Media and Communication Research in Barcelona, Spain (Fuller 2002), beginning with what the *Monitor* presented as almost a primer on "Islam's beginnings and its major sects" (10/18/01) that was intriguing to run by my audience. First, see how well you do answering these questions, and hopefully you will appreciate how *CSM* doesn't talk down to its readers but assumes that we should know about this amazing religion. The community of all adherents of Islam is known as the *ummah* (nation), a term that embraces the sense of one Muslim people, overriding national and cultural boundaries. At its core is the Koran, believed to be the word of Allah (Arabic for God) as revealed to Muhammad, and central to Muslim life are "the five pillars": the affirmation that "there is no god but God, and Muhammad is the messenger of God," five daily prayers, giving alms, dawn-to-dusk fasting during the month of Ramadan, and the pilgrimage to Mecca. Ready for the quiz?

Q: What are the three monotheistic world religions?

A: Judaism, Christianity, and Islam

Q: What does "Islam" mean?

A: Arabic for "submission"

Q: When, where, and by whom did Islam originate?

A: Seventh-century Arabia, by the Prophet Muhammad

Q: How many Muslims are there worldwide?

A: One billion

Q: How many of that number are Arabic?

A: Less than one-fifth

Here, then, is the opener: "One of the three monotheistic world religions, Islam began in 7th century Arabia by the Prophet Muhammad. Today, of the approximately one billion Muslims worldwide, less than one-fifth are Arab." Since 9/11, the *Monitor* has continued its balanced coverage of Islam; for example, how Muslim women in Turkey have gained expanded religious authority (4/27/05); political gains for Iraqi women (5/3/05); book reviews (John Esposito's *The Future of Islam*, 3/23/10), and others. "The Islamic world represses women, spawns terrorism, is prone to war, resists democracy and has contributed remarkably few great scientists or writers to modern civilization," Nicholas Kristof (2002) has written; so, reacting to hate speech and xenophobia in the United States after 9/11, he decided to defend Islam: "It also has admirable qualities that anyone who has lived in the Muslim world observes: a profound egalitarianism and a lack of hierarchy that confer dignity and self-respect among believers; greater hospitality than in other societies; an institutionalized system of charity, *zaket*, to provide for the poor."

SPORTS

The feats of the gymnast prove that latent mental fears are subdued by him. The devotion of thought to an honest achievement makes the achievement possible. Exceptions only confirm this rule, proving that failure is occasioned by a too feeble faith.

—Mary Baker Eddy (1875/1994, 199)

"The *Monitor* began in 1908 and maintained for several years one unexpected policy: It put its sports page in its second-best new position, page three," Erwin D. Canham (1958, 80) detailed in his chronology of the newspaper on the occasion of its 50th anniversary. Then under the direction of Alexander Dodds, the first managing editor, and Archibald McLellan, the first editor and Mother Church director, it seemed a logical source for drawing readers and advertising. Citing Mary Baker Eddy's interest in and praise of "deeds of physical heroism and unusual skill," as they "showed mastery of the human body and material limitations," sport seemed a natural inclusion. Further, *New England Magazine* noted how, within a year, the *Monitor*'s sports page was voted "best in New England" by students at a New England university.

Today, though, after 38 years at the *Monitor*, Ross Atkin, who does the *Daily News Briefing*, finds himself the "last man standing" relative to sport. In 1971, there were four staff members. There were even female sports columnists in the 1930s and 1940s, he disclosed (1/20/10). Raymond Boyle of the Sterling Media Research Institute (UK) has discussed the paradox of how sports journalism "has been traditionally viewed disparagingly as the 'toy department,' a bastion of easy living, sloppy journalism and 'soft' news" (cited in Fuller 2008b, 81).

Leigh Montgomery, librarian, put me on to Margery Miller Welles (1924–1985), one of *Sports Illustrated*'s pioneers who wrote a weekly sports column for *The Christian Science Monitor* from 1946 to 1961. There is a bit of irony here: Her expertise was boxing—she was the first female reporter allowed in world champion Joe Louis's dressing room, owing to her well-received book *Joe Louis: American* (1945)—but she was prohibited from writing about boxing because it was a "blood sport." A boxing buff who earned the nickname "Cauliflower" from her Wellesley College classmates, the "Brown Bomber" was the subject of her senior thesis: "That if one poorly educated Negro, with little opportunity, were able to handle being a celebrity gracefully, what might we expect if we recognized ability, race and color" (cited in Clark 2003). It was very well received, none other than Eleanor Roosevelt choosing to write about it in her *My Day* column of September 21, 1945:

HYDE PARK, Thursday—I have just read in manuscript the book called "Joe Louis, American," by Margery Miller, published by Current Books, Inc. If I had been told beforehand that I would read until 2 a.m. in order to finish a book which in large part deals with boxing matches, I would have smiled and said the person knew very little about my tastes and interests. I have never been willing to go to a boxing match, except for the amateur type that youngsters put on . . .

This book, therefore, will not be of interest to boxing fans alone! Neither will it interest only the Negro people, though they will have a justifiable pride in the story of a man's rise from a cotton field farm in the South to fame and respect throughout the sports world. As I read, I realized that this was not the record simply of the boy who had reached the top in his particular sport. It was also the record of a man who, through his work in sports, wanted to win for his people goodwill among the people of other races and religions with whom his people had to live.

The story is simply told, without embellishments, but I believe many people who would not think of reading about Joe Louis, the champion, will be interested to read about Joe Louis, the man and the citizen.

Where else but in *CSM* might you learn about Afghan girls breaking barriers with "karate jabs, kicks, and punches" (5/4/05); NFL players using prayer "to reach their Sunday best" (2/2/05); Esther Phiri, a Zambian boxer (12/3/07, 7); Japanese women wrestlers (7/23/08); Italian émigrés taking up soccer (10/30/08); gender segregation (1/31/08); and editorials on Tiger Woods (12/5/09, 3) or Super Bowl betting (2/5/10)—noting that sports gambling is a $380 billion annual business. And don't miss the April 5, 2010 cover story in the *Weekly Edition*, "Fans or fanatics?" by Kase Wickman, Scott McLaughlin, and Tom Lakin—it is very telling about the bizarre phenomenon of fandom.

On the eighth day of the eighth month of the year 2008, fireworks for the XXIX (29th) Olympiad began in the opening ceremony at Beijing's Bird's Nest, welcoming 10,500 athletes from 204 countries and a global audience of 1.2 billion (recall: China has 1.3 billion people!). By the end of the event, 43 new world records and 132 new Olympic records had been set, and China had been observed on the world stage. But what is really interesting is what preceded all this activity: the controversies surrounding China as host, Western media perpetuating notions of Tibetan and Taiwanese oppression, Falun Gong suppression, and human rights violations in general. But the most—in fact, the only—unbiased Western reportage of the Beijing Olympic torch came from *The Christian Science Monitor* (Wasserstrom 2008). "Two big China stories you missed this year," it reviewed: "The brief yet radical shift of patriotic fervor into criticism of the government after the Sichuan earthquake and the official revival of Confucius."

During the 2010 Vancouver Olympic Games, Mark Sappenfield maintained a blog[6] to keep readers abreast of key events. At the end, it read, "Mark's Olympics Twitter feed would not get 6.0s, but it's still pretty good."[7] On February 27, 2010 he reported that "The US has virtually guaranteed that it will finish first in the overall Winter Olympics medal count for the first time since 1932, and only the second time ever. The US holds a 34-27 lead on Germany entering the last full day of competition today. It's also now certain that the US will break its record for most-ever medals won in a Winter Olympics (34), set in 2002." Earlier (2/26/10), almost by way of explanation for that success, Sappenfield described so much support: "Every athlete here at the Vancouver Olympics arrived on the world's biggest sports stage thanks to a small army of friends, family, and fans who have buoyed them and bolstered the practical support provided by coaches and technicians." Focusing on a specific athlete, his "Kim Yuna: Record score gives Vancouver Olympics their 6.0 moment" (2/26/10) reportage is top-notch: "For many years, figure skating perfection had a number: 6.0. After Kim Yuna's world-record score Thursday night, it does once again: 150. Yuna gave the Vancouver Olympics their Nadia Comaneci moment in the free skate Thursday, scoring 150.06 points on her way to gold in the women's figure skating competition."

Joined by correspondent Stephen Kurczy, contributor Tyler Maltbie, and staff writer Christa Case Bryant, other outstanding sports reportage was available. Here are some examples of that sports journalism:

- "US ladies at the Vancouver Olympics: Why pink, white, and blue?" (2/25/10): "If you haven't noticed, practically half the U.S. women competing at the Olympics have pink hair. Or pink something. Or at least a very feminine touch. Maybe it's some sort of women's lib movement with an athletic twist—witness snowboarders such as Hannah Teter having her own lingerie line. As in, yes we can be buff—and girly, too."
- "Winter Olympics: Women banned from ski jumping, but women's participation way up" (2/22/10): "Olympic ski jumping is a men-only event according to the International Olympic Committee. Turned down by the IOC for their lack of depth, women ski jumpers took their case to Canada's courts, where a judge agreed that the IOC's refusal to hold women's events in the discipline constituted discrimination. But the Vancouver organizing committee (VANOC) was powerless to rectify the situation, concluded the court—a decision upheld by an appeals court. Still, female participation in the Games has improved dramatically over the past three decades."
- "Why the Winter Olympics beat American Idol's ratings" (2/22/10): We know what Canadians think about their Games, but the IOC—which is more biased, or less, depending on how you look at it, is also quite pleased with the popularity of the 2010 Winter Olympics. In addition to the opening ceremonies capturing the attention of three times more Canadians than when

they hosted the Games in 1988, Olympics coverage did what no TV show has been able to do in six years—beat *American Idol*'s ratings. But Olympic popularity goes beyond the US and Canada. In China, Japan, and South Korea, more people tuned in than in 2006 or 2002. The Olympics also drew modest audiences from six countries participating for the first time: the Cayman Islands, Colombia, Ghana, Montenegro, Pakistan, and Peru. With their involvement, a record 82 countries took part in everything from alpine skiing to speed skating.

From these many and diverse examples of *Monitor* coverage, hopefully you begin to see the value of its balanced reportage. What comes next is a discussion of how it actually does it.

Chapter 5

"Abreast of the Times": The Role of Information Technology (IT)

Awareness of changes in both the national and international political scenes is essential to journalism [and] the Monitor *has also been alert to technological changes . . . As network television and then cable television and then the Internet have become major information resources, the challenge to the* Monitor *to keep "abreast of the times" has only become greater. Technology has also made the world smaller, enabling journalists to gather information in ways never before possible. As a result, the* Monitor *has continued its commitment to delivering an international scope of news, not just US news.*

—Judy Huenneke (2008, 13–14)

Without wanting to talk down to anyone, it may be helpful to construct this chapter in the form of a tutorial for any Luddites out there. For those who don't know what a Luddite is: Back in 1779 Britain, legend has it that Ned Ludd, a mad Leicestershire workman, broke up some stocking frames as a protest against hosiery knitting machines that were feared to be replacing men. So someone today who opposes our ever-growing high-tech world—maybe refusing to become computer literate, or even using an ATM—might be called a (Neo)-Luddite, or a "technophobe."

Actually, the more appropriate subtitle for this chapter would be "Information and Communication Technologies (ICTs)," a term that most of the world uses while the United States tends to just call it IT. What you will hopefully find helpful is a brief review of *CSM* and IT, broken down by print, broadcast, and electronic means, as well as the incorporation of "new media" along the way. What makes this topic all *real*, though, is staff reactions to this evolution in their journalistic profession.

THE CHRISTIAN SCIENCE MONITOR AND INFORMATION TECHNOLOGY

Throughout its 100-plus years, *CSM* has been technologically alert, even an early innovator. Both in Chapter 2 and on the Timeline in Appendix 6, you can see some examples of these experiments. Reviewing "over a century of product evolution, experimentation, and broadening reach," it behooves us to recall that, as early as the 1920s, the *Monitor* began AM transmissions, with shortwave broadcasts by 1935. Color printing began in 1938, tricolor 10 years later. *CSM*'s 15-minute weekday show "News from Everywhere," which premiered in 1943 on the Mutual Broadcasting System, was the first national news program using the resources of an international newspaper. Apollo 14 commander Alan B. Shepard carried microfilm with eight pages of *The Christian Science Monitor* to the moon in 1971, and by 1974 pages were faxed to remote plants and a weekly "International Edition" was launched.

In the mid-1980s, "Monitor Radio Weekend Edition" debuted on American Public Radio, distribution of *Monitor* print content via syndication peaked at 200 subscribers with a combined circulation of about 20 million, and the Christian Science Monitor Syndicate, Inc., bought WQTV Channel 68 in Boston. "The World Service of *The Christian Science Monitor*" began broadcasting on international shortwave radio to Europe, Africa, and Asia, "World Monitor: A Television Presentation of *The Christian Science Monitor*" launched nightly programming, and *World Monitor: The Christian Science Monitor Monthly* magazine began publication while four-color ink and photographs were introduced. *The Monitor Channel* (1991–1992), detailed here, is a fascinating case study of *CSM*'s brief foray into cable television. By 2000, its SciTech blog was one of the first news website blogs. Two years later, *CSM*'s "Treeless edition," a digital replica of its daily newspaper, was deliverable in PDF form. The website was averaging 1.5 million unique visitors per month by 2008.

As the first national newspaper to introduce a Web-first model, the print edition ceased—if supplemented, as of April 12, 2009 with the *Weekly Edition* and, as of April 27, 2009, the *Daily News Briefing*. By 2010, CSMonitor.com had 5.3 million monthly unique users and 14.5 million monthly page views, *CSM Weekly* a circulation of 77,000, and *Daily News Briefing* (*DNB*) claimed 3,000 paying subscribers.

Recall that, not long after its founding in 1908, *The Christian Science Monitor* became involved in the newly-discovered medium of radio in the 1920s—later, going on to establish Monitor Radio, shortwave radio, and cooperation with other radio systems. Hearing his voice on an answering machine, it struck me that former *CSM* editor (1970 to 1979) John Hughes has such a stentorian broadcaster's voice that, when we connected (4/28/10) it was my first question. Sure enough: Hughes began at WBZ "pontificating for 13 minutes about anything that struck me, without interviews or audio interruption," later working on Monitor Radio and the Monitor Channel. *CSM*'s entry into television began in the mid-1980s with the news program "*The Christian Science Monitor* Reports," rising and falling with the Monitor Channel cable television attempt from 1991 to 1992.

Within three decades (1938), the *Monitor*, which began as a broadsheet, added color printing, and by 1960 it became available internationally. The format change to a "compact" tabloid in 1975 was welcomed as an ideal size for commuters and home readers alike. Production, which started by sending copy by airplane to various presses around the country, was greatly facilitated by fax[1] developments in the 1970s, and by 1985 it was being syndicated in some 200 subscribing newspapers. The magazine *World Monitor* premiered in 1988, lasting for five years.

Between microfilm and microfiche, the newspaper became available everywhere aided by critical indexing packages such as ProQuest.

In 1995, spurred on when correspondent David Rohde was taken prisoner in Bosnia, the *Monitor* hastened to help readers keep up with his fate, and so set up an online[2] service—one of the first newspapers to do so.[3] Within a year, the beta[4] website[5] became www.CSMonitor.com. Monitor Radio broadcasts were carried there—thus making it one of the first websites with audio. By 2001, many *Monitor* staffers had blogs[6]—some discussed here.

The digital[7] age began. A "treeless" edition of *The Christian Science Monitor* became available in PDF[8] by 2002, and in 2003, when staff writer Ben Arnoldy covered the war in Iraq for the *Monitor* online,[9] it was a first for a journalist to report via a newspaper using that means. Since CSMonitor.com had done well—drawing some 1.5 million unique visitors per month by 2008—it seemed almost inevitable that *CSM* should try to switch to a Web-first, free[10] model. In April 2009, that is what happened—making the *Monitor* the first national newspaper to do so. Simultaneously, as you undoubtedly know by now, the *Weekly Edition* (in print magazine format) and *Daily News Briefing* (in PDF, delivered by email,[11] were available for paying subscribers.

CSM AND THE INTERNET, THE WEB, AND BLOGS

Although these terms are all interrelated, it may be helpful to put them into perspective as to where they fit in the *Monitor* story.

The Internet

A "network of networks" or "network of computers" whose origin, in 1969, was the U.S. Department of Defense's Advanced Research Projects Agency Network (ARPANET)—linking government, university, military, and commercial sites for email and online databases—the Internet emphasizes interconnectivity. Its evolution since then has been cited as the most important communications development of our times. Relative to *The Christian Science Monitor*, its significance has to do with facilitation of a digital newspaper.

"The Internet can be faulted for many things—pornography and frivolity, to name two—but it is an incredibly powerful tool for communication, democratization of intelligence, and linking people and ideas across the planet," John Yemma stated in an *Editor's View* (*DNB* 6/25/09). "The human capital that the Internet unleashes is ultimately much more valuable than natural resources or manufactured goods. If Twitter and blogs and amateur videos are shut down in the name of social order, a nation also loses conversation, brainstorming, knowledge transfer, and the serendipity that is the concomitant of invention and creativity." Separately, he "provided insights into the new, Internet-centric *CSM* in a webinar[12] organized by the World Editors Forum" (Brown 2009) and, in an interview with *American Editor* (Watson 2009), Yemma pointed out the Internet's journalistic role in storytelling: "Storytelling in this medium has to recognize the habits and preferences of Internet users: fast and simple access, links to related content, enabling of comments and feedback, engaging a social network that can help multiply the eyes, ears, and intelligence brought to bear on a subject (i.e., crowd-sourcing)—and presentations appropriate to the story."

On March 11, 2009, the *Monitor* was featured in a video, "Digital Newspapers: The New Reality," from the Newseum in Washington, D.C.,[13] that echoed many of the issues discussed in Chapter 2 on closings and cutbacks in the industry, with hope for the troubled business model seen in multimedia. John Yemma spoke of the "perfect storm" that led to *CSM's* decision to move beyond its cumbersome, expensive distribution method by going Web-first. "It's a chance to reach new readers, faster," he added—along with the ability to have continuous updates.

THE WEB

While lowercase "internet" refers to a collection of interconnected networks and capital "Internet" to the world's largest internetworking system, lowercase "web" is used for terms like *website, web hosting,*[14] *webmasters,*[15] *web browsers,*[16] and *web space,*[17] and capital "Web" refers to the "World Wide Web" (WWW), a collection of resources and users on the Internet who are using http.[18] Don't miss the fact that Web protocols are sent over the Internet.

Historically, the *Monitor* has been a pioneer, then, in providing online access to its content, being one of the first (inter)national newspapers to have a website, supporting staffer blogs, having RSS feeds[19] and audio reports, enabling podcasting,[20] using wikis,[21] supporting tweets[22] and instant messaging,[23] participating in webinars, being on social networks,[24] and/or using mobile technology.

The move to a Web-based model, Susan Hackney, senior marketing director, predicted to *Wired* (Keane 2008) "should enable the *Monitor* to keep its foreign bureaus open, at the same time lowering costs," adding, "We will be able to apply more resources to the Web, where the future is going. For that reason we will be more competitive." Recognizing the complexity of RSS feeds, continually updated blogs, and all the intricacies of the Internet, Brennon Slattery (2008) of *PC World* applauded *CSM*'s decision to be Web-based, saying, "To me, it's the evolution of modern journalism." Basically agreeing, Mashable Social Media (Hopkins 2008) further suggested it look into social news services such as Digg, Friend-Feed, and Twitter to promote itself.

Since going online, the *Monitor* religious article has included a byline, editor Clare Turner explained to me (2/26/10). They have both a batch of timeless articles (such as about comfort, job loss, loneliness—human issues) and breaking news and current events, with a cache of items in their database. Additionally, Spirituality.com is an online website featuring original articles on Christian Science, as well as reprints from *JSH* and *Christian Science Perspective*. There are biweekly chats on Spirituality.com every Tuesday from 2 to 3 p.m. covering a variety of subjects such as incurability, cancer, addiction to pornography and cybersex, prayer for government, and what spirituality is. Through an outside tracking firm the producers have learned that people—not all Christian Scientists—from about a dozen countries tune in to the chats both when they are live and later in the "reply" mode.

"It's all about the hits" is a frequent refrain heard at *Monitor* headquarters these days. What this means is counts of both page views[25] and unique visitors[26] to its website, CSMonitor.com. These measures are valuable tabulations not only for the editorial staff but also for advertisers. Technorati, a keyword-search website that in 2006 was tracking 31 million sites and more than two billion links at the time of Jill Carroll's kidnapping by Al Qaeda in Iraq, reports there were 193 service videos calling for her release.[27] At this point, *The Christian Science Monitor* ranks as a top news site with ABC News, CNN, Fox News, the *Los Angeles Times*, the *New York Times*, *Time*, *USA Today*, the *Wall Street Journal*, and the *Washington Post*.

Greg Jarboe (2009) of Search Engine Watch has pointed out that *CSM* was "One of the top six sources in Google News in February 2009 and #1 in terms of most appearances on the home page as a percentage of site total." Tom Regan, a 1992 Nieman Fellow and NPR news and politics blogger who worked on the *Monitor*'s website before going to the Online News Association (ONA), reported how the paper benefited from "surf and drill" practices whereby Internet users searched for sites, then dug into potential links, adding, "And they're discovering the printed paper, too. I've had a couple of thousand emails that tell me 'didn't know about your paper' and 'glad you're still in business.' September 11 really changed the outlook on the importance of foreign news to this young audience," he wrote (cited in Shanor 2003, 113).

Like many of his colleagues, David Cook started off as a copy kid, in 1968—a time he recalled in our conversation (2/13/10). In his many roles, including editorial positions in both print (editor of the *Monitor*, 1994–2001) and broadcasting, he came to realize that "the Web is the place for us to be."

Claiming more than 13,000 *Monitor* fans on Facebook, *CSM*'s website[28] reportedly has more than 1,200 followers on its *Horizons* blog (@CSMHorizonsBlog), 1,400 on the National Desk (@CSMNational). In addition, it lists these staff members on Twitter: @CSMonitoronline, the main Twitter site for *The Christian Science Monitor*; @johnyemma, John Yemma, editor; @jimmy_orr, Jimmy Orr, online editor and politics blogger; @davidclarkscott, David C. Scott, international editor; @judydigginit, Judy Lowe, gardening and environment editor and *Diggin' It* blogger; @andrewjh, Andrew Heining, National News Desk editor and blogger by day, Red Sox fan by night.

Early on in the *Weekly Edition*, *CSM* experimented with what were called "SiteSeer" web excursions. Running from April 12 to mid-July 2009, it included articles such as these: "Online with Obama: A new kind of democracy?"; "Christian book expo a 'major disappointment' "; "Twitter as a customer service shortcut" (4/12/09); "Fast wireless Internet coming to rural America"; "Kindle e-book readers rebel"; "EPA and CO2"; "High-speed rail: Can it work in the US?"; "A newspaper disappears in a wired town" (Ann Arbor, MI); "BYU professor: Colleges obsolete by 2020"; "Why textbooks we paid for never reached Afghan schools"; "Is Twitter the next second life?"; "As newspapers struggle, readers seem fine with online"; "Murdoch, no more free lunch"; "Apple, the censor?"; "Leasing solar energy"; "A Facebook, er, book"; "Self-published books"; "President Obama seeks cyber czar"; "Are bigger cars safer?"; "J. D. Salinger sues to block a 'Catcher' sequel"; "Here comes the recession-chic bride"; "Men rule on Twitter"; "Toni Morrison on censored books"; "English language gets its 1 millionth word (Web 2.0)"; "Behind MySpace cutbacks"; "How green is public transportation?"; "Dunkin' Donuts makes an iPhone application"; "When a refugee camp closes—where do refugees go?"; and "Bulldoze the burbs?" (7/5–12). After three months, though, it was decided that SiteSeer was an experiment not worth pursuing. Yemma reported that they "played with the @CSMonitor.com page in the weekly, moving it to the back, downsizing it" and eventually substituted it with his Open Source column on the back page. "I've always been a skeptic of print to Web promotion," he added.

Reading is an offline experience. I know of few people who actually go from the printed page to a Web browser and type in the relatively complex URL of a news story. We need to cross promote, of course, but the most effective (and still not that effective) method is to tease URLs directly out of print news stories. We are somewhat limited in doing this, however, because we don't post all of our content immediately upon publication. At any rate, readers did not particularly value the generalized reference to the Web as seen in @CSMonitor.com, which is where SiteSeer existed.

Blogs

Knowing that a blog is a "log" on the Web (We*b log*), you can appreciate the fact that, by beginning in 2001, *Monitor* blogs in many ways set a standard for other newspapers. Consider, too: "blog" was the most looked-up word in Merriam Webster's online dictionary this year.

And do not miss this crucial fact about the blogosphere: Much of it depends on linkages to stories based on print media.

CSM *Blogs*

Blogs are plentiful relative to *CSM*. What follows are outlines on *Bright Green* (the environment), *Chapter & Verse* (books), *DC Decoder* (the capital, by Peter Grier), *Diggin' It* (gardening), *Eco-renovation* (Alexandra Marks, restoration), *Editor's Blog* (John Yemma), *Global News Blog* (David C. Scott), *Horizons* (innovations), *The New Economy* (*Monitor* reports on money), *Terrorism & Security*, and *The Vote* (Jimmy Orr on politics).

- *Bright Green*: an environmental blog. The day we met (2/16/10) was a bittersweet one for online producer Eoin O'Carroll, as it was the last day for *Bright Green*. His original tagline read: "A future of poisoned oceans, withered crops, and irate polar bears is nobody's idea of a good time. It's clear to anyone who is paying attention that our civilization is due for an upgrade. Bright Green covers the news, ideas, opinions, and trends littering the road to an environmentally sustainable future." Table 5.1, "*Bright Green* fades to black," reveals its requiem.

  "Our decision to discontinue the *Bright Green* blog stemmed from several factors," editor John Yemma (cited in Brainard 2010) explained. "For one thing, the Monitor has a longstanding commitment to science and environmental coverage. That continues. Environmental coverage, however, has become much more mainstream in recent years. We expect all of our reporters to be well versed in environmental issues and to pursue these as a matter of course . . . Eoin O'Carroll, kept the flame alive in the environmental beat while many of our other reporters specialized in regional coverage, legal affairs, politics, etc. But with climate change, cap-and-trade, and a host of other environmental issues in the center of the news, specialized environmental coverage seemed something we could move beyond."

- *Chapter & Verse*: Marjorie Kehe, book editor, has one of the oldest blogs at the *Monitor* with *Chapter & Verse*, begun in 2006. "It just began one day," she reported to me (2/10/10), with articles of about 500 to 600 words and a common theme, and almost instantly got hits. Nowadays, she gets hundreds of books but usually only reviews about a half dozen. Check out books and follow her on Facebook and Twitter.[29]

- *DC Decoder*: Peter Grier on politics. Some staff are still pro-print. Although everyone else is involved with the Web, long-time reporter Peter Grier still thinks, he said (2/19/10), that his *Decoder* column in print grabs readers easier. He has a heartfelt objection to the switchover from venerable tradition, although, as he said in an email (4/29/10), it probably was inevitable. We don't have discussions as much anymore, he thinks, and considers that blogs just take stuff out of the air and add comments—unfiltered through a nonpartisan machine. "Hits are both infuriating and energizing," he concedes, adding that, "People are only interested if they're interested." It is easy to see his style in the cover story for the first issue (4/12/09) of *CSM Weekly*, "The new

Table 5.1
Bright Green Fades to Black

After 22 months and some 500 posts, the *Bright Green* blog is coming to an end.

Even though it's closing down, in many respects *Bright Green* was a roaring success. Back in February 2008, when I first proposed doing a daily, Web-only update on environmental topics, the *Monitor* was a blog-free publication. We didn't even have the technology in place to publish directly to the Web without first running content through our (very buggy and cumbersome) print publication system.

Using WordPress, a free, open-source blogging platform, we built a new Environment section, bolted to our existing site and cloned to create new sections for Gardening, Books, Innovation, and Politics. The realization that we were on to something big came in August 2008, when a post titled "Will Paris Hilton's energy plan work?" that sat atop Google News for more than an hour, the resulting onslaught of traffic ending up bringing down our entire site. After that, it was clear that blogs would play an important role in the *Monitor*'s Web strategy. In April 2009, as my responsibilities shifted from writing to helping the Monitor transform from a primarily dead-tree-and-ink product into a Web-centric news organization, Environment editor Judy Lowe and science writer Moises Velasquez-Manoff joined *Bright Green*.

For this final post, I asked them to list the posts they were most proud of. Judy's are: Video games can be energy hogs; Three tips to cut your power bill; Native grasses an explosive idea for cleaning contaminated soil; Decline in honeybees highlights importance of wild pollinators. Moises's favorites: Community based fishery management and Somali pirates; A warmer world could make current airport runways too short; Climategate, global warming, and the tree rings divergence problem; Could water scarcity cause international conflict?; Audi's "Green Police" Super Bowl ad controversial. And my own favorites: Does closing roads cut delays?; Scientists admit global warming is a hoax; Report: Illicit urban chicken movement growing in US; Are climate-change deniers guilty of treason?; Are climate change deniers like creationists?

Many thanks are in order. First is the late Richard Bergenheim, who first suggested I write a weekly news roundup about global warming; Online editor and politics blogger Jimmy Orr for his unceasing encouragement; Christian Scripter for long hours spent designing and assembling the original Environment site. Thanks also to the thousands of coders in the WordPress community. *Monitor* science writer Pete Spotts has repeatedly filled in as guest blogger and is never too busy answer a science question. And a very big thanks to my editor, Judy Lowe, who has repeatedly made me come off sounding far more intelligent than I actually am. Finally, and most importantly, I'd like to thank all of our readers. Your feedback—the praise, the scorn, and everything in between—has kept me far more thorough and motivated than any editor could. Judy, Moises, and I will continue to appear in these pages, and hope that you'll keep reading—and commenting.

economy: 10 ways it will look different": beginning with a historical overview, he includes a chart comparing countries in terms of GDP renewals, home prices, and unemployment; profiles of an elderly couple in Toronto and a small businessman in Germany; reading signs (big-ticket consumer items, home hair-dye kits, sofa index, housing starts, coffee boutiques, used-car lots, dining out, granite countertops, the stock market, FedEx shipments, and the Conference Board Index), and discusses the 10 changes: value as the new virtue, return of the tightwad, eBay America, money in the mattress, the new Big Three (Detroit automakers), the movable resume, "green new deal," stodgy is chic, D.I.Y. investing, and bust of the boomtowns. Amazing, isn't it, that hardly any of the items predicted in the new economy involve information technology?

- *Diggin' It*: Environment editor Judy Lowe, whose area of expertise is gardening, has 1,000 followers on Twitter for *Diggin' It*, as well as seven dedicated bloggers who freely want to contribute to her blog. Having written 10 books about gardening, she has become known as a "Twitter queen." Check her out on Facebook and Twitter.[30]

- *Eco-renovation*: twice-weekly blogs by Alexandra Marks, billed as "The Practical and Spiritual Guide to Green Renovation," concern her green and budget-friendly restoration of a 1902 farmhouse in Connecticut: Sheep Dog Hollow. "During this project, I've learned an enormous amount. The top lesson, though, is how far green technology has come in the past 30 years in terms of its overall efficiency and, equally as important, its affordability," she wrote me (4/27/10). Using terms like *geothermal wells, spray foam insulation, solar energy, on-demand hot water heaters, energy-efficient windows, wind zones, wind power,* and *wind turbine panels,* it's an amazing example. What a weird coincidence it was that the day we talked (4/26/10) was, in fact, her last day. After 20-some years with *CSM,* including opening the Monitor Radio office in Buenos Aires and working both in the Boston and New York offices—as well as stints at other media outlets—Marks is now focusing on writing a book about her house. And, as I told her, she sure can write! You will see her byline attached to numerous articles cited here.

- *Editor's Blog*: video talks with the editor (John Yemma) on Thursdays at 1 p.m. EST. One of my favorites was this comment from his March 12, 2010 blog: "Searching for the hot new thing? Constantly checking your Twitter stream, RSS feeds, and breaking news alerts? It's great to stay informed, but don't forget what's right in front of you."

- *Global News Blog*: World news with David C. Scott. On Facebook is this message: "The *Monitor* tries to push beyond sensation and contribute thoughtful, solution-oriented news. This Facebook page is a place where readers can comment and help elevate discussion about world events."

- *Horizons*: innovations with Chris Gaylord and others on Facebook and Twitter.[31]

- *The Monitor Breakfast*: coordinated by Washington, D.C., bureau chief Dave Cook, "Washington reporters interview major figures over breakfast in a civilized, comprehensive way. Hosted by *The Christian Science Monitor*, guests have included US presidents, vice presidents, as well as countless cabinet officers and congressional leaders," according to the website. You can both review those newsmakers on http://twitter.com/CSMnational and see a list of interviewees on Appendix 4.
- *The New Economy*: the *Monitor*'s money editor, Laurent Belsie, blogs about economic changes underway in the United States and globally.[32]
- *Terrorism & Security*: billed as "A daily summary of global reports on security issues," it deals with a range of worldly issues.
- *The Vote*: Jimmy Orr's political blog reads, "Government is serious. Democracy is sacred. And then there is politics the way it is actually played. The Vote blog looks at politics the way the players talk about it among themselves after work."

"The Bloggiest"

Dave Wieneke (2008) has pointed out that *The Christian Science Monitor*, loved by bloggers, has been "hailed as the most blogged newspaper (per subscriber) in the world." It has been dubbed, frequently, as the nation's "bloggiest newspaper"—meaning that it "attracts more online links by web logs, in proportion to its print circulation, than any other paper."

When "content strategist, info provocateur" Amy Gahran (2005) inquired how the *Monitor* felt about the discovery that it was the "bloggiest" newspaper on the Web, she received this reply from Tom Regan, then in charge of blogs, which had been a staple for four years already:

We also happen to be a media organization with a slightly different emphasis because of the philosophies of the folks who founded the paper. The people who run this place believe that if you get comprehensive, credible, and fair information into the hands of people (or in front of their eyeballs), that information that helps them better understand what's going on around them, they will make better decisions about important issues.

Technorati has 17,800 links to URLs[33]; for example, usatoday.com has 10,861 sources, giving *USA Today* a link per thousand circulation (LpkC) score of 6.68; in contrast, CSMonitor.com, with a circulation of 71,000 and 9,578 links from 4,636 sources, has a LpkC score of 134.9, more than double its nearest competitor (the *New York Times*). Here is a list of the bloggiest newspapers, showing the *Monitor* as "uniquely influential in the blogosphere in proportion to its paper circulation":

Christian Science Monitor—134.90

New York Times—63.08

Washington Post—58.44

San Francisco Chronicle—38.32

Boston Globe—29.80

Seattle Post Intelligencer—18.56

New York Post—12.48

LA Times—11.21

"I don't think of the *Monitor* as being particularly 'bloggy,' " editor John Yemma told me when we met (12/12/09). He points out how you can see, from looking at CSMonitor.com, that there are about a dozen blogs, whereas sites like Boston.com and NYTimes.com have scores of them. "And some of our blogs were started as 'workarounds'—such as *The Global News Blog*, because of the difficulty of posting articles quickly before we implemented our new content management system."

CSM STAFF AND THE WEB

As might be expected, the transition to being Web-first has made an impression on *Monitor* staff; what follows are some testimonials about it, about one year into the experiment.[34]

Pat Murphy, deputy online editor, came aboard in 2007 from a news and sports broadcasting career at the University of Kansas and many years in the Boston television market as a news and sports writer and producer; now he works for Jimmy Orr with Eoin O'Carroll, Casey Bayer, and Jake Turcotte. Right away, he got involved in compatibility issues, such as the video camera not being "Mac-dedicated." The change was time consuming. Online, he told me (3/12/10), "Reporters don't have time to shoot as much as they used to." For example, they might have an article on African musicians and want a video dealing with Mali condensed—adding that reporter Scott Baldauf sent along some examples of local South Africans playing guitar, and they were able to edit them to go along with an online story. For *CSM Weekly*, he works to make sure there is quality control when items move to the Web—such as photos and search engine optimization (SEO). He also works with social media, making sure the *Monitor* has links from a number of sources. In a one-year anniversary video aired on CSMonitor.com (3/25/10), editor John Yemma, *Weekly* editor Clayton Collins, and deputy online editor Pat Murphy did a review. As moderator, Murphy began by asking how the *Weekly Edition* evolved—the answer being that various teams had thought about a number of different short- and long-term plans. Admitting that it took a while to hit their stride, Collins pointed out how, after lots of experimenting, "Print allows us to do a lot of storytelling." John Yemma, in typical fashion, talked about what they try to do at the *Monitor*—explain what is *behind* the news, how it hadn't gone away, it had just diversified.

Recalling how, when she worked an eight-hour shift with no lunch for KNX, the CBS news radio station in Los Angeles, California, in the 1990s during a six-year stint away from the *Monitor*, reporter Gloria Goodale said she now realizes what good training it is for today's schedule with the Web-first *CSM* (4/11/10).

"My job has changed every year, influenced by new technology and changes in the industry," librarian Leigh Montgomery mused when we met (2/16/10). Clearly, the definition of "librarian" at the *Monitor* has evolved since she came there in 1996—physically, even, as she is now directly integrated into the newsroom. She is the administrator of Merlin, a form of digital asset management (DAM) system that functions as the photo and page archive, as well as the digital light table for the photo department. It is also where PDFs of the daily website editions are archived and, though none have been stored in this system as of yet, Merlin can also accommodate multimedia formats. Montgomery had one of *CSM*'s first blogs: *LibLog*. "Having someone type 'gas prices' into Google and have the Liblog appear was satisfying," she said in an email (4/13/10). "We did get traffic reports, and it enjoyed quite a bit of traffic—even after it wasn't updated any more." It ran for five years, but then had to cease due to editing bottlenecks. "I enjoy being here, wondering what will happen next," she reported, respectful of the understood standard of balance and accuracy that the newspaper employs, linked to sites of authority. The tools, she considers, are still in their infancy, and the key is managing information streams. Next, she would like to launch an archive blog, offering this justification:

One of the great things about the *Monitor* is that it has had a global focus, has been publishing for a century, and has its archives digitized back to the first date of publication—1908. Citizen journalists, history buffs, and students could read it, link to it, mash it up and tell new stories with it. Archives are one of the most valuable assets of any news entity. Also, there are so many amazing archives of publications, of collections, being launched—it could also link to these kinds of repositories. It seems like every entity wants to digitize, curate, and share their archives as widely as possible.

"My job is actually split into two functions: Four days a week, I'm an editor. On Sundays, I'm a blogger," deputy national news editor Mark

Sappenfield told me (1/19/10)—a classic example of how the Web has changed definitions of work.

In terms of media, *Monitor* editorial writer Francine Kiefer reported (2/25/10) that she used to read widely (four or five papers per day), but now she is filing more (both in the *Weekly* and on the Web), so she is not able to read as deeply. Each day she checks out Google News, the BBC website, the *Washington Post*, and the *New York Times*. She tries to catch NPR and the network news (usually Diane Sawyer) or the PBS News Hour; in addition, she keeps a very cursory eye on the *Atlantic Monthly*, *Time*, *Newsweek*, and the *Economist*, and likes the aggregate website realclearpolitics.com. Sundays, she listens to television talk shows, which C-SPAN rebroadcasts then, during lunch or as she is driving around. There is an extra burden in more Web work, but she is willing to experiment; in fact, she is surprised by how much she likes to Twitter. "Blogs are personal, but somehow they still need to be in line with the *Monitor*'s views," she said. "Our editorials need prior board approval. We haven't started blogging yet, and I don't believe they will need such approval." There is lots of emphasis on incorporating links to other *Monitor* stories. Google screens out commentary, so it is difficult to get included there. "The Weekly is pro-active, the Web more reactive," Kiefer has noted. As we were talking, Kiefer was IM-ing her boss, Clay Jones. It encouraged us to discuss the role of the Web, whose advantage is that it is more timely, if disadvantaged in that it is less discriminating and reporters are pressured for hits.

Since the change to a Web-first format, reporter Mark Trumbull finds himself writing more, and more frequently, and shorter—all trying to achieve the same goals as he always has. "What does the average reader/person need to know?" he reported asking himself (4/8/10) as he goes about his beat. There is a lot of pressure with the information flow, which is both exciting and difficult to balance, but "It's all about clicks," he noted. By way of example, he pointed out how he recently saw that even David Brooks (*even* esteemed David Brooks, for heaven's sake, of the *New York Times*) used Sandra Bullock's name in a title piece as a draw.

"The move to the Web has really forced big changes in the newsroom, the biggest I've seen in my 29 years in journalism," economy editor Laurent Belsie wrote me in an email (4/30/10), adding that staffers have to adapt to a new environment. In the Money section, for example, in February 2010 they began running the best pieces from 20 high-powered economists, such as former Labor Secretary Robert Reich, and other financial bloggers. Mirroring their copy online dramatically boosted Web traffic to the Money section. In the old days, *CSM* would have paid for contributors; now, though, bloggers agree to the arrangement because it gives them more exposure. Belsie questions whether this type of non-revenue arrangement is sustainable, but so far, it is a win-win. Another big change he cites is the way that we conceive of news. "In the old days, reporters and editors dreamed up stories and we wrote them. We still do that. But now we also react to hot topics that show up on Google, Yahoo, and other big websites and we react much more quickly—within hours instead of days," he said. One final change that may prove ephemeral: With so many guest bloggers and freelance writers to choose from, news-rooms seem to value editors more than writers right now.

Brad Knickerbocker, a senior writer and editor based in Oregon, reports how he works in real time: Today, his workday world is web-oriented such that his 9-to-5 schedule coordinates with the Boston news-room's latest posting time of 8 p.m. (With major breaking news, that can go later.) He's also the Saturday editor, editing several stories and blog posts that day, as well as writing at least one himself. Whether writing about concern over birds relative to pilot Sully Sullenberger's "Miracle on the Hudson," Al Qaeda's terrorist strategies, Obama's "government transparency" pledge, Montana becoming the third state to legalize physician-assisted suicide, or the Bush administration's "torture memos," he represents how seasoned reporters have bent to the demands of a full range of journalistic technologies and philosophies.

"The 'Web first' model that we have adopted has changed our capacity, as photo staff, to produce work on a timely manner," Alfredo Sosa, direc-tor of photography and multimedia, told me in an email (4/14/10). "Therefore our participation on the Web is basically through work cre-ated for the Weekly that finds its way to the Web. We focus our resources to produce strong visual content for a weekly magazine and multimedia pieces to accompany weekly pieces on the Web."

Like a number of his colleagues, science reporter Peter N. Spotts still pre-fers print and likes writing for the *Weekly*—"a different beast," where you can still write longer, analytical stories. "News has become too event- rather than idea-driven, and it's in danger of becoming too Google-dependent," he argues (2/26/10). Before the changeover, Spotts said he and others typi-cally worked a five-day week, usually submitting an average of two or three articles a week. Now, with a 24/7/365 website, the demands have grown to at least a story a day, two or more if you're really on a roll.

Relative to the Web, Peter Rainer wrote me in an email (4/14/10): "I've been a professional film critic for over 30 years and so I come out of a print tradition, but the great thing now about having my reviews appear-ing online is that it allows them to be read and linked by anybody with a computer anywhere. In terms of getting the word out, that's a tremendous improvement over the past." He gets lots of hits, which he credits to both his and *CSM*'s reputation "and because the reviews are linked throughout many different entertainment-based websites, such as Metacritic and Rotten Tomatoes ... And yes, my readership is global." His online reviews, which include, a week delayed, everything that runs in the *Weekly Edition*, cover everything from studio blockbusters on down. "In short: I love my job," he added.

Midwest bureau chief Amanda Paulson, too, is concerned about changes since the move to the Web: "Thoughtful, analytical, *Monitor*-type news will get lost in a black hole," she worries (2/23/10). The *Weekly* is more like old times for her; now, "there is pressure for shorter stories for the Web." She doesn't like to depend on Google Trends, and bemoans the fact that it is difficult to find a web audience for stories about education.

Linda Feldmann of the Washington, D.C., bureau, who has been with *CSM* for 28 years, thinks that the Web holds the key to the future of journalism. "Now, news is more responsive," she said (2/23/10). She considers herself a neutral journalist, explaining, "I look at it as, What's the story?" Feldman, from her experiences serving in bureaus in Boston, Washington, and Moscow, has learned to put her own views off to the side. The magazine is very satisfying, she thinks, while the Web is short and fast.

Web viewers, columnist Walter Rodgers has pointed out (2/24/10), probably do include many church members and might find much of the material on CSMonitor.com rather high-brow. "Unlike the *Washington Post*, which serves the nation's capital, or the *New York Times*, which serves a scholarly audience, the *Monitor* has its own character—something different as a newspaper. It manifests itself in thought and quality, with first-rate journalism." In terms of the future, Rodgers has serious qualms that the industry would be poorer without *CSM*, telling me in an email (4/22/10) "because a real albeit intangible quality of thought would be lost without that paper."

From his experience of having joined the *Monitor* in 1983, diplomatic correspondent Howard LaFranchi realizes that they are "drawing new eyes," which he values, but he is concerned about losing former readership on the Web.

"There's a different rhythm with the Web," Peter Ford has noted. There might be more pieces, but they are shorter. He has had a varied international career, beginning as a stringer for *CSM* from Central America in 1986, covering Latin America, the Middle East, Moscow, Argentina, and now China. When we talked (1/18/10 at 8 p.m. my time, 9 a.m. his time the next day), Google had just announced it had been the victim of cyber attacks originating there and so, citing a breach of some Chinese human rights activists, said it would no longer continue censoring search engine results. How did he, the Beijing bureau chief, hear about it? On a WBUR (Boston radio station) app on his iPhone! Considering that there are some 360 million Internet users in the country and that Google China was started in 2005, Chen Dongyi (2010, 39) wrote that, "There are few in China that want to see the company leave. In front of Google's headquarters in Beijing, users placed bouquets as a sign of mourning, and online forums broadcast expressions of support from netizens."

TECHNOLOGICAL IMPLICATIONS OF IT FOR *CSM* AND STAFF

There is no question that *Monitor* staff is techno-savvy. For starters, editor John Yemma was named number 14 in Conde Nast's Portfolio.com's "25 Innovators in Technology."[35] Relative to IT, Yemma (2010a) worried in a blog post about hackers using computers for evil purposes: "For all the shock and spectacle of an al-Qaeda terrorist attack, a *Monitor* investigation makes clear that a largely silent war is going on via the Internet and deep within the databases of international companies. The stakes in the global cyber-war are at least as high as those in the global war on terror."

A *DNB* editorial (6/25/09) confirms these cyber-fears, saying, "Dictators these days must resort to ever-trickier ways to prevent the truth of their failings from being made known via digital technology," as does Mark Clayton's article "Cyberattacks a 'wake-up' call for US" (2/5/10, 2): "severely threatened," if largely unreported. Dennis Blair, director of national intelligence, concluded that, "Sensitive information is stolen daily from both government and private-sector networks." Unauthorized presences on networks; networks not being reliably prepared; vulnerabilities to disruptions in banking, power, and water supplies; and cyber-threats are increasing.

"It's better to deliver the *Monitor* by truck than by horse-and-buggy," joked Donal Toole (2/26/10), finance and strategy director, referring to the notion of spreading the word efficiently. Yet, as the Web doesn't promise any kind of loyal audience, it behooves *CSM* to constantly consider economic sources. "The key point here is that, as technology has changed, the *Monitor* has kept up, and will continue to do so in the future as delivery vehicles for its journalism continue to change," he added in an email (4/20/10).

Looking at the role of information technology nearly a year into the experiment to go Web-first, editor John Yemma (2010b) produced a wise memo to news sites: "There is no future in 'Digital Razzle Dazzle,'" including the points in Table 5.2:

Table 5.2
Digital Razzle Dazzle

- As for interactivity, we typically don't invite readers to comment at the bottom of our stories. Don't get me wrong, we want thoughtful comments. But comment-happy sites that don't moderate often allow a brilliant piece to be followed by a string of rotten tomatoes thrown by—how can I put this delicately?—comment jerks;

- Relevance doesn't come easy. Just because a topic is trending on Google (NSDQ: GOOG) doesn't mean you'll win by slapping a together a quick blog post on it. Sure, you can place high in search results and get the initial click, but a dissatisfied reader bounces quickly, which forfeits the chance to point out related content and cheapens our brand. Cheese, after all, is just cheese, and people know it. Technology is the enabler, not the differentiator here;

- One of the reasons our site traffic increased 20 percent from January to February of this year (even though February had 10 percent fewer days) was emphasis on search engine optimization. Everybody who is doing news on the web is thinking SEO, so best practices are—or soon will be—a given. It can be as simple as editors thinking like searchers and writing headlines accordingly. Breaking/developing stories like healthcare reform or the Chile earthquake provide opportunities to drive more readers to our site and keep them there longer. Embedding links to our deeper content (a healthcare reform 101 primer, a science of earthquakes piece) invites readers to understand what we are all about: news for people who are trying to understand the world and are searching for solutions. Paying this sort of attention to content can easily amplify a news story that garners 3,000 page views by a factor of 10;

- The multimedia debate needs a new question: How are we using technology to create a more relevant product? We're not going to "save" media by out-featuring each other. We can and will re-cement media by using the technology to deliver the experience consumers want most: intelligent, meaningful news that's accessible where they are in the moment.

Somehow it seems appropriate to end this chapter by reporting on an article from Scott Baldauf called "Homing pigeon vs. the Internet" (*DNB* 9/11/09, 2): "Sometimes 12th century technology wins. A South African call-center business, frustrated by slow Internet speeds, decided to use a carrier pigeon named Winston to transfer 4 gigabytes of data between two of its offices, just 50 miles apart. At the same time, a computer geek pushed a button on his computer to send data the old-fashioned way, over the Internet. Winston the pigeon won. It wasn't even close." Winston: 2 hours, 6 minutes, 57 seconds, with the Internet download only at 4 percent. The bigger issue for Baldauf, though: "Africans pay some of the highest prices for some of the least reliable Internet services in the world."

Chapter 6

"Journalism Should Reflect the Variety of Life": Findings and Future Considerations

Most of what we know, or think we know, we have never personally experienced. We live in a world erected by the stories we hear and see and tell . . . Stories socialize us into roles of gender, age, class, vocation, and lifestyle, offering us models of conformity or targets for rebellion. Stories weave the seamless web of our cultural environment.

—George Gerbner (1999, ix)

When John Yemma was named as the *Monitor* editor who would oversee its transition from a single Monday to Friday (M–F), print, paid-for newspaper to a free one on the Web, supplemented by subscriptions to the *Weekly Edition* and the *Daily News Briefing*, he explained the title of this chapter by stating that, "Journalism should reflect the variety of life—not just the deep and troubling problems but also the triumphs and breakthroughs" (cited in Cook 2008).

At this stage in the story, because it is so intrinsically interdependent with The Mother Church, it behooves us again to consider the background to the founding and development of *The Christian Science Monitor*, check out its current status, and consider its direction as it enters its second century. Following that are findings from my research on *CSM*, concerns, recommendations, and reflections.

A HISTORICAL (RE-) REVIEW OF *CSM*, *CSM WEEKLY*, AND CSMONITOR.COM

It cannot be underscored enough: In 1908, turned off by the tawdry journalism of the day, Mary Baker Eddy determined to establish an alternative publication for news of public importance, affecting public welfare. Following high idealism, with a mission "To injure no man, but to bless all mankind," it has remained true to the tenets of Christian Science and true to self-enforced "non-hysterical" journalism. In its various iterations, as outlined in this book, *CSM* has taken many forms—experimenting along the way. In a special section on "The *Monitor* at 85," editor Richard J. Cattani (1993b) assessed where it was at that point (italics in the original):

The *Monitor* has three masts: broadcast, print, and electronic publishing. As a *newspaper*, we are driven by *news* (the energized information about society's change), and we are printed on *paper* (which remains the simplest, most portable, most compact vehicle for news communication.) We are an original source of news information: Four-fifths of our reportage is from our own staff and special reporters in two dozen reporting points around the world; one-fifth is from contributors in another three dozen countries. We are a technologically advanced newspaper: Stories, photos, and illustrations move along our own electronic highway and converge in a newsroom editorial production unit in a manner that could not have been anticipated even a decade ago. And we are broadcasters of daily radio programs heard across the United States and around the world.

As it turns out, the 1980s were a complicated time for *CSM* operations. Although its esteemed reputation continued—along with numerous awards—a major melee occurred relative to cutbacks and finances. Circulation issues hit a high of 200,000 at mid-decade, if through cut-rate introductory offers that caused the deficit to rise, and CSPS managers considered draconian steps such that in 1989 there were mass protest resignations, led by editor Kay Fanning and some other key players. Then, following a foray into experiments in broadcasting, more lessons were learned.

It seems appropriate, if perhaps odd, to review how, as part of Newspapers in Education Week 1990, the *Monitor* included a graphic on how the M–F newspaper was produced: "Putting the World Together" (3/5/90, 13), in these steps:

1. Stories and photos from four US and 15 overseas bureaus are sent to Boston editorial headquarters by wire, satellite, courier, and by hand.

2. At each morning's Page 1 conference, editors decide where and when stories and pictures will appear in the newspaper.

3. Working at Atex computers, editors refine and coordinate news and feature stories, adding headlines, picture captions, and so forth.

4. All the text flows into the Visionary page layout, around the pictures and graphics. First proofs are printed, which show complete newspaper pages with everything in place. Corrections can be made before the page file is sent digitally to the Scitex system for electronic assembly.

5. The Scitex computers produce the film from which the plates are made at the printing plants in Massachusetts and Arizona.

Although this production process may have seemed high-tech at the time, and although we might smirk at recalling the old-fashioned way that newspapers were constructed and distributed, we nevertheless know that *CSM* has consistently been forward-thinking and technologically innovative. Soon, as Joe Gandleman (2009) has so eloquently phrased it: "*The Christian Science Monitor*—that longtime oasis of thoughtful, issue oriented, balanced journalism—is now actively marketing its new weekly print edition as the next step as it implements a unique newspaper business model that will be watched to see if a longtime media institution can survive in the Internet age." This was *CSM*'s 2009 timeline for the Web, the weekly, and *DNB*:

March 27:   The last daily print *Christian Science Monitor* newspaper is published and the shift to a Web-first focus begins for *The Christian Science Monitor* on CSMonitor.com.

April 12:   *The Christian Science Monitor Weekly Edition* premieres.

April 27:   *Daily News Briefing* (*DNB*) is available by email for paying subscribers.

Where is *CSM* now, a year after implementing a Web-first, multiplatform publishing strategy, supplemented by the two print publications, you might ask. "Nearly one year after the newspaper presses stopped rolling at *The Christian Science Monitor*, editor John Yemma continues to fine-tune the 102-year-old international news outlet's transformation from a daily into what he calls a 'Web-first' publication," Gabrielle Gurley (2010) has noted. She cites editor John Yemma: "The biggest lesson to me of having a 'Web-first' newsroom is that you begin to think more like some version of a wire service. That means online articles are a little shorter and, of course, publication is only a click away. But while the push for breaking news makes the paper more relevant, it also demands that editors and reporters have to constantly rethink what they're doing and why."

"A year after going to a Web-only format, *The Christian Science Monitor* is reporting increased Web traffic, unique users, page views and revenue for its weekly edition and daily E-newsletter," *Media Matters for America* (Strupp 2010) reported, citing Yemma on the experiment:

This was a pretty major change that we went through. We made it through the transition, we are on budget and we are growing. Monthly unique users are up 64 percent to 5.3 million, with monthly page views up 87 percent to 14.5 million . . . Circulation for the paid weekly print edition is up from 43,000 at its launch to 77,000 today. That is a 79 percent growth and we are getting great reader reaction to it.

But there was a "but": Even though overall revenue since the switch to Web-only is higher than expected, at $4.3 million, online ad revenue for the year was below expectations—$490,000, when projections were for $870,000. Prior to going Web-first, the *Monitor* made a buyout offer to employees, knowing that its workforce—especially on the production side—could be reduced in going from five days a week to one. Editorial staff decreased from 99 to 85.

The following year (February 2010), to pare costs and stay in line with the multiyear budget plan, another, smaller buyout was offered. Four accepted, including the Jerusalem and San Francisco bureau reporters—neither to be replaced, though new arrangements were made with freelancers and staff to provide compensatory coverage from these news spots. At the time, there were three bureaus in the Middle East (Baghdad, Jerusalem, Istanbul) and three on the West Coast (Los Angeles, San Francisco, and Ashland, Oregon) so, despite the cut, *CSM* remained committed to news from these areas. Fortunately, the $20 million subsidy provided by TMC continues, although Yemma is determined that it will be reduced systematically over the next few years and that the *Monitor* will eventually break even. Rick Edmonds of *Biz Blog/PoynterOnline* (2009) assessed *CSM*'s finances from the changes as "close to a wash": The money saved on printing, paper, distribution and a reduced staff balances the lower circulation revenue (subscriptions to the print daily went for $219 a year).

Here is an assessment of the multiplatform formats as this book goes to press:

• CSMonitor.com (Web): monthly unique users number 5.3 million, having increased 64 percent, and monthly page views number 14.5 million, having increased 87 percent.

- *CSM Weekly* (print): starting with a circulation of 43,000 in April 2009, it now boasts a circulation of 77,000, for 79 percent growth.
- *Daily News Briefing* (email): beginning with zero in April 2009, *DNB* has jumped to 3,000 paying subscribers.

Managing publisher Jonathan Wells noted to me (5/4/10) that, in the last year, *Monitor* reporters accounted for more than 325 broadcast appearances, the *Monitor* was syndicating content to over 100 newspapers and that, in the last year, there almost six million visitors to CSMonitor.com per month, and those numbers continue to rise. "Basically, we have doubled expectations," John Yemma reported to me (3/24/10) at nearly the year-end mark: "Our readers are the tipping point. They are thoughtful people," he mused. In an article for the site Paidcontent.com and quoted on the *Burst Media blog* (Coffin 2010), Yemma argued: "There's no evidence that [consumers] want, for instance, a thoughtful interactive map/video/database mashup on Afghanistan or global warming on which they can comment. There's no evidence that users love these things so much that they flock to them, stay around, and convert to a news site's brand because of cool multimedia. So here's my position: There is no future in a pay wall. No salvation in digital razzle dazzle. There is, however, a bold future in relevant content." In three bullet points of a PowerPoint presentation, Yemma summed up a century of the *Monitor* and plotted the path ahead:

- 1908–April 2009: 5-day print, lightly updated website
- March 2009: 24/7 Web, 1-day print
- Between 2009–2013: Grown page views and uniques 5X, break even on print
- Goal: End subsidy, develop sustainable model to pursue journalism mission

When asked by *American Editor* (Watson 2009) what he thought the *Monitor* would look like in 2020, Yemma reportedly hesitated, given the long time frame, before answering: "I do know this: Somewhere over the horizon is another big disruptor not unlike the Internet. It will change everything—how news is delivered, consumed, interacted with. I think the smart phone is doing that right now . . . The main thing is that the *Monitor*'s mission has to be protected so that it can continue, because journalism is crucial to democracy, society, and culture . . . So in 2020, I think the *Monitor* will have journalists still carrying out the *Monitor* mission. They may be doing it with lasers or holograms or nanotechnology. They may be doing it with pixels or even occasionally with print."

What comes next? According to managing publisher Jonathan Wells (2/26/10), it is important to research possibilities for greater reach on e-readers, mobile technology, and other ways of reaching the thoughtful audience the *Monitor* has traditionally appealed to. Of course there is a long-range strategic plan, with the publishing team working with those in editorial. They are going forward and hope for financial stability to be able to do so for a long time to come. "The quality and essence of journalism needs to remain intact," he mused. So the challenge becomes balancing the breaking news power of the Web with the opportunity in print to do longer form journalism. Wells added: "We are experimenting every day. It's an adventure. And this is an excellent test case for anyone committed to quality journalism doing it digitally."

Get used to it: the revolution toward new ways of news gathering, dissemination, and interpretation is on. The amazing thing is that the *Monitor*, if perhaps forced to get on the bandwagon to do something about its finances, ends up looking like a leader in this whole movement.

FINDINGS FROM MY RESEARCH ON *CSM*

After a half century of monitoring the *Monitor*, as such, and then spending a year reviewing media reports and interviewing staff for their interpretations on what difference, if any, the move to Web-first production has made, a number of disparate findings have emerged. What follows are descriptions of the "happy newsroom," an assessment of the role of Christian Science in the *CSM* framework, *CSM* as a resource tool, and issues such as loyalty and content.

The "Happy Newsroom"

It is like coming full circle: just as my study of worker harmony at *The Recorder* (Fuller 1983) involved interviewing staff to understand what lay behind its pleasant atmosphere, as cited in the Preface, this project's overwhelming discovery turned out to be similar. As a social scientist, my approach is always to enter the research arena in as neutral a manner as possible—wondering, looking, identifying, and attempting to understand. But even a Martian would get it: The *CSM* newsroom is a happy place. People bend over backwards to help one another, fact-check and double-check any and everything they can or want to make sure their stories are on target, smile when they see you, and share thoughts and ideas. And that is only from my observations from a half-year's worth of being there on a fairly regular basis.

Take the example of Judy Lowe, environment editor, whom I interviewed on January 20, 2010. She has worked for the *Monitor* for 10 years, encouraged to join by Dave Scott. Although she hesitated transferring, enjoying the weather where she was in Tennessee at the time, the newspaper where she was working had too much office politics and backstabbing to suit her, and it was inevitable that it would be sold. Her experience in Boston has been just the opposite, and she has been pleased with the decision to join—added to the fact that she lived within walking distance and could garden in her condo. "People here *like* the *Monitor*," she noted. "They care about working with one another in a cooperative way, and they also care about the newspaper itself." Judy's only concern was that CSM management seems to be ambivalent about features, or softer issues, while she encourages greater coverage of those areas. Her real area of expertise is gardening—having written 10 books about the topic and having become a Twitter queen on it—with 1,100 followers and seven dedicated bloggers, she hopes it becomes part of regular *Monitor* coverage.

"Family is important here," Rex Nelles, executive assistant, has noted (3/24/10) about the *CSM* newsroom. By way of example, Stacy Teicher Khadaroo and Amanda Paulson, both education reporters who wanted to work part time while their children were young, had maternity leaves such that when Amanda returned Stacy could take her leave; since then, they have managed to divide tasks by means of a "job share" that the *Monitor* worked out for them to cover the education beat. Josh Burek, when we met (2/17/10), had just come off being granted a four-week paternity leave for his second child. He was also appreciative of the *Monitor*'s flexibility during his studies at Harvard Divinity School, when he worked part time for *CSM*'s web team. His specialty is "nitty-gritty" religious articles, such as his recent cover story about the New Calvinists: "Religion in America: Back to basics." As part of his effort to promote the *Monitor* and reach out to the local university community, Burek gives a presentation on effective opinion writing each semester at Harvard Kennedy School.

Kendra Nordin, who has been 10 years at the *Monitor*, now as a staff editor on the *Weekly Edition*, has followed in the footsteps of her father, Ken Nordin, who was on staff for four years as what they called a "cub reporter," with a New England and Canada beat, before she born.

Susan Hackney, senior marketing director, works what is called "part time," but from the difficulties I had getting a hold of her—we started once in person, but she got called away, and then, when I tried so often unsuccessfully to get her during the suggested 8:15 to 9 a.m. commuter time that it felt I was becoming a stalker—it became clear that her life is quite complicated, as she tries to accommodate kids ages 8 and 11. Focused, professional, and organized, it helps that the *Monitor* is supportive, she told me (4/9/10) when we finally connected—and she sure represents today's female employee, juggling it all.

Many people commit to the *Monitor* for their entire careers, and there are a number of staff marriages. Mentors are often cited. For Kendra Nordin, it was Clara Germani, who also encouraged her to take journalism courses at Northeastern University. "Despite constraints on editors' time, a good deal of mentoring or staff development happens on the job," reporter Mark Trumbull disclosed to me (4/8/10).

"Values get handed down to generations," Cheryl Sullivan said (3/25/10) when we talked about her role as writing coach to many young *Monitor* journalists. Several staffers had mentioned her as a mentor, so it was important to learn that this comes from her role as national news editor, instructing new reporters on how to frame stories, develop news judgment, and polish writing styles when she ran a writer training program back in the late 1990s. Nowadays, Sullivan tries to do some of this same kind of training with interns. She used a pioneer analogy: "As we go forward Web-first, we realize that, on the trail, we may not need certain things that we assumed would be needed in the wagon. So as we set off, we are discarding stuff along the way and taking on things we might not have known we would need."

Like many of his colleagues, Laurent Belsie, economy editor, told me (3/12/10) that he has made lots of friendships at the *Monitor*. "There is competition here, but it's not destructive. It's a great place to work."

The Role of Christian Science in *CSM*

Andrew W. Hartsook (1993), a Christian Scientist whose free newsletter, the *Banner*, has followed church membership since the 1950s, has found a 75 percent decrease in the number of church-listed healers along with branch churches around the world continuing to close at a steady rate since it began. Most alarming of all, however, is that, of the remaining churches still open, they are "for the most part, practically empty" (p. 191). Deidre Michell (2009) has pointed out that, despite late twentieth-century interest in the conjunction between women, religion, and healing, by the time of what became known as Second Wave feminism—from the early 1960s until the late 1970s, when the focus turned from inequalities of voting and property rights to inequalities of the home and the workplace, sexuality, and control over one's body—TMC was in decline. Why? She blames the Board of Directors and their "masculinist" doctrines. In fact, Michell goes so far as to say that, by then, it was no more appealing than the Catholic Church: "Both had a

Mary who was honored and revered, and both had men lording it over women" (p. 5).

Pointing out how the Board of Directors is legally bound to follow Mary Baker Eddy's *Manual of The Mother Church, the First Church of Christ Scientist, in Boston, Massachusetts* (1936), Douglas J. Swanson (2001, 2) has pointed out that, "Her church is faced with innumerable threats Mrs. Eddy did not foresee or prepare followers to address. The church needs to stabilize its financial footing, re-energize its organizational structure, add new members, and stem the tide of branch church closings." Its social order, he contends, is in a bind: TMC needs to adapt to "a post-modern interactive multi-media world" (p. 9), but it cannot under its current theological and organizational structure. The *Manual* is key. Designating "overlapping duties" for CSPS and the Board of Directors—for the former responsibility for what literature is published, for the latter responsibility to be sure that what is, in fact, published is "ably edited and kept abreast of the times." The genius of the *Manual,* according to John K. Simmons (1991, 110) lies in the paradox that "Mrs. Eddy designed it such that The Mother Church would morally cease to function under its own covenant upon her death!" To this day, he notes, the *Manual* "remains a viable routinized covenant that, as interpreted by the self-perpetuating Board of Directors, continues to guide the Christian Science Organization" (p. 120). While theology and structure are in place, however, the fact that *CSM* has adapted so well to the multimedia world add to my admiration for its efforts.

Describing the "cultural matrix" making up church members in 1910 "and, for that matter, 1990" Simmons (1991, 121) describes the rank and file being characterized as "a white, middle class, socially conservative American concerned with security and stability in the culture." The newsroom appears to have the same demographic imprint. Although there are some Asian names listed among staff member lists, not a single person of color was identified, and, although my interviews never asked directly whether someone was of the Christian Science faith, through either their claiming and/or implying membership or dropping information such as that they were graduates of Principia College or that they read daily lessons, it was easy to infer that at least 75 percent (or more) are practicing members. Yet John Yemma has assured me (email 5/9/20)that he and his previous editors have tried tirelessly to recruit people of color and non–Christian Science staff and, once hired, to make them feel they are "full partners."

Some 70 percent of the membership in the First Church of Christ, Scientist has consistently been female—Susan Starr Sered (1994, 3) designating it as one of 12 women's religions globally, joining ancestral cultures among Black Caribs in contemporary Belize, the indigenous religion of the Ryukyu Islands, the *zar* culture of Northern Africa, the Sende secret society of Sierra Leone, matrilineal spirit cults in northern Thailand, Korean Shamanism, Shakerism, Afro-Brazilian religions, nineteenth-century spiritualism, the indigenous *nat cultus* of Burma, and the Feminist Spirituality Movement in the twentieth-century United States.

CSM as a Resource Tool

Obviously, this book could not have been written without all my clippings and cartons of various topics throughout all the years *CSM* has been monitored; yet, admittedly, the Web—with its "catch me this minute" transience—brings both nearly unlimited resources and yet limited capabilities for capturing their importance. This is the "Catch-22" of immediacy, or reality—whether in life or in televised episodes. While most of my research has depended on the methodology of content analysis, oftentimes omission is just as critical.

My experience monitoring the *Monitor* continually makes me overwhelmingly impressed with its even-handedness. Its tendency to take a wide(r) perspective, providing historical background, sociopolitical and economic perspectives, philosophical considerations, and then examples of people and processes is exemplary. Its approach, as was my intention here, is holistic. Yet, if *CSM*'s nonopinionated journalism can be faulted, it would be in terms of omission, its editorial decisions continuing to steer clear of breaking headlines and popular pap. In our era of corporate-fed and corporate–led media, it provides a refreshing exemplar.

CSM ON CSM

The five-day-a-week *Christian Science Monitor*, ideally commuter-sized at 11-1/2 by nearly 14 inches, ran 20 pages long. The cover included several front page–appropriate stories, along with a left sidebar story that was usually about particular peoples around the world. "World," on page two, included inside insights such as *Reporters on the Job*, where staff writers would tell about various experiences, and a *Cultural Snapshot* with global significance. World stories started each edition, running about five pages, followed by articles under *USA* for about two pages. The *Op-Ed*, *Readers Write*, and *Opinion* sections came next, for about three pages, followed by *Currents* for four, *Arts & Culture* for three, then *A Christian Science Perspective* and oftentimes a translation of it into a foreign language,

Home Forum, and *Back Story*, each on a single page. Obviously well thought through and well received in print, it nevertheless proved to be a dinosaur in the twenty-first century.

Utility

A key Christian Science term is *utility*, Donal Toole, finance and strategy director, has pointed out (2/26/10): If something is of use, people will pay for it. "At first, the website was updated once a day; now, it is constant," subscriptions for the *Weekly Edition* have exceeded expectations, and *DNB* is produced at a low cost, so it is critical to assess its utility. Circulation brings in $7 million, but Toole thinks they need to ensure that the product is valued enough by readers that they will subscribe at full price: "This will probably mean increasing spending in market research," he added in an email (4/20/10).

Syndication is a consideration. It brought in over $1 million in the financial year ending April 2008, but now is about $700,000 from those same sources, so *CSM* is looking to other reuse of *Monitor* content to make up the difference—mostly expansion of existing content into value-added stand-alone products like the video *Monitor Breakfast*.

Loyalty

Loyalty is key. The *Monitor* has to go mobile, as this is where the market is going, though the timing and format are not yet fully clear. Finance and strategy director Donal Toole suggests the following: Make money on print products, expand Web advertising, have spin-off products, be available on e-readers, and consider other electronic resources. "The archives alone will be valuable," he considers. Overall, as a staff management consultant, he is optimistic: "There is a huge amount of latent value in the *Monitor*; our challenge is realizing it."

With the shift to an emphasis on technology, a veteran reporter confided that he doesn't see enough loyalty from the "bottom tier techies," who seem to only want to use working at *CSM* as a stepping-stone to another job. "Younger staff, not properly schooled in the basics of journalism, scare me," another long-time staff writer admitted, adding that they find the métier of the Web more simplistic—while she worries about the sacrifices it might make to *Monitor* quality. Many of my interviewees, as noted here, have been with the *Monitor* for many decades, most several decades, and even those who are fairly new hires—as evidenced in the "Happy Newsroom" syndrome—are strongly loyal to *CSM* institutionally, philosophically, and personally.

Content

"We see encouraging signs of storytelling in new forms," I have noted (Fuller 1998), "such as the public space of the Internet giving way to web diaries, created from individual hypertext or multi-user domains (MUDs). Futurists predict increasing interactivity in human storytelling." Moving beyond mainstream media, the *Monitor* and its stories allow just such a scenario.

In the *Weekly Edition*, it is not clear what the difference is between *Briefing* and *Spotlight*. Since both seem so similar and analytical, it would seem that only one term is needed. *Briefing* offers background, and *Spotlight* works like a klieg light, true, but it still seems redundant.

Regular polling has confirmed that *Monitor* readers want a "stronger news orientation" rather than off-the-news essays, editor John Yemma has reported (Edmonds 2009), and the new *Monitor* retains the old one's international orientation with eight bureaus abroad. News, then, is what it should be all about.

CONCERNS ABOUT *CSM*

"The newsroom is quiet, like a church," one interviewee pointed out to me. Infused with workers and a work ethic that rests on the caring and compassionate principles of Christian Science, it becomes something of a package. Yet, my prediction is that a paradigmatic shift in the newsroom has already begun: Strong, serious, mostly Christian Scientist staff are automatically doing what they have always done in terms of commitment to the cause—and yet it is taking a toll.

A veteran reporter commented that he has noticed how, "More and more, non–Christian Scientists are leaving the paper. The daily prayer/ lesson speaks to them. Religion informs a lot—if more in the magazine than on the website. They have been trained metaphysically to think, not act, and non-stop work pressures are getting to them." As it turns out, it has been brought to my attention that this is an uninformed observation, as those who have opted to leave and those who have been hired recently have been about 50-50. In her 2004 book *Open the Doors of the Temple: The Survival of Christian Science in the Twenty-First Century*, Nancy Niblack Baxter makes the point that members need to remain mindful of the role of healing in their (meta)physical lives and stick to the spiritual base of the movement.

Privately, quietly, a young female staff member shared her observation that there is still a paternalistic overlay in the *Monitor* newsroom—putting into words a sentiment picked up from several women interviewees.

Although it was noted in Chapter 4, on gender as a case study, that women from MBE on down have played pivotal roles at *CSM*, that old glass ceiling still looms. Mary Baker Eddy had "overcome seemingly insurmountable odds in convincing her uniquely American religious organization out of a male-oriented cultural environment," John K. Simmons (1991, 180) has noted—seeing as all the more amazing her transformation of the church from a charismatic to a bureaucratic institution. Yet, as in so many other professions, journalism tends to privilege men. "A question of whether or not women bring a new, fresh or even different perspective to their work in the media is controversial all over the world," Ammu Joseph (2005, 42) has written. In *The Gendered Newsroom* (2009), Louise North discusses how gender shapes newsroom culture, and Scott Reinardy's (2009) survey of 715 U.S. newspaper journalists found women reporting higher levels of exhaustion and lower levels of professional efficacy than their male counterparts. For his part, editor John Yemma said in an email (5/9/20) that he is not satisfied with the balance of the newsroom in terms of race, gender, or ethnicity, believing the newsroom should reflect the broader society. He acknowledges it skews too much toward white and male: "We have to do better. People from different cultural and gender backgrounds are as much a source of strength to a news organization as to society."

In the old days of newspapering, reporters and editors rarely knew if their articles were being read. Subscribers bought the whole paper and that was that. A story on page 8 may not have been as important as the one on page 1, but there was no way to judge whether readers read it. In a world of news aggregators such as Google and Yahoo, however, journalists know immediately if one of their articles has become popular: people click on it and the page-view numbers ring up. That has its pluses and minuses. "Most of our people get the *Monitor* from news aggregators," a long-time reporter has observed. Lots of news comes from Google Trends, and he worries that this might lead to uniformity in staff worldviews. Like many of his colleagues, Chris Gaylord has found the *Monitor* to be flexible. He is busiest early in the week, he reported (2/10/10). Like his many colleagues, Gaylord doesn't like being so dependent on Google News (google.com/news), realizing that, "It's just a small piece of the pie" (email 4/12/10), nevertheless knowing that the goal is being Number One on a Google search—even if briefly. As schedules, salaries, and equity issues surface, it is imperative that *CSM* realize it must maintain its own style. It reminds me of something online director Jimmy Orr cautioned against (1/20/10): "Don't look inward."

With 10 years experience writing and editing, Mark Guarino is prolific— online every day, producing anywhere from five to seven stories per week.

Working in the Chicago bureau, he finds it less regional and more about getting the pulse of the Midwest. Mark Guarino of the Chicago bureau disclosed (2/9/20) that his best talent is not being used: he is a music critic—doing album, concert, and awards ceremonies reviews. Like his fellow correspondents, Guarino is concerned about the obsession with Google News. And yet, every other news organization is dealing with the same paradigm shift—from a world where news articles were part of a newspaper to a 24/7 pace where individual articles are indexed by search engines and are found individually on aggregator sites. The result is that many more people see articles that are popular, but those readers are not necessarily loyal to the publication that published them. The *Monitor* and other news organizations are trying to find ways to build that loyalty so that "one and done" readers stick around. This is the central challenge of the Web-first business strategy.

Just recently, the film *Shattered Glass* (2003) ran on the Sundance Channel. Based on the true story of Stephen Glass, an ambitious writer who was found to have invented and/or subverted stories at the *New Republic* during 1995 to 1998, it was instructive to review the proofing process in place at that time, where so many staff (the writer, the editor, the fact-checker, the copyeditor) checked and then double- or even triple-checked details. With the frenetic 24/7 pace now in place at *CSM*, one could wonder how long it will take before the easy route might be considered. With shrinking staffs and a faster pace, that kind of belt-and-suspenders editing and fact-checking takes a back seat to speed. Thus, it is imperative that Web-first journalists pay close attention to accuracy from the beginning, since there is little backstopping (although, on the Web, an error can be corrected immediately post-publication in a way that a print article cannot). Yemma's earlier point to Gabrielle Gurley (2010) about Web-first being more like a "wire-service" form of journalism is instructive here. Deadline-every-minute wire services have always edited quickly—and corrected just as quickly if necessary.

"The *Monitor*'s hallmark has always been good, analytical journalism," Pentagon and national security correspondent Gordon Lubold has stated, thinking it is important to answer the question, "Who cares, or why does anyone care about this" in the top of a story. By way of example, he asks and then answers his own question in an email (4/18/10): "Why should we write about Kyrgyzstan? Because there is a US base there that, if closed, will make it a lot harder for operations in Afghanistan to succeed. That's why." Online, though, reporters do not have as much time to take a deep breath and be as analytical. They are writing more—what he describes as "playing Twister, with deadlines." Where it used to take 120 words to make a point, now they have to do it in 10. "While the transition from paper to online has probably freed us of some of the valuable writing conventions to which we used to adhere, now we write quickly about topics that are already in the news, and sometimes we don't have time to take a deep breath before we do. And there is less of a need to justify the story with a why-does-the-reader-care-about-this graph."

In his analysis of what determines journalistic excellence, Leo Bogart (2004, 52) concludes that it is determined "by the pride of the journalists who write and edit their contents." By any measure, as you have read here in their own words, *Monitor* writers have, to date, fit that bill. Hopefully the various concerns listed here will warn *CSM* decision-makers to keep this in mind.

RECOMMENDATIONS FOR *CSM*

In my files is a letter dated June 16, 2004, written to then editor Paul Van Slambrouck as a response to David Cook's article "Annual Meeting 2004: Church focuses on needs of humanity" (6/8/04, 4), asking for suggestions on what to do to increase subscriptions to *The Christian Science Monitor*. Here are my proposals:

1. Offer current subscribers an opportunity to send a brief (say, one- to three-month) subscription to other people.
2. Capitalize on the fact that you have become a frequent citation on CNN's *NewsNight* with Aaron Brown.
3. Make yourselves more visible on other media outlets, whether at workshops or popular venues.
4. Investigate commercial gain possibilities from your large Internet viewership.
5. Consider starting up a "zine" online, containing many of the major themes in the newspaper.
6. Offer internships to journalism, communications, business, and other college students.
7. Construct a major public relations campaign, emphasizing the positive aspects of your work and mission.
8. Use your many Reading Rooms to solicit membership in the organization.
9. Hold an international conference on media ethics.
10. Highlight some of your key personnel; for example, David Sterritt's film reviews are outstanding.

On the one hand, this seems so dated, as Aaron Brown was let go from CNN soon thereafter and David Sterritt retired from the *Monitor* in 2005, after nearly four decades. Yet, complimentary trial subscriptions to the

Weekly Edition or *DNB* are still a good idea, as are free email newsletters telling about the multiplatform formats. It is admirable that staff—especially John Yemma—have made themselves available in the media, as the wider public still seems to be quite ignorant about *CSM* and its activities. By way of example, when people heard about this project, there were two distinct reactions: "Oh, that's the most fantastic newspaper" or "Sure—John Travolta!"—the latter confusing Christian Science, which doesn't have any celebrity spokespersons, with Scientology, which certainly does. (And no, this is not suggesting they get one!)

Relative to the Web, no doubt advertising and marketing are working on expanding commercial revenues, and the "zine" idea is already being dealt with by *CSM*'s blogs. The intern program appears to draw top-quality candidates, and it might be a good idea to highlight it, along with some successful participants. Knowing how Christian Scientists feel about proselytizing, it is doubtful that Reading Rooms would be a potential source for spreading the word, but sponsorship of a conference might serve a similar purpose—such as the *Monitor*'s 2008 "Future of Journalism" gathering, shortly after announcing its changes. The bottom line is realizing its unique value and celebrating it.

As to other recommendations: Several staff, especially from foreign bureaus, told me they thought things would work smoother if the operation were 24/7. While these logistics might seem impossible, and admittedly while Web traffic and advertisers need to make them viable, they are worth investigation. The *Monitor*, along with other news organizations, needs to get beyond a M–F, five-day mindset. Even though *CSM* has some weekend workers, it is difficult to know how many might be needed. Whether this means outsourcing, extra pay, and/or security issues, this is the single most pressing topic as *CSM* enters the twenty-first century. Although most readers and viewers are available during weekdays, and although that is when most news is covered, this is just a suggestion that news producers start thinking along these lines. After all, with so many resources available to a news-hungry population—who have become so used to instant, breaking, headlining news, and who have so many toys and ways of accessing that news—innovators need to take note.

More than one reporter mentioned that the *Monitor* needs some humor—that it takes itself too seriously and that it needs a different texture. One long-time employee pointed out: "My work in the public practice of Christian Science has shown me that humor can play a role in healing . . . It can serve as an instrument for change." Editors would do well to (re)read Colleen Douglass's "Humor's healing effect" (9/22/09, 3); she cited by way of example, as well as pointing out that MBE was able to slip a humorous remark into an otherwise serious subject. For example, Mrs. Eddy warned readers not to buy the media's advertising of maladies, especially so-called seasonal diseases: "A new name for an ailment affects people like a Parisian name for a novel garment. Everyone hastens to get it. A minutely described disease costs many a man his earthly days of comfort. What a price for human knowledge!" (1875/1994, 197).

While this is a tricky topic, and we all know that humor has different appeals to different people at different times, *CSM* already has a role model in Peter Grier. The Washington, D.C.-based reporter joined the *Monitor* in 1978 as an intern and copy kid along with Adam Bellow, son of Saul Bellow. Grier has a great sense of humor, but, he admitted— like Erma Bombeck and Art Buchwald—he works at it, figuring that, in essence, he is more like the serious Russell Baker. He really made me laugh when we talked (2/19/10), and you can see why with his article "Westminster dog show 2010: Why it's better than winter Olympics," which ran on February 15, 2010[1] and appears here as Table 6.1.

One strong suggestion concerns the *Weekly Edition*. If it looks like a magazine and is dealt with for subscribers as a magazine, why not call it a magazine? It is fantastic, and everyone who sees it agrees. Recalling that, from its earliest issue, *The Christian Science Monitor* was available on newsstands (and for home delivery), it would seem natural to return to a model that gives it wide recognition and easy purchase. Of course, the cost to market a magazine on a newsstand is considerable, and many magazines are struggling, including *US News & World Report* (which has decreased from weekly to monthly) and *Newsweek* (which went up for sale in May 2010). The *Monitor* is following what is known as a "controlled circulation" strategy, trying to keep its marketing costs low and trying to avoid the "churn" of new subscribers who come in at a deep discount or because they found a *Monitor* on a newsstand and then don't renew when asked to pay full price at the end of their trial period. Still, better exposure for the weekly would be welcome. The cover would be a great draw, and information about subscriptions could be inserted in individual copies. Amazingly, it is not even available at the MBE Library gift shop.

It strikes me that the *magazine*, billed as "A weekly review of global news and ideas," features the word "MONITOR," with "The Christian Science" smaller above it, on its label. While this is an even stickier subject, and no doubt has been discussed forever in *CSM* boardrooms, it even being a running joke that newspaper and design consultants are all ahead of me suggesting this, staff are committed to keeping MBE's stipulation that it should be very clear who the publisher is and what the underlying values are. Still, it would seem that, once the decision was made to call

Table 6.1
Westminster Dog Show 2010: Why It's Better Than Winter Olympics

The Westminster Dog Show is on TV tonight. So is the Winter Olympics. Which are you going to watch?

On the one hand, NBC in prime time will be showing pairs figure skating and snowboards. On the other, Westminster will have the hound, toy, non-sporting, and herding groups, starting on the cable USA Network (owned by NBC Universal), then shuffling over to CNBC later in the evening.

The human-based competition will probably win this ratings smackdown. After all, it's got glamorous athletes cavorting on snow and ice. Westminster? A bunch of people in tweed walking their dogs indoors.

That's the conventional wisdom, anyway. But for a significant minority of American households, salukis are a bigger draw than skaters. Here are some of their reasons why: *Dogs are cuter than Lindsey Vonn. That flowing hair! Those gleaming teeth! There's nothing like an Irish setter bounding around the ring. US skier Lindsey Vonn is very attractive. But walk a long-haired dachshund down the street, and people will spontaneously coo, "Awww, she's so cute! Look at the hair in her ears! Who's a good dog? Yes you are! You're such a good dog!"; *Dogs are happier than Scott Hamilton. Dogs live for the moment. The tension of competition does not furrow their brow. This is how dogs emote: "Time for a walk? My favorite thing! A judge? My favorite thing! Did I lose? Still my favorite thing!" As the great American humorist and dog observer James Thurber wrote, "Dogs are obsessed with being happy." Figure skating analyst Scott Hamilton—a former gold medal winner himself—is pretty upbeat. But he's not spreading joy around as surely as if he were tossing out gold coins; *New breeds are better than new events. The Olympics has added several new events this year, such as snowboard cross, a type of race that is generally described as winter-sports-meets-NASCAR. But Westminster has added three new breeds. New competitions? That's for amateurs. The folks at the Westminster Kennel Club have got whole new categories of competitors. There's the Norwegian Buhund, which looks like an albino mini-sled dog; the Pyrenean Shepherd, which looks like a cross between a collie and a teddy bear; and the Irish Red and White Setter, which looks like you would expect.

the website CSMonitor.com—admittedly because URLs have to be "short and sweet"—it cannot be too difficult to contemplate the same for what might roll well off the tongue as *CS Monitor Magazine*. And from there, it is not too big a leap to make *DNB* better known by naming it something easier, such as *CSM Daily Briefing* or something similar.

Knowing how far-sighted staff is, no doubt it will be only a matter of time before *CSM* is available as an app(lication) on the iPhone, iPad, and other mobile services, along with e-readers.[2] To make things flow easily, *CSM* could consider incorporating an iTunes-like micropayment system.

Although the website is generally pleasing, it could be made much easier to navigate. For example, it takes two clicks to reach the blog section and, once there, the blog titles need to be more descriptive. *Diggin' It* is leaving, but instead of a gardening term, try "Earth," or "Environment," or something "Eco-" oriented as in Alexandra Marks's blog. This is a niche well worth cultivating—if you'll pardon the pun. Think of the press Michele Obama got for showing inner-city kids how to grow vegetables, think of organic and/or environmentally oriented folks, the push for "sustainability" in organizations ranging from colleges to corporations, and how the target market ranges so demographically. Then, maybe it's just me, but the term "Terrorism & Security" is just a turn-off. Why "The Vote" when it could be many votes? and you need to show me research results showing the "The New Economy" is a draw when something simpler like "Finance" would work as a blog name. While it might not be expected that people will necessarily follow a specific blog as much as certain blog posts— research showing that they tend to "browse around"—the crux is catching them with links to quality journalism.

It surprises me that there are not special sections for the following popular areas (sport, music, animals, travel, and news trivia), which I'm suggesting be added:

- Sports: there are several highly qualified staff who could contribute to this journalistically—not statistics and such, but a wider view of how and where this $39 billion industry impacts our societies. The way the *Monitor* has covered sport in the past on an ad hoc basis encourages me to push them to more.
- Music: include it as a category, maybe even a blog, and many different interested parties will be drawn to the *Monitor*. Of course there are already some outstanding sites on this topic, but in-depth coverage is worth consideration.
- Animals: several staff members discussed their animals, and when the topic of having a blog about pet lovers was raised each one thought it a great idea. Consider Dan Murphy's "Animals feel global warming, too" (12/15/09, 2), where he discusses threats to the koala, emperor penguin, ringed seal, Arctic fox, and the clown fish as a starter for interest.
- Travel: supposedly there is a travel editor, but the single entry in the *Weekly Edition* was on the date of August 30, 2009, including these citations: Mary Mihaly's "Good, to go" (volunteer vacations); Sherry Shahan's "Volunteering at Yosemite is a natural"; Lisa Harris's "Volunteers get wild in Alaska"; and Elizabeth Hansen's "Taking flight on a mission." Why not rename this area "Geography" and have an editor add knowledge points, maps, and such to both national and international articles? This is not to say having a full-time, daily commitment to the topic, but it would enhance *CSM*'s specialty as being a global observer.

- Trivia: how about having a "News Trivia" blog? The staff already includes several ideal bloggers and news junkies.

Since *CSM*'s photographers are so incredible, let me suggest that their work be highlighted more. This is not self-promotion, but validation of various staff. Along those lines, it has been helpful for the "In Pictures" segment to have a title and a theme, rather than just random photos. The *Monitor Photo Store* idea is brilliant, but navigation-wise it needs to be made easier for the potential buyer: What is available? How can it be accessed? Paid for? Used? Shared?

If the *Monitor* wants to indulge in self-promotion, let me suggest that inclusion of a sound bite about its seven Pulitzer Prizes—1950, Edmund Stevens; 1967, John Hughes; 1968, Howard James; 1969, Robert Cahn; 1978, Richard Strout; 1996, David Rohde; and 2002, Clay Bennett—at every opportunity. True, as evidenced on the impressive list of awards outlined in Appendix 2, there have been many other well-deserved recognitions, but most people recognize the name Pulitzer.

Utne Reader set up reading groups around the country a few years ago. Would it be worth investigating geographical places where book editor Marjorie Kehe (or someone involved in books) could do something similar, with *Monitor* book suggestions similar to what is available as this is being written about the vote in the United Kingdom?

No doubt the marketing department has constructed some clever ways to draw and maintain subscribers to the two paying parts of the model (the *Weekly* and *DNB*). If it is not already in place to do so, they should be sure to offer specials for educators (and other professionals), certain age groups (students, seniors), libraries, and institutions of learning. Along those lines, having a long-term renewal (e.g., three-year) process in place appeals to many subscribers.

Although, as a news source with a religious affiliation, there are no legal requirements about discrimination in hiring, nevertheless history shows us that group thinking and team production by diverse peoples adds an important layer. Just as age, gender, and socioeconomic status add to a mix, there is not doubt that including people of different races and religions is critical to sensitivity.

Maybe I missed it, but if *CSM* established a philanthropy fund for helping Haiti or Chile, that is a good way for people to contribute—knowing they are dealing with a respected institution. The *Monitor* has done this in the past, and it is not only good public relations and good works, it is a natural for the organization.

CSM: A REVIEW AND A BLESSING

What is The Christian Science Monitor *anyway? What is it trying to do? How is it guided and controlled? How does it relate to other newspapers and to public affairs of its time?*

—Erwin D. Canham (1958, xiv)

At this point, it is entirely appropriate to repeat the question: What is *The Christian Science Monitor* anyway? In answer, Canham (1958, xvi) wrote that, "By law and public authority, under the federal regulations and taxation rules of city, state, and federal governments it is defined as a religious newspaper," so "The *Monitor* is a 'religious newspaper' in the sense that its fundamental obligation is to a religious purpose, its net revenues are turned over to The Christian Science Board of Directors, and many of its decisions and actions are motivated by profound religious criteria." Yet, he continues, "In a broad, nontechnical and nonlegal sense, the *Monitor* is not a religious newspaper. Down through the years, from the very outset, [it] was designed to be a 'real newspaper,' as its first editor, Archibald McLellan, defined it before it was ever issued."

Clearly not Boston, nor Massachusetts or even New England, can claim *CSM*, as it has made its mark around the globe for more than a century now. Armed with tools of information, along with explanations, it continues to see its role as arousing thinking in its readers.

"Mary Baker Eddy lived in a jingoistic era, when William Randolph Hearst gunned for a war with Spain, but she believed fervently that the purpose of journalism is not to incite war," declared diplomatic correspondent Howard LaFranchi when we talked (4/2/10). We had fun reviewing the fact that he began his journalistic career near me, in Holyoke, Massachusetts, but from there his career took him to Paris, North Africa, Mexico, Iraq, and more. LaFranchi used Mexico as an analogy for the *Monitor* and its staff: the Spanish came to conquer, but the indigenous people exerted their influence and their culture has prevailed. "It may be a crazy idea," he asserted, "but I think in a similar way we should be able to meld the old and new worlds of journalism and see that the old culture, the purpose of the *Monitor*, endures."

The question remains, though: Is *The Christian Science Monitor* a newspaper? Jill Lepore (2009, 72) has brought up an interesting point: " 'The newspaper is dead, long live the newspaper!' has lately become the incantation of advocates of e-journalism, who argue that the twenty-first-century death of the newspaper hardly merits a moment's mourning, since it is no death at all but, rather, a rebirth." But what kind of rebirth might it be for the *Monitor*? The *Chicago Tribune* (Rosenthal 2008), writing about *CSM*'s recent decisions, reported how "a paper without paper is still a paper." In his PowerPoint presentation on "How to Survive," editor John Yemma has suggested this (newspaper?) model: Expect constant change; understand your audience, think like a user, reader, viewer; and learn all forms of storytelling, but stay strong on narrative.

Veteran reporter Peter Spotts made a profoundly simple observation (2/26/10): "When a newspaper is dropped off at the end of my driveway, it's a physical presence. I have to do something with it every morning. I can pick it up and read it, toss it out, or line bird cages with it. But I have to do something with it." The Web does not command attention in the same way, he says. In the midst of our multimediated, technological era, it is important for us to consider where our loyalties will be relative to news sources and—more importantly—relative to sharing ideas with our fellow world citizens.

"What we're learning is that the key to building and keeping traffic is far more prosaic than multimedia and sharing buttons. It rests on overcoming a huge cultural barrier: evolving a serious, experienced, thoughtful newsroom into an audience-first organization" John Yemma (2010b) has noted. "I use the term 'evolving' because this is all about the present tense. Trying to understand our current and future audience is a work in progress that will continue for as long as we publish on the Web."

By way of review, then: According to founder Mary Baker Eddy's instructions, despite enormous hazards and hindrances, the first issue of *The Christian Science Monitor* was produced less that three months later. So, when you think about it, the simultaneous experiments of now publishing this secular "newspaper" on the Web, as a weekly, and on *DNB* are almost expected experiments.

In closing, permit me to say what an honor and a privilege it has been, meeting and talking to so many talented and committed staff members of the *Monitor*, and attempting to tell its story to this point. How often does one get the opportunity to dissect a product and the people behind it, only to find that at its core is a moral sensibility that helps explain its enduring contribution to journalism in general, and human lives in particular.

Appendix 1

Acronyms

ALCTS	Association for Library Collections and Technical Services
APEC	Asia Pacific Economic Cooperation
ARPANET	Advanced Research Projects Agency Network
ASNE	American Society of Newspaper Editors
BBC	British Broadcasting Corporation
BRIC	Brazil, Russian, India, and China
CBO	Congressional Budget Office
CDC	Centers for Disease Control and Prevention
CPJ	Committee to Protect Journalists
CSM	*The Christian Science Monitor*
CSPS	Christian Science Publishing Society
DADT	Don't ask, don't tell
DAM	Digital Archive Management
DAM	Digital Asset Management
DEA	Drug Enforcement Administration
DNB	*Daily News Briefing*
EWA	Education Writers Association
FDA	Food and Drug Administration
FEMA	Federal Emergency Management Agency
FGM	Female genital mutilation
HIV/AIDS	Human Immunodeficiency Virus/Acquired Immune Deficiency Syndrome
HTTP	Hypertext Transfer Protocol
i4d	Information for Development

ICT	Information and Communication Technologies
IM	Instant message/instant messaging
IOC	International Olympic Committee
IT	Information technology
IWMF	International Women's Media Foundation
JEDA	Junior editorial assistant
JSH	*Journal*, *Sentinel*, and *Herald* Editorial Department
LpkC	Link per thousand circulation
MBE	Mary Baker Eddy
M–F	Monday to Friday
MUD	Multiuser domain
NORML	National Organization for the Reform of Marijuana Laws
NRA	National Rifle Association
OMMA	Online Media Marketing and Advertising
ONA	Online News Association
Op-Ed	Opinion/Editorial
PDF	Portable Document Format
PMAD	People Making a Difference
PRC	People's Republic of China
RSS	Really Simply Syndication
SARS	Severe Acute Respiratory Syndrome
SEO	Search engine optimization
SND	Society of Newspaper Design
SPJ	Society of Professional Journalists
TMC	The Mother Church
URL	Uniform Resource Locator
UVP	Unique value product
VOA	Voice of America
WHO	World Health Organization
WIC	Women, Infants, and Children
WNBA	Women's National Basketball Association
WPGA	Women's Professional Golf Association

Appendix 2

Awards Granted to *The Christian Science Monitor*

The Mary Baker Eddy Library (research@marybakereddylibrary.org) has a 34-page listing of 434 awards that have been granted to *The Christian Science Monitor*, including seven Pulitzer Prizes:

1950	Pulitzer Prize for International Reporting: Edmund Stevens, "This is Russia uncensored"
1967	Pulitzer Prize for International Reporting: R. John Hughes, "Transition to the New Order"
1968	Pulitzer Prize for National Reporting: Howard James, "Crisis in the courts"
1969	Pulitzer Prize for National Reporting: Robert Cahn, "The future of our national parks and methods that may help to preserve them"
1978	Pulitzer Prize Special Citations and Awards, Journalism: Richard Strout, distinguished commentary from Washington
1996	Pulitzer Prize for International Reporting: David Rohde, onsite reporting of the massacre of thousands of Bosnian Muslims in Srebrenica
2002	Pulitzer Prize for Editorial Cartooning: Clay Bennett

In 1914, *The Christian Science Monitor* won the National Star Spangled Banner Tercentennial, and since then numerous organizations, expos, conferences, and prizes have recognized *CMS*, such as the Bookman Prize, American Humane Education Society, Wilson Library, University of Missouri School of Journalism, U.S. Treasury War Saving Program, Helms Athletic Foundation, National Board of Fire Underwriters, U.S. Coast Guard, U.S. Treasury Award for Patriotic Services, Sigma Delta Chi, U.S. Navy, U.S. Treasury Payroll Savings Plan, U.S. War Department,

French Legion of Honor, Community Chests of America, Institute of American Democracy, Medaille de la Reconnaissance, Press Photographers, American Society of Newspaper Editors, Education Writers Association, News Executive Association, American Society of Travel Agents, English-Speaking Union, Freedom Foundation, United Nations, New England Women's Press Association, American Association for State and Local History, American Heritage Foundation, American Federation of Arts, National Conference of Christians and Jews, World Council of Churches, Kiwanis Club, National Safety Council, National Management Association, Overseas Press Club, U.S. Commission on Civil Rights, American Bar Association, U.S. Department of Commerce, New England Citizens Crime Commission, American Political Science Association, Boy Scouts of America, Editor & Publisher Newspaper Promotion, Yankee Quill, Americans United for Separation of Church and State, International Reading Association, American Trial Lawyers, Interamerican Press Association, Journalism Education Association, Future Farmers of America, Harvard Business School, NAACP, Distinguished Service in Conservation, National Council for Advancement of Educational Writing, Religious P/R Council, Scripps-Howard Foundation, Associated Press Managing Editors, Science in Society Journalism, Women in Communications, World Hunger Media, Media Research Institute, National Association of Black Journalists, Publick Occurrence, Best Overall U.S. Newspaper Online Service, National Cartoonists Society, World Calendar, American Society of Journalists and Authors/Editors, and hundreds more.

Appendix 3

Editors of *The Christian Science Monitor*

1908–1914	Archibald McLellan, editor
1914–1922	Frederick Dixon, editor
1922–1927	Willis J. Abbott, editor
1927–1939	Editorial board (Note: Roscoe Drummond was editor, unmentioned, from 1934 to 1939)
1939–1941	Roland Harrison, administrative editor
1941–1944	Erwin Canham, managing editor
1945–1964	Erwin Canham, editor
1964–1970	DeWitt John, editor
1964–1974	Erwin Canham, editor-in-chief
1974	Erwin Canham, editor emeritus
1970–1979	John Hughes, editor
1979–1983	Earl Foell, editor
1983	Earl Foell, editor-in-chief
1983–1988	Katherine W. Fanning, editor
1988–1994	Richard Cattani, editor
1994–2001	David Cook, editor (also editor of *Monitor* broadcasting)
2001–2005	Paul Van Slambrouck, editor
2005–2008	Richard Bergenheim, editor
2008–	John Yemma, editor

Source: Monitor library card file, revised, with thanks to John Hughes, David Cook, and John Yemma.

Appendix 4

CSM Interview Schedule

Date	Method[a]	Staff Member
1/18	[T]	Brad Knickerbocker, senior writer/editor (Oregon)
1/18	[T]	Peter Ford, Beijing bureau chief
1/19		Marshall Ingwerson, managing editor
1/19		David C. Scott, World editor
1/19		Mark Sappenfield, deputy national news editor
1/20		Judy Lowe, environment editor
1/20		Ross Atkin, *Daily News Briefing* editor
1/20		Abe McLaughlin, product manager
1/20		Jimmy Orr, online director
1/20		Melanie Stetson Freeman, photographer
2/9	[T]	Mark Guarino, National Bureau (Chicago)
2/9	[T]	Gordon Lubold, reporter (Washington, D.C., Pentagon)
2/10		Chris Gaylord, Innovation editor
2/10		Amelia Newcomb, world news
2/10		Marjorie Kehe, book editor
2/10		Clay Jones, chief editorial writer
2/11		Rosalie Dunbar, news editor, Christian Science magazines
2/11		Gregory Lamb, *PMAD* editor/reporter

(*continued*)

2/12	[T]	Stacy Teicher Khadaroo, education editor
2/13	[T]	Dave Cook, Washington, D.C., bureau chief
2/16		Gillian Charters, copyeditor
2/16		Kendra Nordin, *Weekly* assistant editor
2/16		Leigh Montgomery, library
2/16		Eoin O'Carroll, online producer
2/17		Alfredo Sosa, photo editor
2/17		David R. Francis, columnist
2/17		Josh Burek, Op-Ed
2/19	[T]	Peter Grier, *Decoder*/reporter (Washington, D.C.)
2/19	[T]	John Kehe, design director
2/22	[T]	Mike Farrell, San Francisco bureau
2/22	[T]	Peter Rainer, film critic
2/23	[T]	Amanda Paulson, national bureau (Chicago)
2/23	[T]	Ed Blomquist, copyright administrator
2/23	[T]	Linda Feldmann, Washington, D.C. bureau
2/24	[T]	Walter Rodgers, columnist
2/25		Patty Collingsworth, circulation marketing director
2/25		Haide Bolanos, marketing manager, *CSM*
2/25		Amanda Gustin, researcher, MBE Library
2/25	[T]	Francine Kiefer, editorial writer
2/26		Donal Toole, finance and strategy director
2/26		Clare Turner, *Monitor* religious article
2/26	[T]	Jonathan Wells, managing publisher
2/26	[T]	Peter Spotts, reporter
3/12		Clara Germani, cover editor
3/12		Owen Thomas, deputy *Weekly* editor
3/12		Heather Ehmke, copyeditor
3/12		Pat Murphy, deputy online editor
3/12		Laurent Belsie, economy editor
3/23		Cindy Anderson, manager, planning and administration
3/23		Cheryl Sullivan, national news editor
3/23		Judy Huenneke, MBE Library senior archivist
3/24		Rex Nelles, executive assistant
3/24		John Yemma, editor
3/26	[T]	Howard LaFranchi, diplomatic correspondent
4/2	[T]	Bob Hanna, ad sales director
4/8	[T]	Mark Trumbull, reporter
4/9	[T]	Susan Hackney, marketing director
4/11	[T]	Gloria Goodale, reporter (Los Angeles bureau)
4/13	[E]	Clay Collins, *Weekly* editor
4/26	[T]	Alexandra Marks, *Eco-renovation* blogger
4/28	[T]	John Hughes, columnist

[a][T] = telephone; [E] = email; otherwise, personal interview

Appendix 5

Christian Science–Related Websites

The Bookmark

http://www.thebookmark.com
Books and transcripts on Christian Science by early and contemporary writers
Christian Science Community Board

http://www.lii.net/tcscb
Provides a forum for discussions on religious and secular topics
Christian Science Healing with MBE

http://christianscience.rolf-witzsche.com
A research presentation by Rolf A. F. Witzsche
Christian Science Index

http://www.christianscience.net
Links to the Aequus Institute and Christian Science places
Christian Science Research Books Series

http://science.rolf-witzsche.com
Christian Science Website

http://www.christianscience.com
Official website of The Mother Church, the First Church of Christ, Scientist
Christian Science on Beliefnet

http://www.beliefnet.com/index/index_10123.asp

Christian Science Endtime Center

http://www.endtime.org

Explores the teachings of Christian Science as taught and explained by MBE

Christian Scientist at the Leading Edge

http://christianscientist.rolf-witzsche.com

What it means to be a Christian Scientist

CSE News

http://www.csenews.com

Directory of businesses and Bible study resources

Emergence International

http://www.emergence-international.org

Provides support for lesbians, gay men, and bisexual and transgendered people

Exploring practical spirituality

http://www.spirituality.com

Interactive community sharing healing solutions

Healing Unlimited

http://www.christianscience.org

Historical Christian Science Bible Lessons

http://biblelessons.rolf-witzsche.com

Online collection of 26 historic (1898) Christian Science Bible lessons

Marlene F. Johnson Fund for Scholarly Research on Christian Science

http://www.johnsonfund.org

Information on grants for scholarly writings concerning Christian Science

Largest Christian Science Communities

http://www.adherents.com/largecom/com_chrsci.html

Statistics on U.S. states with most Christian Science branches

The Mary Baker Eddy Library for the Betterment of Humanity, Inc.

www.marybakereddylibrary.org

Rock and Feathers, LLC

http://www.rockandfeathers.com

Bible study materials, books, recordings, and gifts relating to Christian Science

Note: URLs compiled from http://www.google.com/Top/Society/Religion_and_Spirituality/Christianity/Denominations/Christian_Science/.

Appendix 6

The Christian Science Monitor: A Timeline

CSM's history represents over a century of product evolution, experimentation, and broadening reach.

1897:	The Christian Science Publishing Society (CSPS) is incorporated.
1908:	*The Christian Science Monitor* begins publication on November 25.
1920s:	The *Monitor* joins other newspapers in distributing worldwide news via radio: AM transmission in 1922, adding programming and expanding to shortwave broadcasts by 1935.
1938:	Color printing is used (three-color printing tested in 1948).
1943:	The *Monitor* joins the Mutual Broadcasting System to broadcast "News from Everywhere," a 15-minute weekday show—the first nationwide news program to use the resources of an international newspaper.
1960:	A daily London Edition of *CSM* is launched.
1961:	The last year the *Monitor* is profitable.
1971:	Microfilm containing eight pages of *The Christian Science Monitor* is carried by Apollo 14 commander Alan B. Shepard to the moon.
1973:	*CSM* switches to weekday publication, eliminating the Saturday edition.
1974:	Pages are sent by fax to remote plants—at an average speed of five minutes per page—eliminating the need to fly plates to presses in Chicago and California. A weekly International Edition replaces the London Edition.
1975:	Format changes from a broadsheet to a compact tabloid.
1977:	The *Christian Science Monitor* Radio News Service broadcasts around the world.
1983:	A relaunch standardizes all editions, eliminating several regionals.

1984:   "Monitor Radio Weekend Edition" makes its debut on American Public Radio. "Conversations with *The Christian Science Monitor*" offers half-hour, in-depth interview programs to commercial radio stations in the United States.

1985:   Distribution of *Monitor* print content via syndication peaks at some 200 subscribing papers, with a combined circulation of about 20 million. A monthly syndicated TV news program, "The *Christian Science Monitor* Reports," begins.

1986:   Christian Science Monitor Syndicate, Inc., buys WQTV Channel 68, Boston.

1987:   "The World Service of *The Christian Science Monitor*" broadcasts by shortwave radio to Europe and Africa from WCSN in Scotts Corners, Maine, then to Japan, Korea, and China from station KYOI on Saipan, Mariana Islands.

1988:   *World Monitor: A Television Presentation of The Christian Science Monitor* launches nightly programming, and *World Monitor: The Christian Science Monitor Monthly* magazine begins publication for a five-year run.

1989:   Four-color ink and photographs are introduced in daily and international editions. New TV programs première in Boston: "One Norway Street," "Today's *Monitor*," "*Monitor* de Hoy," "*Monitor* Forum," "Inner City Beat," and "Affairs of State."

1989:   "Monitor Radio Early Edition" premières on American Public Radio stations. Shortwave expands to Latin America and the Pacific Rim. *World Monitor: A Television Presentation of The Christian Science Monitor* begins international distribution.

1991:   The Monitor Channel, a national cable television service, starts.

1992:   The Monitor Channel cable network closes.

1995:   A beta website is built to circulate news about reporter David Rohde, captured during the Balkan War but fortunately released after nine days.

1996:   Debut of CSMonitor.com, carrying complete Monitor Radio broadcasts—one of the first websites to feature audio.

1997:   Monitor Radio shuts down and shortwave is scaled back.

1998:   A significant redesign of the newspaper is introduced.

2000:   *MonitorWeek*, a national insert for local papers, is launched as a 12-page color publication, and *MonitorWorld* becomes *CSM*'s weekly international edition. Its SciTech Blog, one of the first news website blogs, begins.

2001:   "Terrorism & Security: A Daily Update" begins Web publication shortly after the September 11 terrorist attacks. By year-end, other blogs are produced by the Web team, Washington bureau chief, and library staff.

2002:   The Treeless Edition, a digital replica of the daily newspaper, is first delivered in PDF form.

2003:   *CSM* staff writer Ben Arnoldy goes to Iraq—the first journalist sent to cover a war for a newspaper's online edition.

2008:	CSMonitor.com averages 1.5 million unique visitors per month. The *Monitor* is the first national newspaper to introduce a Web-first model and announces its intent to end daily print edition. A new print weekly edition is unveiled.
2009:	The last daily *Christian Science Monitor* newspaper is published (March 27). The *Christian Science Monitor Weekly* premières (April 12), along with *Daily News Briefing* (April 27).
2010:	*CSMonitor.com* has 5.3 million monthly unique users and 14.5 million monthly page views; *CSM Weekly* has a circulation of 77,000; *Daily News Briefing* (DNB) claims 3,000 paying subscribers.

Note: This is a revised version of a timeline compiled by Leigh Montgomery and Stephanie Frueh (November 25, 2008) for *The Christian Science Monitor*'s centennial (http://www.csmonitor.com/USA/2008/1125/p99s01-usgn.html), Hoover's profile of the Christian Science Publishing Society (http://www.hoovers.com/company/The_Christian_Science_Publishing_Society/htrfri-1.html), and assorted other histories.

Appendix 7

Film Reviews

Date	Title	Director	Country
2009			
4/12	*Sugar*	Anna Borden, Ryan Fleck	Dominican Republic
4/19	*Goodbye Solo*	Ramin Bahrani	Senegal
4/26	*American Violet*	Tim Disney	United States
5/3	*Tyson*	James Toback	United States
5/10	*The Limits of Control*	Jim Jarmusch	Spain
5/17	*Adoration*	Atom Egoyan	Canada
5/24	*O'Horten*	Bent Hammer	Norway
5/31	*Easy Virtue*	Stephan Elliott	England
6/7	*Summer Hours*	Olivier Assayas	France
6/14	*Seraphine*	Martin Provost	France
6/21	*Whatever Works*	Woody Allen	United States
6/28	*Cheri*	Stephen Frears	France
7/5, 12	*The Unmistaken Child*	Nati Baratz	Nepal
	Food, Inc.	Robert Kenner	US
	Throw Down Your Heart	Sascha Palladino	Uganda, Tanzania, The Gambia, Mali
	Herb and Dorothy	Megumi Sasaki	United States
7/19	*The Stoning of Soraya M.*	Cyrus Nowrasteh	Iran
7/26	*The Beaches of Agnes*	Agnes Varda	France
8/2	*Afghan Star*	Havana Marking	Afghanistan
8/9	*The Cove* (dolphins)	Louie Psihoyos	Japan
8/16	*Lorna's Silence*	Jean-Pierre and Luc Dardenne	Belgium
8/23	*A Woman in Berlin*	Max Farberbock	Germany
8/30	*Five Minutes of Heaven*	Oliver Hirschbiegel	Northern Ireland

9/6	*Still Walking*	Hirokazu Koreeda	Japan
9/13	*Art & Copy*	Doug Pray	United States
9/20	*Baader Meinhof Complex*	Uli Edel	Germany
9/27	*Paris*	Cedric Klapisch	France
10/4	*Capitalism*	Michael Moore	United States
10/11	*Disgrace*	Steve Jacobs	South Africa
10/18	*Coco before Chanel*	Anne Fontaine	France
10/25	*Araya*	Margot Benacerraf	Venezuela
11/1	*The Yes Men Fix the World*	Bonanno, Bichlbaum	United States
11/8	*The Maid*	Sebastian Silva	Chile
11/15	*The Wedding Song*	Karin Albou	Tunisia
11/22	*The Messenger*	Oren Moverman	United States
11/29	*La Danse: Paris Opera Ballet*	Fred Wiseman	France
12/13	*Broken Embraces*	Pedro Almodovar	Spain
12/20	*Crazy Heart*	Scott Cooper	United States
12/27–1/3	*The Imagination of Dr. Parnassus*	Terry Gilliam	United Kingdom
2010			
1/10	*A Town Called Panic*	Aubier, Patar	Belgium
1/17	*The Last Station*	Michael Hoffman	Russia
1/24	*Police, Adjective*	Cornelui Porumboiu	Romania
1/31	*The Girl on the Train*	Andre Techine	France
2/7	*Mine* (Katrina pets)	Geralyn Pezanoski	United States
2/14	*Fish Tank*	Andrea Arnold	United Kingdom
2/21	*Ajami*	Scandar Copti, Yaron Shani	Israel
3/1	*A Prophet*	Jacques Audiard	French-Arabic
3/8	*Terribly Happy*	Henry Ruben Genz	Denmark
3/15	*Harlan*	Felix Moeller	Germany
3/22	*Vincere*	Marco Bellocchio	Italy
3/29	*Walking Sleeping Beauty*	Don Hahn	United States (Disney)
4/5	*The Warlords*	Peter Ho-Sun Chan	China
4/12	*The Art of the Steal*	Don Argott	United States

Appendix 8

Book Reviews

8/16	Pat Conroy, *South of Broad*; Paul Collins, *The Book of William*
8/23	Tracy Kidder, *Strength in What Remains* (Burundi refugee); John Updike, *The Maples Stories*
8/30	Janet Soskice, *The Sisters of Sinai*
9/6	E. L. Doctorow, *Homer & Langley*; Doug Stanton, *Horse Soldiers* (vs. Taliban)
9/13	Rebecca Solnit, *A Paradise Built in Hell*; Danny Wallace, *Friends Like These*
9/20	Michael Meyer, *The Year That Changed the World* (1989, Berlin Wall); Kazuo Ishiguro, *Nocturnes*; Kate DiCamillo, *The Magician's Elephant*
9/27	Nicholson Baker, *The Anthropologist*; Carol Berkin, *Civil War Wives*
10/4	Timothy Egan, *The Big Burn: Teddy Roosevelt and the Fire That Saved America*; Simon Carr, *The Boys Are Back* (single dad)
10/11	Karen Armstrong, *The Case for God*; Jeannette Wells, *Half Broke Horses*
10/18	Taylor Branch, *The Clinton Tapes*; Eckhart Tolle, *Guardians of Being*
10/25	Barbara Ehrenreich, *Bright-Sided: How the Relentless Promotion of Positive Thinking Has Undermined America.*
11/1	A. S. Byatt, *The Children's Book*; Malcolm Gladwell, *What the Dog Saw*
11/8	Ken Auletta, *Googled: The End of the World as We Know It*
11/15	Jonathan Safran Foer, *Eating Animals*
11/22	George Packer, *Interesting Times: Writings from a Turbulent Decade*; Barbara Kingsolver, *The Lacuna*
11/29	Children's books: Peter H. Reynolds, *The North Star*; Jerry Pinkney (illustrator), *The Lion & the Mouse*; Gilliam Shields, *When the World Is Ready for Bed*; Carmen Agra Deedy, *14 Cows for America*; Richard Peck, *A Season of Gifts*; Patricia McCormick, *Purple Heart*; Suzanne Collins, *Catching Fire*; Grace Lin, *Where the Mountain Meets the Moon*; Katherine Paterson, *The Day of the Pelican*
12/13	Photography: Steve McCurry, *The Unguarded Moment*; Nick Brandt, *A Shadow Falls*; Annie Leibowitz, *A Photographer's Life, 1990–2005*; Eugene Richards, *The Blue Room*
12/20	Terry Teachout, *Pops: A Life of Louis Armstrong*; P.D. James, *Talking about Detective Fiction*
12/27–1/3	Joshua Ferris, *The Unnamed*; Don DeLillo, *Point Omega*; Zachary Mason, *The Lost Books of the Odyssey*; Anna Lawrence Pietroni, *Ruby's Spoon*; Sam Lipsyte, *The Ask*; Chang-rae Lee, *The Surrendered*; Martin Cruz Smith, *The Golden Mile*; Hillel Cohen, *Good Arabs*; Oe and Boehm, *The Changeling*; David Maraniss, *Into the Story*; Robert Harris, *Conspirata*
2010	
1/10	Anne Tyler, *Noah's Compass*
1/17	Mark Hudson, *Titian: The Last Days*; Martin Jacques, *When China Rules the World*
1/24	Richard Reeves, *Daring Young Men* (Berlin airlift); Robin Okrant, *Living Oprah*
1/31	A. N. Wilson, *Our Times: The Age of Elizabeth II*
2/7	David R. Dow, *The Autobiography of an Execution*; Eric Siblin, *The Cello Suites*
2/14	John Bowe (Ed.), *Us: Americans Talk about Love*

2/21	Kevin and Hannah Salwen, *The Power of Half* (the Hunger Project); Andrew Porter, *The Theory of Light and Matter*
3/1	Peter Hessler, *Country Driving*
3/8	Garry Wills, *Bomb Power*
3/15	Brenda Peterson, *I Want To Be Left Behind: Finding Rapture Here on Earth*
3/22	Michael Shelden, *Mark Twain: Man in White*
3/29	Henry M. Paulson, *On the Brink*; David Wessel, *In Fed We Trust*; Andrew Ross Sorkin, *Too Big to Fall*; John Cassidy, *How Markets Fall*
4/5	David Remnick, *The Bridge: The Life and Rise of Barack Obama*; Philip Zaleski, *The Best Spiritual Writing of 2010*
4/12	John L. Esposito, *The Future of Islam*; Helen Simonson, *Major Pettigrew's Last Stand*

Appendix 9

CSM Editorial and Publishing Staff

STAFF WRITERS

Scott Armstrong, senior editor

Ben Arnoldy, staff reporter, New Delhi

Ross Atkin, *Daily News Briefing*

Scott Baldauf, staff reporter, Johannesburg

Laurent Belsie, Money

Christa Case Bryant, Middle East

Josh Burek, Op-Ed, Commentary

Gail Russell Chaddock, staff reporter, Washington, D.C.

Dante Chinni, staff reporter, Washington, D.C.

Matthew Clark, Africa and Americas

Mark Clayton, staff reporter

Clayton Collins, *Weekly Edition* editor

David T. Cook, bureau chief, Washington, D.C.

Judy Nichols Douglass, international staff

Mike Farrell, staff reporter, San Francisco

Linda Feldman, staff reporter, Washington, D.C.

Jenna Fisher, assistant Op-Ed

Peter Ford, staff reporter, Beijing

David R. Francis, *Economic Scene*

Melanie Stetson Freeman, staff photographer

Chris Gaylord, Innovation and *Horizons*

Clara Germani, senior editor

Gloria Goodale, staff reporter, Los Angeles

Peter Grier, staff reporter, Washington, D.C.; *Decoder*

Mike Guarino, staff reporter, Chicago

Jim Hagengruber, Europe

Andrew Heining, online news editor

Carol Huang, Asia

Marshall Ingwerson, managing editor

Patrik Jonsson, staff reporter, Atlanta

Clayton Jones, chief editorial writer, *Inklings*, crossword puzzle

Marjorie Kehe, book editor

Stacy Teicher Khadaroo, staff reporter, Midwest

Brad Knickerbocker, international staff

Howard LaFranchi, staff reporter, Washington, D.C.

Gregory Lamb, *PMAD* editor and reporter

Sue Leach, *Home Forum* editor

Sara Miller Llana, staff reporter, Mexico City

Judy Lowe, Environment editor

Gordon Lubold, staff reporter, Washington, D.C.

Bob Marquand, staff reporter, Paris

Mary Knox Merrill, staff photographer

Leigh Montgomery, librarian

Pat Murphy, deputy online editor

Amelia Newcomb, world news

Kendra Nordin, *Weekly* assistant editor

Eoin O'Carroll, online news editor

Jimmy Orr, online editor

Amanda Paulson, staff reporter, Chicago

Scott Peterson, staff reporter, Istanbul

Ilene Prusher, staff reporter, Israel

Peter Ranier, film critic

Warren Richey, staff reporter, Washington, D.C.

Tracey D. Samuelson, correspondent

Mark Sappenfield, national news

Ron Scherer, staff reporter, New York

David Clark Scott, international section editor

Matthew Shaer, *Horizons*

Peter Spotts, staff reporter

Cheryl Sullivan, national news editor

Owen Thomas, deputy editor, *Weekly Edition*, crossword puzzle

Mark Trumbull, staff reporter

Jake Turcotte, multimedia producer, graphics editor

Moises Velesquez-Manoff, staff reporter

Robert Veneman-Huges, online news editor

Ruth Walker, *Home Forum*

Dan Wood, staff reporter, Los Angeles

John Yemma, editor

CORRESPONDENTS

Jonathan Adams, Rondi Adamson, Issam Ahmed, Josh Allen, Heba Aly, Cynthia Anderson, Christopher Andrese, Lindsey Arkley, Jane Arraf, Iason Athanasiadis, Tony Azios, Oliver Bach, Taylor Barnes, Julien Barnes-Dacey, Michael Benanav, Nicholas Blanford, Jennifer Bleyer, Susan Bourette, Christina Boyle, Amy Bracken, Sibylta Brodzinsky, Andres Cala, Nancy Humphrey Case, Julius Cavendish, Lucien Chauvin, Kimberly N. Chase, Daniella Cheslow, Kristen Chick, Anuj Chopra, David Conrads, Rob Crilly, Erin Cunningham, Bob Deans, Frederick Deknatel, Max Delany, Isabelle de Pommereau, Charlie Devereux, Peter DiCampo, Steve Dinnen, Randy Dotinga, Judy Nichols Douglass, Andrew Downie, Jesse Emspak, Ian Evans, Amy Farnsworth, Lucy Fielder, Robin Forestier-Walker, David Francis, Rafael D. Frankel, Heather Vogel Frederick, Marilyn Gardner, Nicholas Gilman, Elisabeth Ginsburg, Bill Glauber, A. J. Goldman, Jacqui Goddard, Anand Gopal, Alex Halperin, Stephanie Hanes, Nicole Hano, Elizabeth Hansen, Husna Haq, Danna Harman, Lisa Harris, Hilary Heuler, Bridget Huber, Stephen Humphries, Nicole Itano, Marilyn Jones, Michael J. Jordan, Takehiko Kambayashi, Lois Kapila, Jeff Kass, Ashraf Khalil, Jennifer Kho, Donald Kirk, Jeremy Kitner, Kathie Klarreich, Robert Koehler, Tibor Krausz, Stephen Kurczy, Jeremy Kutner, Blake Lambert, Jane Lampman, Kurt Lancaster, Jonathan

Landreth, Patti Lane, Christina Larson, Clare Leschin-Hoar, Sara Miller Llana, Chrissie Long, Elizabeth Lund, Richard Luscombe, G. Jeffrey Mac-Donald, Matthew MacLean, Alexandra Marks, Kathy Marks, Eric Marx, James Mason, Judith Matloff, Joseph Mayton, Sarah More McCann, Mary Beth McCauley, Christianna McCausland, Tristan McConnell, Patti McCracken, Kitty McKinsey, Lourdes Medrano, Richard Mertens, Mary Mihaly, Sean J. Miller, Joshua Mitnick, Aunohita Mojumdar, Anna Momigliano, David Montero, Simon Montlake, Elizabeth Armstrong Moore, Jina Moore, Jason Motlagh, Rolf Mowatt-Larssen, Annie Murphy, Caryle Murphy, Dan Murphy, Yuriko Nagano, Ayesha Nasir, Richard O'Mara, Josh Penry, Tom A. Peter, Mike Pflanz, Evan Pondel, Alessandra Prentice, Margaret Price, Ben Quinn, Mark Rice-Oxley, Mian Ridge, Linda Rodriguez, Jonathan Roeder, Tim Rogers, Yereth Rosen, Susan Sachs, Bikash Sangraula, Yigal Schleifer, Lisa Schroeder, Michael Seaver, Nicholas Seeley, Sherry Shahan, Danielle Shapiro, Ben Simon, Jordan Michael Smith, Nick Squires, Liam Stack, Carol Strickland, Sushma Sub-ramanian, Tom Sullivan, Roshanak Taghar, Kevin Taylor, George Tombs, James Turner, Vuaysree Venkatraman, Christopher Wallenberg, Norman Weinstein, Fred Weir, Jeffrey White, Brian Whitley, Jocelyn Wiener, Todd Wilkinson, Mary Wiltenburg, Duncan Woodside, Lina Yoon, Huma Yusuf, Eilene Zimmerman, Yvonne Zipp

CONTRIBUTORS

Valerie Criscione, Ezra Fieser, Erik German, Ritt Goldstein, Andrea Gregory, John Hearne, John Hughes, Drew Hinshaw, Aidan Jones, Laura Kasinof, David Khattak, Savious Kwinika, Julie Masis, John McLean, Rehmat Mehsud, Mxolisi Noube, Walter Rodgers, Sara Shahriari, Kosha-nak Taghavi, Sarah A. Topol, Karl Wilson, Patrick Winn, Benjamin Witte

PUBLISHING STAFF

Cindy Anderson, *Daily News Briefing*

Patti Carter, assistant production manager, graphics and layout

Gillian Charters, copy desk manager

Joanne Ciccarello, staff photographer, assistant photo editor

Rich Clabaugh, graphics

Patty Collinsworth, circulation director

Rosalee Dunbar, *Christian Science Perspective*

Heather Ehmke, copy desk editor

Julie Fallon, assistant production manager, graphics and layout

Bob Hanna, advertising director

John Kehe, print design director

Abe McLaughlin, product manager

Leigh Montgomery, librarian

Lily Mui, production manager, operations manager, technology coordinator

Rex Nelles, executive assistant

Alfred Sosa, director of photography

Notes

CHAPTER 1

1. See Appendix 1: Acronyms.
2. The Mary Baker Eddy Library (www.mbelibrary.org), at 200 Massachusetts Avenue in Boston, is open six days a week. Since opening in September 2002, it allows the public access to an impressive collection of papers. Housed in the 1934 building constructed for CSPS, it shares office space with both TMC and the CSPS. It occupies portions of three floors (40,000 square feet) and cost $50 million for its (re)design and renovation. the president and executive manager is Lesley Pitts, who reports to the Library's Board of Trustees.

In addition to archival collections of Eddy's articles, manuscripts, and correspondence dating from approximately 1835 to 1910, the Library also includes the Mapparium, a three-story, stained-glass globe representing the world of 1935, which visitors walk through on a 30-foot glass bridge. More recent additions include the interactive Quest Gallery (a multimedia exploration of spirituality and MBE's life), rotating exhibits, and a café and museum shop. Reference and research services are available for the casual visitor and the serious scholar.

3. See Appendix 2: Awards Granted to the *Christian Science Monitor*.
4. http://www.youtube.com/watch?v=RPRtv3KqdXI). Also, see Appendix 3: Editors of the *Christian Science Monitor*.
5. This *knol* ("a unit of knowledge") was created by Kevin Curley, a senior web marketing associate at *CSM* (http://knol.google.com/k/the-christian -science-monitor).
6. There are 162 datelines from the USA section, plus "guesstimates" from others.
7. http://www.csmonitor.com/About/The-Monitor-difference.
8. http://www.csmonitor.com/About/The-Monitor-difference.
9. http://abell.austincollege.edu/Abell/Elinfor/eresources/csm.html.

10. www.english.aljazeera.net/news/middleeast.
11. http://www.poynter.org/content/content_view.asp?id=58937.
12. http://www.globalethics.org/mission-and-values.php.
13. www.proquest.com.
14. http://www.csmonitor.com/multimedia.
15. http://view.fdu.edu/default.aspx?id=3324.

CHAPTER 2

1. RSS: "Really Simple Syndication."
2. See http://www.marybakereddy.org.
3. Biographies of Mary Baker Eddy include the following: Bates and Dittemore 1932; Beasley 1963; Carpenter 1997; CSPS 1911/1993; Clemes 1924; Dakin 1929; Ferguson 2001; Gardner 1993; Gill 1999; Grekel and Grekel 1999; Johnston 1946; Kennedy 1947; Keyston 2007; Knapp 1947/1991; Knee 1994; Nenneman 1997; Orcutt 1950; Pickering 1974; Powell 1930; Ramsay 1935/1991; Silberger 1980; Smaus 1966;. Smillie 2007; Smith 1941; Smith 1991; Snowdon 1920; Springer 1930; Thomas 1994; Tomlinson 1945; von Fettweis and Warneck 1998/2009; Wilbur 1908; Wright 1998.
4. Angola, Argentina (16), Australia (33), Austria, Bahamas, Barbados, Belgium, Benin, Bermuda, Brazil (15), Burundi, Cameroon, Canada (38), Chile, China, Colombia, Democratic Republic of the Congo (18), Cuba, Czech Republic, Denmark, Ecuador, Egypt, Finland, France, Germany (62), Ghana, Greece, Grenada, Guam, Guatemala, Haiti, India, Indonesia, Ireland, Italy, Ivory Coast, Jamaica, Japan, Kazakhstan, Kenya, Korea, Latvia, Malawi, Mexico, Namibia, Netherlands, New Zealand (13), Nigeria (25), Peru, Philippines, Poland, Portugal, Puerto Rico, Russia, Rwanda, Sierra Leona, Singapore, South Africa (19), Spain, Sweden, Switzerland (20), Tanzania, Thailand, Togo, Trinidad and Tobago, Uganda, Ukraine, United Kingdom (101), Uruguay, Venezuela, Zambia, Zimbabwe.
5. Alabama, Alaska, Arizona (20), Arkansas, California (179), Colorado (25), Connecticut (19), Delaware, District of Columbia, Florida (67), Georgia, Hawaii, Idaho, Illinois (56), Indiana (26), Iowa, Kansas, Kentucky, Louisiana, Maine, Maryland, Massachusetts (51), Michigan (37), Minnesota, Mississippi, Missouri (22), Montana, Nebraska, Nevada, New Hampshire, New Jersey (20), New Mexico, New York (58), North Carolina, North Dakota, Ohio (40), Oklahoma, Oregon (26), Pennsylvania (33), Rhode Island, South Carolina, South Dakota, Tennessee, Texas (51), Utah, Vermont, Virginia (23), Washington (43), West Virginia, Wisconsin (27), Wyoming.
6. http://en.wikipedia.org/wiki/List_of_Christian_Scientists_%28religious_denomination%29.
7. http://christianscience.com/beliefs.html.
8. See Appendix 5: Christian Science–Related Websites.
9. http://www.csmonitor.com/About/The-Monitor-difference.

10. See Appendix 6: *The Christian Science Monitor*: A Timeline.

11. http://www.csmonitor.com/About/The-Monitor-difference.

12. http://www.poynter.org/column.asp?id=101&aid=125651.

CHAPTER 3

1. http://www.ustream.tv/recorded/3809510.

2. http://www.ustream.tv/recorded/3809510.

3. http://www.claybennett.com.

4. http://www.CSMonitor.com/globalwarming.

5. See Appendix 7 for a list of film reviews by Peter Rainer, as well as occasional contributions by Andy Klein, in the first year of the weekly.

6. http://www.*CS*Monitor.com/Commentary/editors-blog/2010/0401/Talk-to-the-Editor-for-April-1-Monitor-books-coverage.

7. See Appendix 8: Book Reviews.

CHAPTER 4

1. "Against the Neo-liberal Tide: Media and Democracy in the 21st Century."

2. http://www.pbs.org/mediashift/2010/01/best-online-resources-for-following-haiti-news-taking-action014.html.

3. http://www.twitter.com/csmlibrary.

4. http://christianscience.com/blogs/articles-monitor/prayers-of-love-for-haitis-people.

5. http://www.csmonitor.com/atcsmonitor/specials/women.

6. http://www.csmonitor.com/World/Olympics/Olympics-blog.

7. http://twitter.com/sappenfieldm.

CHAPTER 5

1. For "facsimile," a telecommunications method for transmitting textual and/or graphically documented information over telephone lines.

2. "Online" means hosted by a computer network.

3. http://www.csmonitor.com/USA/2008/1125/p99s01-usgn.html.

4. Meaning it was still in a state of development.

5. A website is a page on the World Wide Web with information about its owner(s).

6. Blogs are personal Web logs—techno-chat dealing with everything from the mundane to the monumental.

7. "Digital" refers to discrete, computer-readable information.

8. Portal Document Format, a file for document exchange.

9. Logged onto a computer or network.

10. Not charging subscribers access fees.

11. Electronic mail.

12. Live web conferencing via the Internet.

13. http://www.newseum.org/news/newseum_videos/video.aspx?item=nv_DIGI090311.

14. Made possible by Internet Service Providers (ISPs).

15. People who create and manage information content.

16. Software used to find Internet information.

17. A cyberspace environment.

18. Hypertext Transfer Protocol—how Web browsers communicate with servers.

19. "Really Simple Syndication," allowing you to see a number of headlines and news.

20. From Apple's iPod, a means of creating and/or delivering digital files by the Internet for online programs or syndicated talk shows.

21. Web pages created and edited via a web browser.

22. Messages on the social networking/microblogging service known as Twitter.

23. IM: real-time, text-based communication between two or more people on personal computers (PCs).

24. Individuals or groups interdependently connected through websites such as Facebook, YouTube, LinkedIn, Twitter, OurMedia, or MySpace.

25. Overall number of "hits"—i.e., anyone coming as many times as he or she wants.

26. A count of individuals coming only once to the site.

27. http://www.csmonitor.com/specials/carroll/index.html.

28. http://www.csmonitor.com/About/Find-Us-Online.

29. http://www.facebook.com/pages/Marjorie-Kehe/235853723852 and http://twitter.com/MarjorieKehe).

30. http://www.facebook.com/ChristianScienceMonitor and http://twitter.com/JudyDigginit.

31. http://www.facebook.com/ChristianScienceMonitor and http://twitter.com/csmhorizonsblog.

32. http://www.csmonitor.com/Money/new-economy.

33. Uniform Resource Locator, which shows where a resource is available.

34. See Appendix 9 for a list of *CSM* publishing staff, staff writers, columnists, and correspondents relevant to this study.

35. http://www.portfolio.com/executives/features/2009/02/11/25-Innovators-in-Technology?page=3#listItem14.

CHAPTER 6

1. http://www.csmonitor.com/USA/Society/2010/0215/Westminster-Dog-Show-2010-Why-it-s-better-than-Winter-Olympics.

2. Electronic "books".

References

Alia, Valerie. 2004. *Media Ethics and Social Change.* New York: Routledge.

Allan, Stuart. 2006. *Online News: Journalism and the Internet.* Open University Press.

Allen, Eric W. 1942. "The Newspaper and Community Leader." In *The press and society: A book of readings,* edited by George L. Bird and Frederic W. Merwin (1951), 146–48. New York: Prentice Hall.

Alterman, Eric. 2008. "Out of Print." *The New Yorker* (March 31): 48–59.

Altschull, J. Herbert. 1990. *From Milton to McLuhan: The Ideas behind American Journalism.* New York: Longman.

Armstrong, Joseph and Margaret Williamson. 1980/2009. *Building of The Mother Church: The First Church of Christ, Scientist, in Boston, MA.* Boston: The Christian Science Publishing Society.

Auletta, Ken. 2010. "Non-stop News." *The New Yorker* (January 25): 38–47.

Austin, April. 1998. "A User's Guide to the e-Monitor." *The Christian Science Monitor* (April 1): 10–11.

Bankoff, Greg, Georg Frerks, and Dorothea Hilhorst, eds. 2004. *Mapping Vulnerability: Disasters, Development and People.* Earthscan Publications.

Bates, Ernest Sutherland and John V. Dittemore. 1932. *Mary Baker Eddy: The Truth and the Tradition.* New York: Alfred A. Knopf.

Bauder, David. 2007. "Study Finds Conservatives Dominate Editorial Pages." *The Republican* (Springfield, MA) (September 13): D15.

Baxter, Nancy Niblack. 2004. *Open the Doors of the Temple: The Survival of Christian Science in the Twenty-First century.* Hawthorne Publishing.

Beam, Alex. 2005. "Appealing to a Higher Authority." *Boston Globe.* Available: http://www.boston.com/ae/media/articles/2005/06/09/appealing_to_a _higher_authority.

Beam, Alex. 2008. "Monitoring the Future of Newspapers." *Boston.com.* Available: http://www.boston.com/ae/media/articles/2008/08/26/monitoring _the_future_of_newspapers?mode=PF.

Bearden, Michelle. 2008. "*Christian Science Monitor* Changes How It Delivers the News." *Tampa Bay Online* (November 8). Available: http://www2.tbo.com/ content/2008/nov/08/na-christian-science-monitor-is-changing-the-way-i.

Beasley, Norman. 1952. *The Cross and the Crown: The History of Christian Science.* New York: Dual, Sloane and Pearce.

Beasley, Norman. 1963. *Mary Baker Eddy.* New York: Dual, Sloan, and Pearce.

Birkland, Thomas A. 2006. *Lessons of Disaster: Policy Change after Catastrophic Events.* Washington, D.C.: Georgetown University Press.

Blanding, Michael. 2010. "Re-writing the Future." *Suffolk Alumni Magazine* 5 (2) (Winter): 14–19.

Boczkowski, Pablo. 2005. *Digitizing the News: Innovation in Online Newspapers.* Cambridge, MA: MIT Press.

Bogart, Leo. 2004. "Reflections on Content Quality in Newspapers." *Newspaper Research Journal* 25 (1) (Winter): 40–53.

Bradlee, Ben. 1995. *A Good Life: Newspapering and Other Adventures.* New York: Simon and Schuster.

Brainard, Curtis. 2010. "Monitor-ing the Environment." *Columbia Journalism Review* (March 9). Available: http://www.cjr.org/the_observatory/ monitoring_the_environment.php.

Bridge, Susan. 1998. *Monitoring the News: The Brilliant Launch and Sudden Collapse of the Monitor Channel.* Armonk, NY: M. E. Sharpe.

Brown, Melinda. 2009. "Christian Science Monitor Bids Adieu to Print Edition." *Media News International* (March 25). Available: http://www.mnilive.com/ 2009/03/christian-science-monitor-bids-adieu-to-print-edition.

Bruns, Axel. 2005. *Gatewatching: Collaborative Online News Production.* New York: Peter Lang.

Business Wire. 2008. "*The Christian Science Monitor* Announces Shift from Print Daily to Online Daily and Launches Weekly Print Publication." *FindArticles.com* (October 28). Available: http://findarticles.com/p/articles/ mi_m0EIN/is_2008_Oct_28/ai_n30939873/?tag=content-inner;col1.

Campbell, W. Joseph. 2003. *Yellow Journalism: Puncturing the Myths, Defining the Legacies.* Westport, CT: Praeger Publishing.

Canham, Erwin D. 1958. *Commitment to Freedom: The Story of the Christian Science Monitor.* Boston: Houghton Mifflin.

Carpenter, Gilbert C. 1997. *Mary Baker Eddy: Her Spiritual Footsteps.* Aequus Institute Publications.

Cather, Willa and Georgine Milmine. 1909/1993. *The Life of Mary Baker G. Eddy and the History of Christian Science.* Lincoln: University of Nebraska Press.

Cattani, Richard J. 1993. "The *Monitor* at 85: Where We've Been, Where We're Going." *Christian Science Monitor* (November 24): 9.

Chen Dongyi. 2010. "Google's China Operations: Search Problems." *NewsChina* (February 5): 38–39.

Christian Science Publishing Society. 1947. *The Story of Christian Science Wartime Activities, 1939–1946.* Boston: Christian Science Publishing Society.

Christian Science Publishing Society. 1984. *Understanding Our Century.* Boston: Christian Science Publishing Society.

Christian Science Publishing Society. 1988. *The Christian Science Monitor: The First 80 Years.* Boston: Christian Science Publishing Society.

Christian Science Publishing Society. 2008. *Engaging with the Christian Science Monitor.* Boston: Christian Science Publishing Society.

Christians, Clifford G., Mark Fackler, Kathy Britain McKee, Peggy J. Kreshel, and Robert H. Woods. 2008. *Media Ethics: Cases and Moral Reasoning,* 8th ed. Allyn and Bacon.

Clark, Roy Peter. 2003. "Cauliflower and the Champ." *St. Petersburg Times* (June 1). Available: http://www.sptimes.com/2003/06/01/Perspective/Cauliflower_and_the_C.shtml.

Clemes, William Montgomery. 1924. *The Ancestry of Mary Baker Eddy.* Pompton Lakes, NJ: Biblio Company.

Coffin, Jarvis. 2010. "Life after Newspapers: Editor, John Yemma, Checks in a Year after the *Christian Science Monitor* Became the CSMonitor.com." *Burst Media* (March 29). Available: http://burstmedia.wordpress.com.

Cohen, Daniel. 2000. *Yellow Journalism: Scandal, Sensationalism, and Gossip in the Media.* Brookfield, CT: Twenty-First Century Books.

Cook, David. 2008. "John Yemma Named *Monitor* editor." *Christian Science Monitor* (June 9). Available: http://www.csmonitor.com/layout/set/print/content/view/print/229066.

Coville, Liz. 2009. "Is Nonprofit Status the Future of Newspapers?" *Finding Dulcinea* (March 26). Available: http://www.findingdulcinea.com/news/business/2009/march/Is-Nonprofit-Status-the-Future-of-Newspapers-.html.

Cowen, Robert C. 1984. "Natural Science Shapes a New World View. In *Understanding our century*, 75–89. Boston: Christian Science Publishing Society.

Curtiss, Richard H. 1997. "As U.S. Media Ownership Shrinks, Who Covers Islam?" *Washington Report on Middle East Affairs* (December): 60–61.

Dakin, Edwin Frander. 1929. *Mrs. Eddy: The Biography of a Virginal Mind.* New York: Charles Scribner's Sons.

Danziger, Jeff. 1988. *Used Cartoons.* Boston: Christian Science Publishing Society.

de Villiers, Marq. 2008. *The End: Natural Disasters, Manmade Catastrophes, and the Future of Human Survival.* Thomas Dunne Books.

Eddy, Mary Baker. 1875/1994. *Science and Health with Key to the Scriptures.* Boston: First Church of Christ, Scientist.

Eddy, Mary Baker. 1936. *Manual of The Mother Church, the First Church of Christ Scientist, in Boston, Massachusetts.* Boston: First Church of Christ, Scientist.

Eddy, Mary Baker. 1995. *Prose Works, Other than Science and Health with Key to the Scriptures.* Writings of Mary Baker Eddy.

Eddy, Mary Baker. 2002. *Mary Baker Eddy, Speaking for Herself.* Writings of Mary Baker Eddy.

Eddy, Mary Baker. 2006. *Essays and Other Footprints: Left by Mary Baker Eddy, Discoverer and Founder of Christian Science.* Healing Unlimited.

Edmonds, Rick. 2009. "Online Focus Is Working for *Christian Science Monitor.*" *Biz Blog/PoynterOnline* (October 23). Available: http://www.poynter.org/column.asp?id=123&aid=172295.

Ehrlich, Matthew C. 2006. *Journalism in the Movies.* Urbana: University of Illinois Press.

Ferguson, Isabel. 2001. *Come and See: The Life of Mary Baker Eddy.* Lincoln, MA: Small Rain Press.

Foell, Earl W. and Richard A. Nenneman, eds. 1986. *How Peace Came to the World.* Cambridge, MA: MIT Press.

Foell, Earl W. 1990. "Harding to Reagan with Dick Strout." *Christian Science Monitor* (August 22): 19.

Frankel, Max. 2000. *Times of My Life and My Life with the Times.* New York: Delta.

Friend, Cecilia and Jane B. Singer. 2007. *Online Journalism Ethics: Traditions and Transitions.* Armonk, NY: M. E. Sharpe.

Fuller, Linda K. 1983. "The *Recorder*: An Observational Study of a Community Newspaper." *Newspaper Research Journal* 4 (Spring): 25–32.

Fuller, Linda K. 1988a. "Terrorism vis-à-vis the *Christian Science Monitor*, l977–l987." Paper presented to the Terrorism and News Media Research Project, Boston, MA.

Fuller, Linda K. 1988b. "Terrorism as Treated by the *Christian Science Monitor*, l977–l987." *Political Communication and Persuasion* 5: 121–37.

Fuller, Linda K. 1988c. "Tiananmen as Treated by the *Christian Science Monitor.*" Paper presented to the Media and Crisis Conference, Quebec City, Canada.

Fuller, Linda K. 1991. "Tiananmen as Treated by the *Christian Science Monitor.*" *Political Communication and Persuasion* 8: 79–91.

Fuller, Linda K. 1992. "*Monitoring* the Soviet coup." Paper presented at the Conflict and Diversity Conference, Temple University, Philadelphia, PA.

Fuller, Linda K. 1996. "The Ideology of the 'Red Scare' Movement: McCarthyism in the Movies." In *Beyond the Stars V: Themes and Ideologies in American Popular Film*, edited by Paul Loukides and Linda K. Fuller, 229–247. Bowling Green, OH: Popular Press.

Fuller, Linda K. 1997. "*Monitoring* the O. J. Simpson Case vis-à-vis Domestic Violence." Paper presented to the Northeast Popular Culture Association, Wentworth Institute of Technology, Boston, MA.

Fuller, Linda K. 1998. "Saving Stories: A Goal of the Cultural Environment Movement." *Gazette: The International Journal for Communication Studies* 60 (2) (April): 139–153.

Fuller, Linda K. 1999. "From Tramps to Truth-Seekers: Images of the Homeless in Motion Pictures." In *Reading the Homeless: The Media's Image of Homeless Culture*, edited by Eung Jun Min, 159–173. Westport, CT: Greenwood Press.

Fuller, Linda K. 2002. "Resilience and Restraint: Coverage of 9/11 by the *Christian Science Monitor.*" Paper presented to the International Association for Media and Communication Research Conference, Barcelona, Spain.

Fuller, Linda K., ed. 2003. *Media-Mediated AIDS.* Cresskill, NJ: Hampton Press.

Fuller, Linda K. 2004a. "Gay Bishops, Gay Marriages, Gay News: The Treatment of 'Homosexuality' in the *Christian Science Monitor.*" Paper presented to the Northeast Popular Culture Association, Newbury College, Boston, MA.

Fuller, Linda K. 2004b. "An International Newspaper with Unique Reportage on Women and Women's Issues: The *Christian Science Monitor.*" Visiting Scholar lecture, Northeastern University.

Fuller, Linda K. 2007. Interview. *Nobody Knows Us.* Directed by Max Lewontin. Available: http://nobodyknowsus.blip.tv.

Fuller, Linda K. 2008a. *African Women's Unique Vulnerabilities to HIV/AIDS: Communication Perspectives and Promises.* New York: Palgrave Macmillan.

Fuller, Linda K. 2008b. *Sportscasters/Sportscasting: Practices and Principles.* New York: Routledge.

Fuller, Linda K. 2009. "Framing a Flaming Issue: The Beijing Olympic Torch Issue." Paper presented to the Popular Culture Association, New Orleans, LA. Available: http://www.LKFullerSport.com.

Fuller, Linda K. 2010a. "A Tsunami of News Coverage: The *Christian Science Monitor* on the 12/27 disaster." In *Tsunami Communication: (Inter)personal/Intercultural, Media, Technical, Ethical, Philanthropic, Development, and Personal Responses*, edited by Linda K. Fuller, 101–21. Cresskill, NJ: Hampton Press.

Fuller, Linda K. 2010b. "Matters of Communication from the Tsunami of 2004: (Inter)personal/Intercultural, Mass Media, ICTs, and Other Responses." Panel for the International Communications Association, Singapore.

"Future of Newspapers Looks Dim, Experts Agree: Various Solutions Offered." 2009. *PR Log* (April 22). Available: http://www.prlog.org/10222399 -future-of-newspapers-looks-dim-experts-agree-various-solutions-offered .html.

Gahran, Amy. 2005. "Christian Science Monitor Loves Its 'Bloggiest' Status." *Contentious.* Available: http://www.contentious.com/2005/04/22/ christian-science-monitor-loves-bloggiest-status.

Gandleman, Joe. 2009. "*Christian Science Monitor* Begins Marketing Weekly Print Edition." *The Moderate Voice* (June 30). Available: http://themoderatevoice .com/37426/christian-science-monitor-begins-marketing-weekly-print -edition.

Gardner, Martin. 1993. *Healing Revelations of Mary Baker Eddy: The Rise and Fall of Christian Science.* UK: Prometheus Books.

Garfield, Bob. 2005. "When the Eddy Breaks." Interview with Marshall Ingwerson. *On the Media* (May 27). Available: http://www.onthemedia.org/ yore/transcript/transcripts_052705_eddy.html.

Gelb, Arthur. 2004. *City Room*. New York; Berkley Trade.

Gerbner, George. 1993. "Instant History: The Case of the Moscow Coup." *Political Communication* 10 (Spring): 185–194.

Gerbner, George. 1999. "What Do We Know?" In *Television and Its Viewers: Cultivation Theory and Research*, edited by James Shanahan and Michael Morgan, ix–xiii. New York: Cambridge University Press.

Gill, Gillian. 1999. *Mary Baker Eddy*. New York: Da Capo Press.

Good, Howard. 1989. *Outcasts: The Image of Journalists in Contemporary Film*. Metuchen, NJ: Scarecrow Press.

Good, Howard and Sandra L. Borden, eds. 2010. *Ethics and Entertainment: Essays on Media Culture and Media Morality*. McFarland and Co.

Gopnik, Adam. 2010. *Angels and Ages: A Short Book about Darwin, Lincoln, and Modern Life*. Vintage.

Gottschalk, Stephen. 1974. *The Emergence of Christian Science in American Religious Life*. Berkeley: University of California Press.

Gould, John. 1992. "Eyah, it's been 50 years." *Christian Science Monitor* (October 23): 16–17.

Graham, Katharine. 1997. *Personal History*. New York: Alfred A. Knopf.

Gray, Stephen T. 1999. "Readers and the *Monitor* Difference." *Christian Science Monitor* (August 12): 11.

Grekel, Doris and Morris Grekel. 1999. *The Founding of Christian Science: The Life of Mary Baker Eddy, 1888–1900*. Healing Unlimited.

Gross, Terry. 2009. "Christian Science Monitor Shifts Focus to Web." Interview with John Yemma. *Fresh Air on WHYY/NPR* (January 12). Available: http://www.npr.org/templates/player/mediaPlayer.html?action=1&t=1& islist=false&id=99239994&m=99247853.

Gunther, Barrie. 2003. *News and the Net*. Mahwah, NJ: Lawrence Erlbaum.

Gurley, Gabrielle. 2010. "The Monitor's Web-First Approach." *INCSpot* (February 23). Available: http://www.massinc.org/INCSpot/The-Monitors -web-first-approach.aspx.

Halberstam, David. 1979. *The Powers That Be*. Urbana: University of Illinois Press.

Hanusch, Folker and Jan Servaes. 2010. "Death on the Front Page: 'Awesome Things' and This Thing Called Humanity." In *Tsunami Communication: (Inter)personal/Intercultural, Mass Media, Philanthropic, Ethical, and Developmental Responses*, edited by Linda K. Fuller, 47–60. Cresskill, NJ: Hampton Press.

Harsch, Joseph C. 1993. *At the Hinge of History: A Reporter's Story*. Athens: University of Georgia Press.

Hartill, Lane. 2001. "How the *Monitor* works." *Christian Science Monitor* (May 8): 22–23.

Hartsook, Andrew W. 1993. *Christian Science after 1910*. Zanesville, OH: The Bookmark.

Heckler, Cheryl. 2007. *An Accidental Journalist: The Adventures of Edmund Stevens, 1934–1945*. Columbia, MO: University of Missouri Press.

Heinz, Teresa L. 2004. "The Homeless as Criminals or Consumers: A Critical Discourse Analysis of the *Christian Science Monitor* and the *Washington Post*'s Coverage of Homelessness Legislation." Paper presented to the National Communication Association conference, Chicago, IL.

Herther, Nancy. 2008. "The *Christian Science Monitor* Moves to a Web-based Model—Is This the Future of News?" *KM World* (November 10). Available: newsbreaks.infotoday.com/...christian-science.../is-this-the-future-of-news-51495.asp.

Hirschman, David. 2010. "So What Do You Do, John Yemma, Editor of the Christian Science Monitor?" *Media Bistro* (March 31). Available: http://www.mediabistro.com/articles/cache/a10833.asp.

Hoffman, David. 1993. "Broadcasting, Press Play Vital Roles in New Russia." *Christian Science Monitor* (May 19): 19.

Hoffman, Susanna M. and Anthony Oliver-Smith. eds. 2002. *Catastrophe and Culture: The Anthropology of Disaster*. School for Advanced Research Press.

Hopkins, Mark "Rizzn." 2008. "The Christian Science Monitor transitions to new media." *Mashable Social Media* (October 28). Available: http://mashable.com/2008/10/28/christian-science-monitor.

Huenneke, Judy. 2008. " 'To Enlighten Mankind': 100 Years of the *Christian Science Monitor*." *Engaging with the Christian Science Monitor*, 11–14. Boston: Christian Science Publishing Society.

Ini, Gilead. 2009. "The Unseen Bias in Middle East Reporting." *Christian Science Monitor* (September 20): 28.

Ivan, Robert. 2008. "*Christian Science Monitor* Editor John Yemma Explains Print and Online Costs." *Metaprinter* (December 2). Available: http://blog.metaprinter.com/2008/12/christian-science-monitor-editor-john-yemma-explains-print-and-online-costs.

Jamieson, Kathleen Hall and Paul Waldman. 2004. *The Press Effect: Politicians, Journalists, and the Stories That Shape the Political World*. Oxford University Press.

Jarboe, Greg. 2009. "Death of Newspapers or New Era of Online Journalism?" *SearchEngineWatch.com* (March 28). Available: http://blog.searchengine watch.com/090328-181359.

Johnston, Julia Michael. 1946. *Mary Baker Eddy: Her Mission and Triumph*. Boston: Christian Science Publishing Society.

Joseph, Ammu. 2005. *Making News: Women in Journalism*. New Delhi: The Media Foundation.

Kaslow, Amy. 1995. "Cartoon Lovers Salute the Funny Pages." *Christian Science Monitor* (May 4): 10–11.

Keane, Meghan. 2008. "Christian Science Monitor Goes All In on the Web." *Wired* (October 28). Available: http://www.wired.com/epicenter/2008/10/christian-scien.

Keil, Richard. 2004. "With the President: A Reporter's Story of 9/11." *Rochester Review*, 67 (1) (Fall). Available: http://www.rochester.edu/pr/Review/V67N1/feature1.html.

Kennedy, Dan. 2009. "Second Life: The *Christian Science Monitor* Reinvents Itself for the Digital Age." *CommonWealth Magazine* (January 20). Available: http://www.commonwealthmagazine.org/Departments/Mass-Media/2009/Winter/The-Christian-Science-Monitor-goes-digital.aspx.

Kennedy, Dan. 2010. "Chile and Earthquake Fatigue." *Media Nation* (March 1). Available: http://www.dankennedy.net/tag/christian-science-monitor.

Kennedy, Hugh A. Studdent. 1947. *Mrs. Eddy: Her Life, Her Work, and Her Place in History*. San Francisco: The Farallan Press.

Kenny, Herbert A. 1987. *Newspaper Row: Journalism in the Pre-television Era*. Chester, CT: Globe Pequot Press.

Keyston, David L. 2007. *The Healer: The Healing Work of Mary Baker Eddy*. Healing Unlimited.

Kidder, Rushworth M., comp. 1987. *An Agenda for the 21st Century*. Cambridge, MA: MIT Press.

Knapp, Bliss. 1947/1991. *Destiny of The Mother Church*. Boston: Christian Science Publishing Society.

Knee, Stuart E. 1994. *Christian Science in the Age of Mary Baker Eddy*. Westport, CT: Greenwood Press.

Kramer, Linda S. 1999. *The Religion That Kills: Christian Science: Abuse, Neglect, and Mind Control*. Bookworld Services.

Kraus, Clifford. 1998. "Remember Yellow Journalism." *New York Times* (February 15): WK2.

Kristof, Nicholas D. 2002. "Bigotry in Islam—and Here". *New York Times* (July 9).

Lavoie, Denise. 2008. "Christian Science Monitor to End Daily Publication." *USA Today* (October 28). Available: http://www.usatoday.com/money/media/2008-10-28-csmonitor_N.htm.

Lepore, Jill. 2009. "Back Issues: The Day the Newspaper Died." *The New Yorker* (January 26): 68–73.

Li, Xigen. 2006. *Internet Newspapers: The Making of a Mainstream Medium*. Mahwah, NJ: Lawrence Erlbaum Associates.

Lipstadt, Deborah E. 1983. "A Road Paved with Good Intentions: The *Christian Science Monitor*'s Reaction to the First Phase of Nazi Persecution of Jews." *Jewish Social Studies* 45 (2) (Spring): 95–112.

Maddocks, Melvin. 1984. "The Arts' Search for What Is Real. In *Understanding our century*, 91–105. Boston: Christian Science Publishing Society.

Madigan, Charles M., ed. 2007. *-30-: The Collapse of the Great American Newspaper*. Lanham, MD: Ivan R. Dee.

Marks, Alexandra. 1995. "Former Monitor Reporter Recalls Capture during Vietnam War." *Christian Science Monitor* (November 10). Available: http://www.csmonitor.com/1995/1110/10111.html.

Marks, Alexandra. 2004. "Different News for Different Views." *Christian Science Monitor* (July 19). Available: http://www.csmonitor.com/2004/0719/p01s01-uspo.html.

Marks, Alexandra. 2009. "Newspapers' Troubles Escalate in Recession." *Christian Science Monitor* (March 16): 2.

"McClatchy, *Christian Science Monitor* to Exchange Stories." 2008. *McClatchy* (December 1). Available: http://www.mcclatchydc.com/2008/12/01/56807/mcclatchy-christian-science-monitor.html.

McLellan, Archibald. 1908. "The Christian Science Monitor." *The Christian Science Journal* (November).

Meyer, Philip. 2004. *The Vanishing Newspaper: Saving Journalism in the Information Age.* Columbus: University of Missouri Press.

Michell, Deidre. 2009. *Christian Science: Women, Healing, and the Church.* Lanham, MD: University Press of America.

Mnookin, Seth. 2005. *Hard News: Twenty-one Brutal Months at the New York Times and How They Changed the American Media.* New York: Random House.

Mollmann, Megan. 2009. "When Career and Faith Collide." *Sects in the City* (November 24). Available: http://medillsectsinthecity.com/?p=19.

Montlake, Simon. 2008. "Newspapers Thriving? Yes—in Asia." *Christian Science Monitor* (January 24): 6.

Mott, Frank Luther. 1941. *American Journalism.* New York: Routledge.

Mullaney, Tom. 2009. "Read All about It (Somewhere)." *University of Chicago Magazine* (November–December): 30–35.

Mutter, Alan. 2009. "Presses Stopped Forever at 140+ Papers in 2009." *Reflections of a Newsosaur* (December 21). Available: http://newsosaur.blogspot.com/2009/12/presses-stopped-forever-at-140-papers.html.

Nenneman, Richard A. 1984. "Economic progress in a complex world." In *Understanding Our Century*, 41–55. Boston: Christian Science Publishing Society.

Nenneman, Richard A. 1997. *Persistent Pilgrim: The Life of Mary Baker Eddy.* Boston: Christian Science Publishing Society.

Nenneman, Richard A., Richard J. Cattani, and John H. Hoagland, Jr. 1989. "To the readers of the *Christian Science Monitor*." *The Christian Science Monitor* (January 5): 15.

Neuharth, Allen. 1989. *Confessions of an S.O.B.* New York: Doubleday.

Nichols, John and Robert W. McChesney. 2009. "The Death and Life of Great American Newspapers." *The Nation* (March 18).

Nichols, John and Robert W. McChesney. 2010. "How to Save Journalism." *The Nation* (January 25).

North, Louise. 2009. *The Gendered Newsroom.* Cresskill, NJ: Hampton Press.

O'Carroll, Eoin. 2010. "Bright Green fades to black." *Christian Science Monitor* (February 16). Available: http://www.csmonitor.com/layout/set/print/content/view/print/279856.

Orcutt, William Dana. 1950. *Mary Baker Eddy and her Books.* Boston: Christian Science Publishing Society.

Ordonez, Sandra. 2009. "So . . . What Is the Future of Citizen Journalism and Social Media?" *Online Journalism Review* (July 28). Available: http://www.ojr.org/ojr/people/ordonez/200907/1764.

Parr, Ben. 2010. "The Dire State of the Newspaper Industry." *Mashable: The Social Media Guide* (March 26). Available: http://mashable.com/2010/03/26/the-dire-state-of-the-newspaper-industry-stats.

Patterson, Phillip and Lee Wilkins. 2007. *Media Ethics: Issues and Cases*, 6th ed. McGraw-Hill.

Peel, Robert. 1966/1972. *Mary Baker Eddy: The Years of Discovery*. New York: Holt Rinehart and Winston.

Peel, Robert. 1971/1977. *Mary Baker Eddy: The Years of Trial*. Boston: Christian Science Publishing Society.

Peel, Robert. 1977/1982. *Mary Baker Eddy: The Years of Authority*. Boston: Christian Science Publishing Society.

Peel, Robert. 1984. "Religion's Emerging Role." In *Understanding our century*, 107–119. Boston: Christian Science Publishing Society.

Pelton, Richard. 1995. *R. F. Outcault's The Yellow Kid: A Centennial Xelebration of the Kid Who Started the Comics*. Northampton, MA: Kitchen Sink Press.

Pew Project for Excellence in Journalism. 2010. *The State of the News Media: An Annual Report on American Journalism*. Available: http://www.stateofthe media.org/2010/overview_intro.php.

Pickering, George White. 1974. *Creative Malady: Illness in the Lives and Minds of Charles Darwin, Mary Baker Eddy, Sigmund Freud, Florence Nightingale, Marcel Proust, and Elizabeth Barrett Browning*. London: Allen & Unwin.

Powell, Lyman P. 1930. *Mary Baker Eddy: A Lifesize Portrait*. New York: Macmillan.

Prasad, Kiran. 2009. *e-Journalism: New Media and News Media*. New Delhi: B. R. Publishing Corporation.

"The Press: Monitor's *Monitor*." 1949. *Time* (November 21). Available: http://www.time.com/time/magazine/article/0,9171,856323,00.html.

"ProQuest Completes *Christian Science Monitor* Digital Archive." (2003, April 10). Available: http://www.il.proquest.com/enUS/aboutus/pressroom/03/20030410.shtml.

Ralston, Richard E., ed. 1991. *Communism: Its Rise and Fall in the 20th Century. From the Pages of the Christian Science Monitor*. Boston: Christian Science Publishing Society.

Ramsay, E. Mary. 1935/1991. *Christian Science and Its Discoverer*. Writings of Mary Baker Eddy.

Regan, Tom. 2008. "Where the Monitor Is Going, Others Will Follow." *Nieman Reports* (Winter). Available: http://www.nieman.harvard.edu/reportsitem .aspx?id=100668.

Regan, Tom. 2009. "Newspaper Failures Are Old News. Time to Focus on Solutions." *Christian Science Monitor* (March 12): 16.

Reinardy, Scott. 2009. "Female Journalists More Likely to Leave Newspapers." *Newspaper Research Journal* 30 (3) (Summer): 42–57.

Riley, Patricia and Nikki Usher. Work in progress. *Organizational Capacity for Change in the Digital Environment*.

Robards, Brooks. 1990. "Newshounds and Sob Sisters: The Journalist Goes to Hollywood." In *Beyond the Stars: Stock Characteristics in American Popular Film*, edited by Paul Loukides and Linda K. Fuller, 131–145. Bowling Green, OH: Popular Press.

Roberts, Gene. 2004. *Leaving Readers Behind: The Age of Corporate Newspapering*. Fayetteville: University of Arkansas Press.

Roberts, Johnnie L. 2008. "The Paperless Paper." *Newsweek* (October 28).

Roosevelt, Eleanor. 1945. *My Day*. (September 21). Available: http://www .gwu.edu/~erpapers/myday/displaydoc.cfm?_y=1945&_f=md000136.

Rosan, Rohab. 2010. "Future of Journalism Is Hyperlocal." International Media Conference: Community Voices Create the Difference (February 19). Available: http://www.inwent-iij-lab.org/projects/2010/wordpress/2010/ future-of-journalism-is-hyperlocal.

Rosenberg, Jerry M. 1982. *Inside the Wall Street Journal: The History and the Power of Dow Jones and Company and America's Most Influential Newspaper*. Macmillan.

Rosenthal, Phil. 2008. "*Christian Science Monitor*: A Paper without Paper Is Still a Paper." *Chicago Tribune* (October 29). Available: http://newsblogs .chicagotribune.com/towerticker/2008/10/a-paper-without.html.

Rowe, Chip. 1992. "Hacks on Film." *Washington Journalism Review* 7: 27–29.

Schuette, Kim M. 2008. *Christian Science Military Ministry 1917-2004*. Indianapolis, IL: Brockton Publishing.

Sered, Susan Starr. 1994. *Priestess, Mother, Sacred Sister: Religions Dominated by Women*. New York: Oxford University Press.

Shanor, Donald R. 2003. *News from Abroad*. New York: Columbia University Press.

Silberger, Julius. 1980. *Mary Baker Eddy: An Interpretive Biography of the Founder of Christian Science*. Boston: Little, Brown.

Silverman, Ben. 2009. "The Demise of 'Dead Tree Media' and the Future of PR." *PR Fuel* (January 14). Available: http://www.ereleases.com/prfuel.

Simmons, John K. 1991. "Charisma and Covenant: The Christian Science Movement in Its Initial Post-charismatic Phase." In *When Prophets Die: The Post-charismatic Fate of New Religious Movements*, edited by Timothy Miller, 107–123. Albany, NY: SUNY Press.

Simmons, Thomas. 1991. *The Unseen Shore: Memories of a Christian Science Childhood*. Boston: Beacon Press.

Slattery, Brennon. 2008. "Christian Science Monitor Goes Online-only." *PC World* (October 31). Available: http://www.washingtonpost.com/wp-dyn/ content/article/2008/10/29/AR2008102901960.html.

Smaus, Jewel Spangler. 1966. *Mary Baker Eddy: The Golden Days*. Boston: Christian Science Publishing Society.

Smillie, Paul. 2007. *In Defense of Mary Baker Eddy and the Remnant of Her Seed: A Compilation of His Articles*. BookSurge Publishing.

Smith, Clifford. 1941. *Historical Sketches from the Life of Mary Baker Eddy*. Boston: Christian Science Publishing Society.

Smith, Louise A. 1991. *Mary Baker Eddy: Discoverer and Founder of Christian Science.* New York: Chelsea House.

Smith, Wesley J. 2006. "*Christian Science Monitor* shows journalistic integrity." *Secondhand Smoke* (February 9). Available: http://www.firstthings.com/blogs/secondhandsmoke/2006/02/09/christian-science-monitor-shows-journalistic-integrity.

Snowdon, James H. 1920. *Truth about Christian Science: The Founder and the Faith.* Philadelphia: F. M. Braselman.

Solnit, Rebecca. 2009. *A Paradise Built in Hell: The Extraordinary Communities That Arise in Disaster.* New York: Viking.

Spencer, David R. 2007. *The Yellow Journalism: The Press and America's Emergence as a World Power.* Chicago: Northwestern University Press.

Spencer, Michael. 2009. "The Coming Evangelical Collapse." *Christian Science Monitor* (March 11). Available: http://richarddawkins.net/article,3652, The-coming-evangelical-collapse,The-Christian-Science-Monitor-Michael-Spencer.

Springer, Fleta Campbell. 1930. *According to the Flesh: A Biography of Mary Baker Eddy.* New York: Coward McCann.

Squires, James D. 1994. *Read All about It!: The Corporate Takeover of America's Newspapers.* New York: Times Books.

Storch, Gerry. 2010. "The Future of Journalism." *OurBlook.com* (March 25). Available: http://www.ourblook.com/The-Future-of/The-Future-of-Journalism.html.

Stores, Bruce. 2004. *Christian Science: Its Encounter with Lesbian/Gay America.* New York: iUniverse, Inc.

Strout, Lawrence N. 1999. *Covering McCarthyism: How the Christian Science Monitor Handled Joseph R. McCarthy, 1950–1954.* Westport, CT: Greenwood Press.

Strupp, Joe. 2010. "*Christian Science Monitor* Calls First Web-only Year a Success." *Media Matters for America* (April 6). Available: http://mediamatters.org/strupp/201004060013.

Swanson, Douglas J. 2001. " 'Standing Porter at the Door of Thought': The Social Order of the Christian Science Church." Paper presented to the Western Social Science Association conference, Reno, NV.

Sylves, Richard. 2008. *Disaster Policy and Politics: Emergency Management and Homeland Security.* Washington, D.C.: CQ Press.

Talese, Gay. 1969. *The Kingdom and the Power: Behind the Scenes of the New York Times: The Institution That Influences the World.* New York: Random House.

Thomas, Robert D. 1994. *With Bleeding Footsteps: Mary Baker Eddy's Path to Religious Leadership.* New York: Alfred A. Knopf.

Thompson, Katherine. 2008a. "*Christian Science Monitor* Interview Part I: Why the Move Away from Print?" *Editors Weblog* (November 19). Available: http://www.editorsweblog.org/analysis/2008/11/christian_science_monitor_interview_part.php.

Thompson, Katherine. 2008b. "*Christian Science Monitor* Interview Part II: Preparing the Newsroom for a Paperless Future." *Editors Weblog* (November 19). Available: http://www.editorsweblog.org/analysis/2008/11/christian_science _monitor_interview_part_1.php.

Thornton, Patrick. 2008a. "*Christian Science Monitor* to Cease Publishing Print Newspaper." *Endemic* (October 28). Available: http://patthorntonfiles .com/blog/2008/10/28/christian-science-monitor-to-cease-publishing-print -newspaper.

Thornton, Patrick. 2008b. "Interview with John Yemma about the CS *Monitor*'s Future." *BeatBlogging.org* (October 30). Available: http://beatblogging.org /2008/10/30/interview-with-john-yemma-about-the-cs-monitors-future.

Tifft, Susan E. and Alex S. Jones. 1999. *The Trust: The Private and Powerful Family behind the New York Times.* Boston: Little, Brown.

Tomlinson, Irving C. 1945. *Twelve Years with Mary Baker Eddy: Recollections and Experiences.* Boston: Christian Science Publishing Society.

Tributes from the Press: Editorial Comments on the Life and Work of Mary Baker Eddy. 1911/1993. Boston: Christian Science Publishing Society.

Twain, Mark. 1907/1993. *Christian Science.* Prometheus.

Vetter, Lara. 2007. "Theories of Spiritual Evolution, Christian Science, and the 'Cosmopolitan Jew': Mina Loy and American Identity." *Journal of Modern Literature,* 31 (1) (Fall): 47–63.

von Fettweiss, Yvonne Cache and Robert Townsend Warneck. 1998/2009. *Mary Baker Eddy: Christian Healer.* Boston: Christian Science Publishing Society.

Walker, Channing. 2008. "The *Monitor* and You." *Christian Science Journal* (11): 47.

Walker, David E. 1957. *Lunch with a Stranger.* London: Wingate.

Wasserstrom, Jeffrey. 2008. "Two Big China Stories You Missed This Year." *Christian Science Monitor* (December 17). Available: http://www.csmonitor .com/2008/1217/p09s01-coop.html.

Watson, Warren. 2009. "John Yemma, Editor of the *Christian Science Monitor*." *The American Editor* (March 28). Available (ttp://tae.asne.org/Default .aspx?tabid=65&id=456.

Wendt, Lloyd. 1982. *The Wall Street Journal: The Story of Dow Jones and the Nation's Business Newspaper.* Chicago: Rand McNally.

Wickman, Kase, Scott McLaughlin, and Tom Lakin. 2010. "Sports in the US: Year-round Madness." *Christian Science Monitor* (April 3). Available: http://www.csmonitor.com/layout/set/print/content/view/print/291180.

Wieneke, Dave. 2008. "The *Christian Science Monitor*'s 'Middle Road' to Greater Utility." *Online Law Blog* (October 29). Available: http://usefularts .us/2008/10/29/christian-science-monitor-takes-a-middle-road-to-greater -utility.

Wilbur, Sibyl. 1908. *The Life of Mary Baker Eddy.* New York: Concord Publishing Company.

Winchester, Mark D. 1995. "Hully Gee, It's a WAR!!!: The Yellow Kid and the Coining of 'Yellow Journalism.' " *Inks: Cartoon and Comic Art Studies* 2 (3) (November): 22–37.

Witt, Leonard. 2008. "Christian Science Monitor Will Publish on \$12 Million a Year." *Public Journalism Network* (November 17). Available: http://pjnet .org/post/1931.

Wolseley, Roland E. 1948. "A National Religious Daily." In *The Press and Society: A Book of Readings*, edited by George L. Bird and Frederic W. Merwin (1951), 613–618. New York: Prentice-Hall.

Wright, Helen M. 1998. *Star of Boston: The Life of Mary Baker Eddy*. Aequus Institute Publications.

Yemma, John. 2009a. "Editor's Message about Changes at the *Monitor*." *The Christian Science Monitor* (March 27). Available: http://www.csmonitor .com/Commentary/Opinion/2009/0327/p09s01-coop.html.

Yemma, John. 2009b. "Going Web-first at the *Christian Science Monitor*: A New Approach for a New Century." Available: http://74.125.93.132/search? q=cache:XncmLZVwm14J:www.americanbusinessmedia.com/images/ abm/images/events/DigitalVelocity/2009/John%2520Yemma%2520Preso .pps+Going+Webfirst+at+The+Christian+Science+Monitor:+A+new +approach+for+a+new+century&cd=3&hl=en&ct=clnk&gl=us&client =firefoxa.

Yemma, John. 2010a. "When Cyber-Attacks Hit US Energy Companies, We All Pay." *Huffington Post* (January 26). Available: http://www.huffingtonpost .com/john-yemma/when-cyber-attacks-hit-us_b_437056.html?view.

Yemma, John. 2010b. "Memo to News Sites: There Is No Future in 'Digital Razzle Dazzle.' " *paidContent.org* (March 29). Available: http://paidcontent.org/ article/419-memo-to-news-sites-there-is-no-future-in-digital-razzle-dazzle.

Zelizer, Barbie. 2004. *Taking Journalism Serious: News and the Academy*. Newbury Park, CA: Sage.

Zelizer, Barbie. 2009. *The Changing Faces of Journalism: Tabloidization, Technology and Truthiness*. New York: Routledge.

Zelizer, Barbie and Stuart Allan. 2002. *Journalism after September 11*. New York: Routledge.

Zuckerman, Ethan. 2005. "Is *Christian Science Monitor* the World's Bloggiest Newspaper?" *My Heart's In Accra* (April 21). Available: http://www .ethanzuckerman.com/blog/2005/04/21.

Index

About the Author

LINDA K. FULLER (B.A., Skidmore College; M.A., American International College; Ph.D., University of Massachusetts), professor of communications at Worcester State University and currently a senior fellow at Northeastern University, is the author/(co)editor of some 20 books and more than 300 professional publications and conference reports, including these from Greenwood/Praeger: *The Cosby Show: Audiences, Impact, Implications* (1992); *Community Television in the United States: A Sourcebook on Public, Educational, and Governmental Access* (1994); *Dictionary of Quotations in Communications* (1997); and *National Days/National Ways: Historical, Political, and Religious Celebrations around the World* (2004). The recipient of Fulbright awards to teach in Singapore (1996) and to do HIV/AIDS research in Senegal (2002), Linda has been monitoring the *Monitor* for half of its 100-year history and feels privileged to tell its recent Web-first story.